MW01002309

from DARKNESS *to* LIGHT

Demonic Oppression and the Christian

AREON POTTER

TATE PUBLISHING & *Enterprises*

Endorsements

The fact of creatures called demons and what they can do to people was established once and for all by the Lord Jesus Christ. I recommend this book to all who desire to broaden their knowledge of demons and their activities in the lives of believers.

Keith Fredrickson
Th.M., Counselor

This subject of demons relating to Christians has too long been over-looked or hushed up—even by Bible-believing spiritual leaders. The supposition that Satan and his hoards are defeated and are not a real threat to those who are in Christ is exploded in this thorough scriptural presentation. Areon Potter has dealt with many people (saved and lost) who have been oppressed by Satan and his demons and has seen many delivered by the power of God in Christ Jesus.

I highly recommend this scholarly work which is laced with scripturally-oriented prayers and a reverent and worshipful spirit toward the Triune Godhead!

Dr. Paul E. Hume, Adjunct Professor of Bible
Colorado Christian University

From Darkness to Light
Demonic Oppression and the Christian
Areon Potter

'But arise and stand on your feet;
for this purpose I have appeared
to you, to appoint you a minister
and a witness not only to the things
which you have seen, but also to
the things in which I will appear to
you; delivering you from the Jew-
ish people and from the Gentiles,
to whom I am sending you, to open
their eyes so that they may turn

From Darkness To Light

and from the dominion of Satan to
God, in order that they may receive
forgiveness of sins and an inheritance among those who have been
sanctified by faith in Me.'

Acts 26:16-18

TATE PUBLISHING
& Enterprises

Tate Publishing is committed to excellence in the publishing industry. Our staff of highly trained professionals, including editors, graphic designers, and marketing personnel, work together to produce the very finest books available. The company reflects the philosophy established by the founders, based on Psalms 68:11,

"THE LORD GAVE THE WORD AND GREAT WAS THE COMPANY OF THOSE WHO PUBLISHED IT."

If you would like further information, please contact us:
1.888.361.9473 | www.tatepublishing.com
TATE PUBLISHING & Enterprises, LLC | 127 E. Trade Center Terrace
Mustang, Oklahoma 73064 USA

Scripture quotations marked "KJV" are taken from the Holy Bible, King James Version, Cambridge, 1769.

All other scripture quotations are taken from the New American Standard Bible ®, Copyright © 1960, 1962, 1963, 1968, 1971, 1972, 1973, 1975, 1977, 1995 by The Lockman Foundation. Used by permission. All rights reserved.

Book design copyright © 2006 by Tate Publishing, LLC. All rights reserved.
Cover design by Taylor Rauschkolb
Interior design by Lindsay B. Behrens

Published in the United States of America

ISBN: 1–5988631–1-8

08.12.08

Dedication

To my wife, Carol,

who has been an ever-present encourager to me.

An excellent wife, who can find? . . . The heart of her husband trusts in her . . . She does him good and not evil all the days of her life. . . . Strength and dignity are her clothing, and she smiles at the future. She opens her mouth in wisdom, and the teaching of kindness is on her tongue. She looks well to the ways of her household, and does not eat the bread of idleness. Her children rise up and bless her; her husband also, and he praises her, saying: Many daughters have done nobly, but you excel them all. . . . but a woman who fears the Lord, she shall be praised.

Proverbs 31

Selected

ⵁ

Acknowledgment

I am deeply appreciative to the following people for their contributions toward the writing of the original manuscript:

Judy Fredrickson for the many hours she spent reading, editing, researching, and critiquing the manuscript prior to publishing. Her effort has made a significant impact on the quality of this book.

Keith Fredrickson for his Foreword, his theological input, and his patience with Judy while she worked on editing the original manuscript.

"Mrs. Jay" for the feedback she provided as I first began to learn about the forces of darkness working in the lives of believers.

My wife, Carol, for the preliminary editing and invaluable critique she provided at each stage of the work and for her patience as I worked on the manuscript.

Troy Potter for his technical assistance with the computer and software.

Those who have come for counseling and by their spoken and living testimony have encouraged the writing of this book.

Those who support the work of Adonai Resources prayerfully and financially.

I extend my personal "Thank you!" to each of you for your contribution. You have played an important part in the writing of this book. You also will be contributing to the lives of those who shall read this book.

Areon Potter

Table of Contents

About the Author

From *Darkness to Light* is a chronicle of the information God taught author Areon Potter. In 1980, Areon moved his family to Denver, Colorado, and worked five years as a counselor for Dr. Charles Solomon at Grace Fellowship International. While there, he became aware of how Christians can be influenced by the kingdom of darkness. In August of 1985, Areon and Carol sensed God leading them to begin the ministry of Adonai Resources. In order to teach Areon what he needed to know concerning demonic activities and entities, God began to bring an increasing number of believers across Areon's path—believers who were experiencing the work of the enemy in their lives. As he learned to deal effectively with harassing, demonic forces, Areon gathered valuable insight into the enemy's various schemes and tactics. Areon organized the information and his efforts have brought forth this book—*From Darkness to Light*.

Areon Potter was born and raised in California. After serving four years with the United States Air Force, he earned his Bachelor of Arts degree in psychology from Northwest Nazarene College, where he met and later married his wife, Carol. He worked as a counselor and teacher at a state correctional facility for delinquent boys in Nevada for nearly nine years. Areon and Carol have two married sons, Ryan and Troy, and two granddaughters.

Foreword

The fact of creatures called demons and what they can do to people was established once and for all by the Lord Jesus Christ. Demonized people were found throughout the years of Jesus' ministry. Those events were recorded in the Christian Bible for all to read. Yet, Biblical evidence of demons seems not to be sufficient for many who are leaders in the evangelical Christian church. A pastor of a large Baptist church once said to me, "I don't know what I believe about demons." An evangelical Christian psychiatrist declared that in all of his years of counseling he had never encountered a demon or a demonized person.

Areon Potter is sure of what he believes about demons because he knows what the Bible teaches concerning them. He encounters them regularly oppressing Christians he counsels. Areon's writing represents an excellent balance of solid Scriptural teaching, blended with his considerable experience with demons.

I have known Areon Potter for twenty-five years, and for several of those years worked together with him as a colleague in a Denver counseling center. I was a witness to the Lord's working in his and his wife Carol's lives as the Lord gently but firmly called them into their present ministry. In the testing, trying, and refining they have experienced through the years, they have grown even more convinced of the Lord's call and provision in this special ministry. Areon and Carol Potter are authentic Christians by every measure.

I recommend this book to all who desire to broaden their knowledge of demonic activity in the lives of Christians.

Keith Fredrickson, Th. M.
Counselor in Arizona

Preface

I became personally aware of the reality of demons working in the lives of believers in 1982. Since that time, there has rarely been a week go by in counseling that I have not encountered people seeking release from oppressive, demonic forces.

Every born-again believer would benefit from being better educated. The Scripture tells us that God's people are destroyed for lack of knowledge (Hosea 4:6). They are destroyed because they don't know God's truth in this area. Ignoring the issue of demonic oppression will not solve the problem—it will still exist. Learning about demonic oppression will not increase the problem—it will only help identify the problem so it can be dealt with. In order to effectively deal with demonic oppression in our own lives, we must take the initiative and be willing to be taught by the Holy Spirit, and thus become better equipped.

My prayer for you, the reader, would be, "That the God of our Lord Jesus Christ, the Father of glory, may give to you a spirit of wisdom and of revelation in the knowledge of Him. I pray that the eyes of your heart may be enlightened, so that you may know what is the hope of His calling, what are the riches of the glory of His inheritance in the saints" (Ephesians 1:17, 18).

Part of a believer's inheritance includes freedom from demonic harassment. Just as the children of Israel had to possess their inheritance, so must we. Knowledge about—and freedom from—demonic oppression can be a reality in your life!

Introduction

We are exhorted in Scripture to forgive "in order that no advantage be taken of us by Satan; for we are not ignorant of his schemes" (2 Corinthians 2:11). Too many Christians know some things about our enemy but are woefully ignorant of how he operates in our lives. Many believe that if they will leave Satan alone, he will leave them alone. The Apostle Paul seemed to have a different perspective. He told the Ephesian Christians that they needed to be strong in the Lord and in the strength of His might. He told them that even while strong in the Lord they needed to put on the full armor of God because there is an on-going battle taking place in the Christian life. Some people would certainly agree with that, and would quickly point to their spouse as proof!

Paul said our battle is not against flesh and blood, but against demonic forces. These forces are being led by their ruler, Satan, a schemer whose purpose is to steal, kill, and destroy. The main focus of his attack is the Christian. Therefore, Paul told these believers to put on all of God's armor.

But exactly how do Satan and his demonic forces work today? Does the Bible speak to this question? Are we as Christians to be under Satan's attack and left to our own measures in dealing with him? Or are there Scriptural guidelines which teach us about the devices or methods he uses? I believe when God, speaking through Paul, said we are not ignorant of Satan's devices, He said it because He has given us all the information we need in His Word. It is essential to study and "be diligent to present yourself approved to God as a workman who does not need to be ashamed, handling accurately the word of truth" (2 Timothy 2:15). With this purpose in mind, I will be sharing with you some of the things God has taught me in the area of spiritual warfare.

Chapter 1

Identifying the Problem

Some people would prefer not to be involved in spiritual warfare. They are afraid that in paying attention to Satan they might lift up, glorify, or somehow give honor to him; this they do not want to do. Nor is that my intention. My purpose is to do what Scripture says: to expose the deeds of darkness and uncover the way Satan and his kingdom operate. In that way the reader's eyes may be opened so they may turn from darkness to light and from the dominion of Satan to God. Satan is active and has a despicable purpose—to steal, kill, and destroy. If we do not stand against him, he is going to obstruct and hinder us. We must learn how to keep him from devouring us. We need to know what his schemes are. We have to gain knowledge of what it means to be equipped. We need to know how to apply that knowledge and how to effectively resist Satan and his demonic forces.

I recall a cartoon I once saw. There was a little demon sitting on the curb outside a church, crying. Someone came by and asked the little demon why he was crying. He pointed to the church and said, "People in there blame me for everything!"

There is more truth in that cartoon than many Christians would care to acknowledge. I've heard people give credit to Satan or demons for things for which they are not responsible. In giving them recognition for these things, it could be considered as lifting up, glorifying, or honoring Satan and his demonic forces. Only God knows how often Satan or a demon gets credited when someone is simply walking after the flesh.

On the other hand, I've also heard people say their problems were caused by every excuse from A to Z. They should have been open to exploring the area of demonic oppression to determine whether that was a factor in their lives.

The Profitability Factor of Scripture

In the third chapter of his second letter to Timothy, Paul tells us that . . .

3:16 All Scripture is inspired by God and profitable for teaching, for reproof, for correction, for training in righteousness;

3:17 that the man of God may be adequate, equipped for every good work.

These verses say that Scripture is profitable for teaching. *Teaching* means "to give instruction, to provide facts, and to define and clarify information for application."

This verse also says that the Scripture is profitable for reproof. *Reproof* means "to find a fault; to convict, or to expose error." When we as God's people are doing something in our battle against the enemy that is faulty, we need to know what we are doing wrong so it can be corrected. Unless we realize the way that seemed right was wrong, we will not seek God's way, which is right.

Correction means "to change from wrong to right." We must accept what is right if we desire correction. Unless we receive His ways as right, we can never realize the experience of victory and maturity. This is God's process of renewing our mind that we may learn to agree with Him and His ways.

Training means "to instruct in order to make proficient or qualified." Training shows how to efficiently carry out instruction and how to respond to reproof until it becomes an automatic way of living in our experience. Then believers will be more proficient and qualified in putting the enemy to flight in their own lives.

Jesus Used Parables to
Help People Understand Spiritual Truth

When working with people, I have found that some have a problem believing in the reality of demons and how they work in the lives of believers. Some are not positive a demon can afflict people—especially believers. Jesus spoke in parables in order to help us understand what He was saying. He would take a familiar truth and compare it to one not yet understood. A *parable*, according to Webster, is "a statement or comment that conveys a meaning indirectly by the use of comparison, analogy, or the like."

For example, Scripture states in Luke Chapter 13,

13:18   Therefore He was saying, "What is the kingdom of God like, and to what shall I compare it?

13:19   "It is like a mustard seed, which a man took and threw into his own garden; and it grew and became a tree; and the birds of the air nested in its branches."

13:20   And again he said, "To what shall I compare the kingdom of God?

13:21   "It is like leaven, which a woman took and hid in three pecks of meal, until it was all leavened."

I would like to share an illustration of my own with you—a physical description of a spiritual phenomenon. Let's consider the world of bacteria and see how it relates to the demonic realm.

The Similarity between Bacteria and Demons

We all know what bacteria are. We know that they are all around us and that they cannot be discerned by the senses. We can not hear them, see them, smell them, touch them, or taste them. For example, have you ever seen a bacterium pneumococcus? These bacteria cause meningitis and pneumonia. If a bacterium pneumococcus was moving around in your house, you could not hear it. If it came into the room where you were reading this book, you could not see it. If it came right up in front of you, you couldn't even smell it. If it were to land on your hand, it would be touching you, but you would not be aware of it. If it were to make contact with a taste bud, you couldn't even taste it.

The same is true of demons. Generally, most people cannot hear them or see them. Neither are they able to smell them, touch them, or taste them.[1] A woman who earlier in her life had been involved with an occult group, told me something very interesting. At night she would see two red eyes glaring at her. They had done so every night for years, but no one had been able to get rid of them, so we addressed the issue. The next time I saw her, she reported—much to her amazement—the two red eyes had gone. However, as a general rule, demons do not reveal themselves physically.

Bacteria can cause waterborne disease. That is why people boil contaminated water in foreign countries. We use chlorine in the United States for the same purpose. We have to use something, or do something, to kill the germs. Even if you wanted to drink water from a clear mountain stream, you would want to take precautionary measures to protect against giardia. You would not want to contract these microorganisms, since they can cause severe digestive tract complications. To protect yourself in the mountains, you would either need to boil the water, add a chemical to it, or filter it.

Demons can also cause a person to be sick. Scripture tells us in Luke 13 about a woman who had a sickness caused by a spirit.

Bacteria are not visible to the naked eye, but a microscope and light can expose them. A microscope visually increases the size of a microscopic object when it is placed on a small glass plate, positioned under the lens, and exposed to light. Only then is it visible.

Neither are demons normally visible. As you read this book, we want to take the reality of demonic oppression, put it under God's microscope, and enlarge it so we can more easily see. Then we want to expose the reality of demonic oppression to the light of God's Word, so the enemy's deeds will be disclosed.

Studying demonic oppression is like looking at a drawing of a microbe. That drawing is simply an enlarged part of the whole. The drawing makes the small section easier to see. By taking a section of the Christian life and enlarging it, demonic oppression will be easier to look at and recognize.

Bacteria create poisons that get into our bloodstream. Bacteria in our food will grow, and when eaten can affect our stomach and intestines, causing headaches, nausea, chills, diarrhea, and various other symptoms. A person contacting bacterium pneumococcus may contract meningitis, which affects the membranes of the brain or the spinal cord.

Communicable bacteria are transmitted from a carrier to another person. If someone had a cold and sneezed around you, their germs would be around you. You could breathe them in and could catch a cold from the carrier.

The same is true in the area of the demonic. If someone around you is oppressed by demons, those demons would relish a chance to afflict your life.

We have learned how to control bacteria. One way is by sterilizing or purifying contaminated articles. Another is by washing those articles thoroughly with hot water and soap. We are aware of the dangers of bacteria. That is why we wash our hands before we eat and after we use the bathroom. In general, cleaners and disinfectants are used regularly without consciously thinking about it. Did you get up this morning thinking, "My goodness, there are bacteria in my house!" Due to their presence in your home, do you put on a sterilized space suit like astronauts wear before you go to work? No! We don't do that, though we know these bacteria are lurking in the shadows. We simply take proper precautions.

It is the same with demons. We should not be paranoid about them. We do need to be aware of them, however. We each need to know what we can do to keep demons from afflicting us.

Three Important Factors

Three factors determine whether a person will contract a disease and how serious that disease will be. The first factor is the number of germs involved. The fewer the germs, the smaller the chance a person will succumb to a disease. The second factor is the strength of the germ. If the germ is strong, it takes fewer to affect a person. The third factor is the physical condition of the person hosting the germ. If the person is very weak, or if he is very susceptible to environmental factors, or if his immune system is not functioning properly, then he may be more vulnerable to that germ.

However, when a person has accurate knowledge about how bacteria work, has a healthy immune system and takes preventive action against germs, that person can ward off most unwanted and unnecessary illness.

When an individual cuts his finger, he should wash and disinfect the wound. He might need a tetanus shot, along with any necessary stitches. If he bandages his finger and keeps it clean, that finger will heal. If he doesn't keep it clean, the possibility continues for that finger to become infected. If the conditions are right, a dirty, infected finger can cause illness or even death if it is not given proper care. However, if that individual knows how bacteria work, he can take preventive action and prevent unnecessary illness.

In like manner, when a person has accurate knowledge about how demons work, has a healthy spiritual immune system, and takes preventive action against demonic forces, he can ward off a great deal of unwanted and unnecessary spiritual and physical illness caused by Satan's kingdom.

So keep the illustration of bacteria in mind as you read about demonic oppression. Bacteria exist in the physical realm in which we live. We have learned how they work; we know how to deal with them and no longer fear them. Remember, we can respond to demons in the same way.

Initial Warfare Prayer

We are considering a very serious subject. Before proceeding any further, it will be wise for you, the reader, either to pray in your own words or to use the following warfare prayer:

Father, in the name of the Lord Jesus Christ, I acknowledge that I do not know as much about spiritual warfare as You would like me to know. If there are any truths in the pages of this book You want me to learn, I'm asking Your Holy Spirit to begin to teach them to me. I desire to be better equipped to effectively put the enemy to flight in my own life.

I take authority over and bind any demonic forces that would try to hinder my understanding. I bring the finished work of the Lord Jesus Christ on the cross between me and all demons that have any legal ground to oppress me in any way. I command those demons to leave me and to go wherever the Lord Jesus Christ wants them to go.

Father, I ask for Your Holy Spirit to search my heart and to make me tender to Your truth, whatever that truth may be. I commit the time I spend reading this book to You, and I ask You to honor and bless it.

All this I pray in the name, the power, and the authority of the Lord Jesus Christ.

Review: Identifying the Problem

In this first chapter we have identified the problem of demonic oppression. We have seen . . .

1. the profitability factor of Scripture.

2. that Jesus used parables to help people understand spiritual truth.

3. the similarity between bacteria and demons.

4. three factors that increase the probability of being oppressed.

5. the importance of beginning our journey by using an initial warfare prayer.

Ignoring the issue of demonic oppression will not solve the problem—it will still exist.

Learning about demonic oppression will not increase the problem—it will help identify and solve the problem.

Chapter 2

Defining Oppression

Demons do oppress believers. They try to oppress us physically, mentally, and emotionally. Their goal is for us to exercise our will in agreement with their will. Demonic oppression involves manipulation. By planting their thoughts into a person's mind, their intent is for the person to accept the bogus thoughts as though they had originated from within the person's own mind. Once accepted, the person's thinking has unintentionally aligned with that of a demon.

To learn about oppression, we need to understand what the word means. Vine says that to *oppress* means "to exercise power over."[2] Acts Chapter 10 says,

> 10:38 "You know of Jesus of Nazareth, how God anointed Him with the Holy Spirit and with power, and how He went about doing good, and healing all who were oppressed by the devil; for God was with Him."

The word *oppressed* in that verse is used in the passive voice, which means the subject is the receiver of the verb's action—the subject is a victim. If we take the sentence "The dog was beaten," the *dog* is the subject. *Was beaten* is the verb. What is on the receiving end of the beating? The dog is the one receiving the beating; the dog is the victim.

When we are oppressed, we are the receiver of the spirit's action. Luke 6:18 tells us that Jesus healed all those who were troubled with unclean spirits. Oppression is the exercising of power over another person.

Strong defines the word *oppress* as meaning "to exercise dominion against."[3] It is exercising the power or right to govern or control. That is precisely what demons want to do. They want to somehow gain the legal right to exercise power over us or to govern us without our knowledge or consent. I have talked to many demonically oppressed Christians who had no clue they were being oppressed from the demonic realm. I worked as a Christian counselor for approximately five years before I learned anything about demonic oppression.

Webster's New Encyclopedic Dictionary defines *oppress* as meaning "to load or burden with cruel, unjust, or unreasonable impositions; to treat with unjust severity, rigor or hardship; to overburden, overwhelm, subdue; to sit or lie heavy upon."[4] A person who is demonically oppressed is a victim.

An Example of Oppression

Dan was saved around the age of 12.[5] At the time I counseled with him, he was a deacon and lay counselor in a fundamental church. He enjoyed working with people who experienced marital problems, were using drugs, or were down and out. Dan wanted to be all that God wanted him to be. As I worked with him, he told me of a very real fear that had victimized him for twelve years; he was afraid of being demon possessed.

He explained that he had recurring nightmares. He dreamed demons were after him, or that somebody was trying to kill him. Some nights he would have to awaken his wife so she could pray and help him recover from his tormenting fear.

Dan felt unworthy. He had continuing feelings of guilt, although he had confessed his sins to God numerous times.

Although he was a roofer, Dan had a fear of heights. As he worked on a roof, he would not walk around like you might expect. When Dan approached the edge of the roof, he had to sit and scoot because of his fear.

During church, thoughts of wanting to hurt somebody or of wanting to kill the pastor would come to his mind. Can you imagine sitting in church and thinking of killing your pastor?

As I began explaining to Dan what could be done to solve his problem, he began experiencing various symptoms. He became nervous, his heart began beating rapidly, and he became fearful. He also started physically shaking and became very tense. He then revealed his most recent thought by telling me that I should die. When he had told me about having thoughts of killing his pastor, I had simply written it in my notes. However, when he told me he had thoughts of killing me, that gave it new meaning.

As I read some verses of Scripture, he interrupted me by pointing out a small knife I had clipped to the pocket of my pants. He said, "Areon, you know that knife you have clipped to your pocket?"

I said, "Yes, I am aware of the knife you are talking about."

He asked, "Would you take that knife and put it inside your pocket?"

I responded by asking, "Why would you want me to do that?"

Dan quickly remarked, "Because I keep getting these thoughts that I want to take that knife and stab you with it!"

The man was obviously being oppressed, and since I didn't want to upset him, I put the knife *deep* inside my pocket! I don't know if he felt any better, but I certainly did.

I also had a glass of water on the table. He said, "Would you take that glass and set it behind you somewhere?"

I asked him if there was any particular reason he wanted me to do that.

He replied, "Yes. I keep getting this thought that I want to grab that glass of water and throw it on you!"

So again, to keep from upsetting him, I took the glass of water and moved it out of the way!

The Result of Dan's Warfare

During that session, Dan learned what to do in the area of spiritual warfare. As a result, he has not experienced any more symptoms. I talked with Dan about a year and a half later; he reported that fear no longer bothered him, even as he worked on a roof.

Dan also related that he had had a pain in his ankle before I'd worked with him and that he'd had it for over a year. He said that after I had worked with him, the pain had begun to subside and within a week it was completely gone. He explained that it had been similar to having pain disappear once a splinter has been removed from your finger.

Dan's story is just one example of how oppression commonly operates in a person's life.

Power on the Side of Their Oppressors

Ecclesiastes Chapter 4 says,

4:1   Then I looked again at all the acts of oppression which were being done under the sun. And behold I saw the tears of the oppressed and that they had no one to comfort them; and on the side of their oppressors was power, but they had no one to comfort them.

During the time I have been counseling, I've seen many people with demonic problems who have been to psychologists, psychiatrists, pastors, and various counselors. In their search for help, they had not fully gotten all the help they needed because no one had dealt with the demonic element that was present in their lives. These people were crying out for someone to help them.

Certainly, not all people needing counsel have a demonic problem, but some do. If the problem is demonic, the counselor must deal with that element if the person is to receive lasting help.

The Similarity between Grizzly Bears and Demons

The above verse in Ecclesiastes says, "And on the side of their oppressors was power." Let me give you an example of how an oppressor can be powerful. Put yourself in the shoes of a Yukon Indian guide for a moment. This story, told by Jack O'Connor, comes from the book *Man and Bear* and is entitled "How to Handle a Grizzly."[6]

In the spring of 1950, the late Field Johnson, a Yukon Indian guide with whom I hunted on several occasions, was out in the bush near the Indian village of Champagne. He had his beat-up old .30/30 carbine with him and he was probably looking for a moose. Suddenly something struck him a tremendous blow that sent his .30/30 flying and knocked him end over end. He was dazed by the blow, but an instant later he realized he was being mauled by a grizzly. He also knew that his only chance to survive was to feign death—and he did. Presently the grizzly decided Field was dead, so he dug a shallow hole and buried him.

Field was bruised and bleeding and in great pain, but he lay there for about an hour. For a time he could hear the bear shuffling around and sniffing. Then all was quiet. He decided that the grizzly had gone, pushed up through the loose earth and brush that was his grave, lurched to his feet, and started off.

But the crafty bear had been hiding nearby, silent and vindictive, waiting and watching to make sure the hated man was dead. With a roar he was on Field again. Once more he knocked him down with a tremendous blow. Then he chewed on him some more. Again Field played dead, with less difficulty this time, because he had spells of unconsciousness from pain and loss of blood. This time the grizzly decided to bury him in a better place. So he took him by the feet and dragged him a half-mile. Then he dug another and deeper hole and covered Field with brush and loose earth.

When Field regained consciousness he could tell that many hours had passed. He was weak, in desperate pain, and burning with thirst. He once more staggered out of his grave, knowing that if he was to live he must have help. This time, the grizzly certain that he had done his job and that Field was dead, had gone. Field managed to make it to the Alaska Highway, got a ride into Whitehorse, and with the aid of sulfa and penicillin and skillful surgery he pulled through.

In spite of good medical care, the terrible ordeal eventually proved too much for him. He went insane and eventually died. He was one of the nicest guys I have ever known.

You say, "Ok, what does that story have to do with demonic oppression?"

If you were in the hills and knew a grizzly bear might be around, what would you do? You would probably begin to implement some type of safeguard.

What if you were out fishing by your cabin in some remote wilderness where a year earlier a friend of yours was mauled by a bear? As you're fishing, you catch a glimpse of something moving off to your side. You look in the direction of the movement and you see a bear—a grizzly bear! Your mind tells you that it is a bear. Your emotions tell you it is not good that a bear is there. When the bear sees you and heads your way, your will says, "This would be a good time to return to the cabin!" So you drop your fish and your equipment and head for the safety of your very sturdy cabin. You would take precautions and make certain no bear would come between you and the safety of your cabin!

The grizzly in the above story almost killed the Yukon Indian guide. Demons are just as dangerous as grizzly bears. Spiritually, however, demons are more dangerous and crafty than grizzly bears; their primary purpose is to kill, steal, and destroy.

Knowing that demons are around us, we need to carry out spiritual safeguards, not allowing anything of a suspicious nature to come between us and the Lord Jesus Christ, our source of safety. Maybe that is why the Scripture warns us in 1 Thessalonians 5:22 to abstain from every form of evil.

One Woman's Bout with Oppression

At one seminar in which I taught on spiritual warfare, an attending woman talked to me during a break. She wondered if part of her problem was due to demonic oppression, so she set up an appointment.

When she arrived for her appointment, she shared the last twelve-month period of her life with me. She'd been in a car accident, had been seriously hurt, and had since experienced a great deal of pain. She had also lost over 300 hours of work. Sometime after the accident, her respiratory system was affected and she had experienced choking sensations. The doctors had given her medication, but her respiratory system had difficulty for a second time. This time she had been hospitalized and had not been expected to live through the night. During her eight-day stay in the hospital she had also contracted viral pneumonia. Once she had returned home, she found herself totally exhausted. She had gone back to work, developed severe diarrhea, and had been hit with a high fever. She had become sick to her stomach, and then contracted bacterial colitis. The doctors had prescribed antibiotics, which killed off the beneficial bacteria, and further complicated the issue. She had changed to a less stressful job. The new job paid no overtime; her salary had dropped by fifty percent.

When she had come to the office for counseling she said, "I feel beat and bloodied to a pulp. I'm very tired."

She explained that she had almost canceled her appointment due to her fatigue. We discovered oppressing demons afflicting her from her parents' bloodlines. The accident had weakened her and given her demonic attackers an advantage.

By the time we were through with that appointment she said, "You know, I don't feel tired anymore. Right now I feel physically normal."

She called me several months later to let me know that she was still doing well, both physically and emotionally.

Oppression Originated with Adam and Eve

Genesis Chapter 1 says,

1:26   Then God said, "Let Us make man in Our image, according to Our likeness; and let them rule over the fish of the sea and over the birds of the sky and over the cattle and over all the earth, and over every creeping thing that creeps on the earth."

1:28   And God blessed them; and God said to them, "Be fruitful and multiply, and fill the earth, and subdue it; and rule over the fish of the sea and over the birds of the sky, and over every living thing that moves on the earth."

Was there anything on the face of the earth over which God had not given man authority? No! He said man was to rule over all the earth. Did that include man having authority over the serpent? Yes! But for the moment, let's assume that God had not given Adam authority over the serpent. Consider this illustration:

A Rattlesnake and a Mouse

Suppose you had a glass cage; in that cage you place a rattlesnake and a little gray mouse. Then you put the lid over the cage. What chance does the mouse have of escaping the jaws of the snake? None. Perhaps the snake is not presently hungry. But when his appetite returns, he's going to view that mouse much like you might look at a Big Mac. The mouse can run, jump, or try to hide, all to no avail; it is dead meat. The mouse does not stand a chance against the hungry rattlesnake.

If God put Adam on earth with the serpent and did not give him authority over the serpent, then God should have protected him. Man in his own strength is no match for Satan. If God had not given man authority over Satan, then God would have been negligent. God would have been putting Adam in a situation in which he would have had no recourse and no defense. We know, however, that God is not negligent and that He did give man authority over the serpent.

Man Given Authority over the Serpent

Look at Genesis Chapter 3:

3:1   Now the serpent was more crafty than any beast of the field which the Lord God had made. And he said to the woman, "Indeed, has God said, 'You shall not eat from any tree of the garden'?"

3:2   And the woman said to the serpent, "From the fruit of the trees of the garden we may eat;

3:3   but from the fruit of the tree which is in the middle of the garden, God has said, 'You shall not eat from it or touch it, lest you die.'"

3:4   And the serpent said to the woman, "You surely shall not die!

3:5   "For God knows that in the day you eat from it your eyes will be opened and you will be like God, knowing good and evil."

Looking at this situation, we see that the serpent and Eve were having a conversation, which the serpent had initiated. This shows one of Satan's methods. The serpent did not haphazardly enter this dialogue. He knew what he wanted to accomplish before he started the conversation. His devious scheme had the purpose of causing mankind's downfall. At the end of their conversation, Eve reached up, took the fruit, and ate it. Where was Adam during this time? Most people think he was somewhere in the Garden naming animals or counting bugs. But look at verse 6 to test this theory.

3:6　　When the woman saw that the tree was good for food, and that it was a delight to the eyes, and that the tree was desirable to make one wise, she took from its fruit and ate; and she gave also to her husband with her, and he ate.

Where was Adam? He was right there with her! Did Adam take authority over the serpent? No! He didn't say a thing. Yet it was to Adam that God had given the command in Genesis Chapter 2:

2:16　　"From any tree of the garden you may eat freely;

2:17　　but from the tree of the knowledge of good and evil you shall not eat, for in the day that you eat from it you shall surely die."

Adam heard God speak those words. Yet from what we read in Genesis Chapter 3 verse 6, Adam must have heard the conversation between the serpent and his wife. He must have known the serpent was referring to the tree of the knowledge of good and evil. Adam knew what was taking place, but still did not exercise his authority over the crafty serpent.

Who sinned first, Adam or Eve? The ladies have taken the brunt of the accusations here, but was Eve really the first one to sin? 1 Timothy says,

2:14　　And it was not Adam who was deceived, but the woman being quite deceived, fell into transgression.

Adam heard the serpent talking to his wife. Eve would not have been deceived if Adam had taken authority over the serpent and said, "Mr. Serpent, did I hear you tell my wife that it was all right to eat fruit from the tree of the knowledge of good and evil?"

"Yes, that is what I told her!" the serpent might have replied.

"Mr. Serpent, God personally told me that if we eat from that tree we are going to die. To add emphasis, He told me we would die on the very day we ate from that tree. Mr. Serpent, I will not allow you to speak to my wife and say things that do not coincide with God's personal, spoken instruction. God has given me authority over every thing that moves on the earth. Therefore, I'm telling you to leave!"

If Adam had said that, do you know what the serpent would have had to do? He would have had to swiftly vacate the premises. We have the same authority over demonic spirits today!

Pay Attention, Men!

The same thing that went on with Adam and Eve is going on today in homes all across our world. The enemy is talking to our wives and children. How often do we as men specifically take authority over the enemy of our households? How often do we let him know we will not permit his incursion upon our territory? How many times do we provide evidence in the form of action to show that we are standing against him in a waged war? If we don't do so, then we are as guilty as Adam. Adam's passivity resulted in the fall of man. Our passivity can contribute to the enemy's oppression and the destruction of relationships in our own home.

We are not Ignorant of his Schemes

In 2 Corinthians Chapter 2 Paul said,

2:10   But whom you forgive anything, I forgive also; for indeed what I have forgiven, if I have forgiven anything, I did it for your sakes in the presence of Christ.

Paul is saying forgiveness is an essential precaution and tells us why it is important in our lives as Christians in the next verse.

2:11   in order that no advantage be taken of us by Satan; for we are not ignorant of his schemes.

Because the Scriptures say, "we are not ignorant of his schemes," some people interpret that verse as referring to the fact that Paul was not ignorant of Satan's schemes. Paul *was* familiar with Satan's schemes. He *knew* how Satan worked. However, we also need to know how the enemy schemes. Therefore, it would be beneficial to study some examples of how Satan and demons are planning our destruction. Our investigation will begin in the next chapter.

Review: Defining Oppression

In this chapter we have . . .

1.   defined oppression.

2.   looked at two examples of oppression accompanied by the results of warfare.

3.   seen that our oppressors have power.

4.   looked at an illustration showing the importance of God giving man authority over the serpent.

5.   investigated how oppression originated.

6.   admonished men to exercise their headship authority in their homes against the enemy.

> Oppression makes a wise man mad.
>
> Ecclesiastes 7:7

Chapter 3

How Satan and Demons Scheme: Old Testament

Part 1: Job

There was a blameless, upright man that lived in Uz, an area southeast of the Dead Sea.[7] This man feared God and had nothing to do with evil. He was the father of ten children: seven boys and three girls. His estate was known to consist of 7,000 sheep, 3,000 camels, 500 yoke of oxen, and 500 female donkeys. He also employed many servants. He was noted to be the greatest of all the men from the east. This man's name was Job. Job was a conscientious family man; he would fast for his children, in case any of them had sinned or cursed God in their hearts.

Job awoke one morning greeting a day which seemed to be as normal as any other. However, there was a difference in the spiritual realm of which Job was totally unaware; the sons of God and Satan had presented themselves before God that day.

The Lord initiated a conversation with Satan, asking him if he had noticed Job as he was walking about and roaming around on the earth. Satan was familiar with Job. He told God that there were only two reasons Job gave Him the time of day. First, the hedge of protection He had set around Job had protected his family and his possessions. Second, He blessed everything that Job had done.

Then Satan set forth a challenge. He told God that if He would back off and allow the hedge to fall away from Job, His servant would curse God to His face. God accepted the challenge; He gave Satan authority over everything Job owned. The only restriction God imposed on Satan at this point referred to Job himself; Satan could not touch Job's person.

It did not take Satan long to take advantage of his newly-acquired freedom to test Job. As Satan began working, Job's life began crumbling around him. It all began on what appeared to be a normal day as Job's sons and daughters had gathered for one of their routine feasts. Out of the blue, a messenger came with the first wave of bad news: the Sabeans had attacked, taken the oxen and donkeys, and killed all the servants except the one delivering the message. As this message was being delivered, the second messenger came on the run with more bad news: fire from heaven had fallen, burning up the sheep and all but one of the servants that were tending them.

As the second servant was giving his message, another of Job's servants arrived on the scene. This one told him the Chaldeans had made a raid on the camels, taking them and killing all the servants, save one.

The fourth bearer of tragedy brought the most devastating news that day: a strong wind had come across the wilderness. It had blown the house down upon his feasting sons and daughters. The toll? Every one of them had died. Only this one servant bearing the tragic news had escaped the crushing blow.

Job's response was immediate. In grief he tore his robe and shaved his head. He then fell to the ground and worshipped. The book of Job makes this entry into the annals of history concerning Job.

1:21 And he said, "Naked I came from my mother's womb, and naked I shall return there. The LORD gave and the LORD has taken away. Blessed be the name of the LORD."

Although Job was deeply grieved, he did not sin nor was he bitter toward God for what had happened. Job had just gone through a great deal of turmoil in his life. He had lost most of his belongings and all of his children. In our natural reasoning, we would think that Job's trial should be over. In reality, however, the suffering had only begun.

For the second time in recorded Biblical history, the sons of God and Satan met to present themselves before God. Again the Lord spoke directly to Satan, who afresh told God that he had been strolling around on the earth. God wanted to know if Satan—in all of his strolling around—had observed Job, who was still a man of integrity even after he had suffered so intensely. Satan became a little snippy at that point. He told God that Job would give all the remainder he owned just to save his own hide. He then suggested that if God were to let that last protective hedge down so he might touch his body, Job would certainly curse God to His face.

God had seen what Satan had previously done concerning Job's possessions and his family. He saw when Job had torn his clothes and shaved his head in tremendous grief and emotional pain. God knew that Satan was ruthless and that he would go just as far as he was allowed to go. Knowing all, God told Satan He was placing Job under his evil power, but quickly added that he could not take his life.

After Satan left God's presence, it did not take him long to find Job. When he did, his attack left a painful effect: Job was covered with boils from the top of his head to the bottoms of his feet.

Earlier Satan had enlisted the help from the Sabeans, from lightning, from the Chaldeans, and from the wind itself to bring disaster to Job. In his second attack on Job, he even used Job's wife, who belittled him for his integrity and suggested he just curse God and die.

To Satan and most believers today, Job's response to his wife must seem incredible. He told her she was speaking very foolishly and reminded her that they had willingly accepted the good things that God had sent them. Then he announced that they should also accept any adversity that might come their way. The Bible is careful to note that in all this turmoil, Job did not slip into sin.

Job's Friends

Job was a man of integrity and had many friends. The book of Job records what next took place when three of his friends heard about Job's adversity and came to sympathize and comfort him. When they first saw Job, he was sitting on an ash heap. They did not even recognize him because his physical appearance had changed so drastically. Once they realized that the man on the ash heap was Job, they agonized with him in silence for seven days.

Job's Attitude Surfaces

Then Job broke the silence by opening his mouth, and cursing the day of his birth. He said, "Let the day perish on which I was to be born, and the night which said, a boy is conceived.[8] May that day be darkness; let not God above care for it, nor light shine on it.[9] . . . because it did not shut the opening of my mother's womb, or hide trouble from my eyes.[10] Why did I not die at birth, come forth from the womb and expire."[11]

Then Eliphaz, one of Job's friends who had come to visit, spoke. He recalled that Job had given instruction to a number of people, had strengthened the weak, and helped the feeble to stand on their own feet. Then he began giving Job some counsel, which he later discovered did not please God.[12] In Job Chapter 4 we find the beginning of this bogus counsel:

4:7   "Remember now, who ever perished being innocent? Or where were the upright destroyed?

4:8   "According to what I have seen, those who plow iniquity and those who sow trouble harvest it."

Eliphaz was inferring that Job was not suffering without reason, and that he apparently was not as innocent as he portrayed himself to be. If he were, he would not be suffering in this way, since Eliphaz had never seen the upright go through anything like this. According to what Eliphaz had seen, those who had sown their wild oats would one day harvest a similar crop.

There are many people today who are going through some of the toughest times of their lives. They have friends that try to give them "comfort." They tell them they must be guilty of some known, unconfessed sin. Otherwise, God would not be allowing them to go through the suffering they endure.

When God is working on an individual's life, God may put that person through some of the most trying times he's ever been through in his entire life. God is not doing it, as Eliphaz seemed to think, because there is some known sin that the person is hanging onto and is just not willing to confess and release. He will do it because the person does not have any idea of what is blocking the process of spiritual growth in their life. God has to take the individual through His breaking process before he will experience spiritual maturity.

Scriptural Indicators of Spiritual Oppression

In the following verses of Job Chapter 4, Scripture gives some significant details that will help us better understand demonic oppression. These verses might also give us an indication of where Eliphaz's counsel to Job might have originated.

4:12   "Now a word was brought to me stealthily, and my ear received a whisper of it.

4:13   "Amid disquieting thoughts from the visions of the night, when deep sleep falls on men,

4:14   Dread came upon me, and trembling, and made all my bones shake.

4:15   "Then a spirit passed by my face; the hair of my flesh bristled up.

4:16   "It stood still, but I could not discern its appearance; a form was before my eyes; there was silence, then I heard a voice:

4:17   'Can mankind be just before God? Can a man be pure before his Maker?

4:18   'He puts no trust even in His servants; and against His angels He charges error.

4:19   'How much more those who dwell in houses of clay, whose foundation is in the dust, who are crushed before the moth!

4:20   'Between morning and evening they are broken in pieces; unobserved, they perish forever.

4:21   'Is not their tent-cord plucked up within them? They die, yet without wisdom.

Looking back to verse 12, notice that Eliphaz is not wanting or seeking anything, yet this word was brought to him. So he is the receiver of the action. It says, "This word was brought to me stealthily." *Stealth* means "secret or unauthorized." It means "executed with secrecy or conceal-ment especially for the purposes of deception or causing the downfall, ruin, or destruction of." In demonic oppression, stealth is used to deceive one's heart or understanding. If we were to paraphrase this with full amplification it might say: "Information was brought to me without my request or consent. The purpose of this word was to deceive me in order to bring about my downfall, my ruin, or my destruction. I listened to a whisper of it; what I heard went into my mind."

Eliphaz said, "A word was brought to me stealthily, and my ear received a whisper of it." Demons do not have physical bodies like we do. The words they speak do not pass through the air. If they did, you could use a tape recorder and a microphone to record demons speaking to each other in the spiritual realm. When a demon speaks, he speaks directly into a person's mind.

The Patch Cord Method

An illustration may help clarify what I mean. You can record from a radio to a tape recorder using a microphone. If you record in that manner, you and others around you could not only hear what is being recorded, but additional data could be inserted.

Another way to record is by using a patch cord which enables you to record directly from the radio to the recorder. If you use this method, you are not able to hear what is being recorded unless you purposely monitor through headphones or a speaker.

When a demon speaks to a person, he uses the patch cord method without the monitor. He speaks directly into the mind. A microphone, or someone's ear, could not pick up what the demon had been saying.

Verse 13 of Job Chapter 4 says, "Amid disquieting thoughts. . . ." Disquieting thoughts are those kinds of thoughts that cause anxiety and uneasiness; they are disturbing thoughts. They are thoughts which divide and distract the mind, agitating it. "Amid disquieting thoughts from the visions of the night. . . ." Strong says these *visions of the night* refer to a "revelation, especially by dream."[13] Eliphaz is dreaming.

Verse 14 says, "Dread came upon me. . . ." To *dread* means "to fear greatly; to be in extreme apprehension of, terror." "Dread came upon me and trembling. . . ." *Trembling* means "to tremble or shake involuntarily." " . . . and made all my bones shake." Bones refer to substance; bones are the foundation upon which the body is built.

In essence Eliphaz has said, "As I was sleeping one night, I heard a disturbing revelation. In my sleep I felt anxious and uneasy. In great fear my body involuntarily trembled."

Verse 15 gives us some insight into why he felt that way in his sleep. It records, "Then a spirit passed by my face; the hair of my flesh bristled up." Have you ever had the hair on your arm or the back of your neck rise up? Did you sense the presence of a demon? Most people have had hair rise up; not all have sensed the attendance of a demon in the situation. While Eliphaz was sleeping, he was aware that a spirit had come to visit.

Verse 16 says, "It stood still, but I could not discern its appearance . . ." To *discern* means to "become aware of, to know or to identify by means of the senses: sight, hearing, smell, taste, touch, or by the intellect." When we discern something, we recognize it or become acquainted with it. Eliphaz reported a form before his eyes; there was a moment of silence—then he heard a voice.

Verse 17 registers what the voice asked, "Can mankind be just before God?" This spirit has posed a question to Eliphaz in his sleep asking if it is possible for mankind to be righteous in God's sight. For a Scriptural answer to that question, look at Genesis Chapter 6.

6:9   These are the records of the generations of Noah. Noah was a righteous man, blameless in his time; Noah walked with God (NASB).

        These are the generations of Noah: Noah was a *just* man and perfect in his generations, and Noah walked with God (KJV).

Now examine Genesis Chapter 7.

7:1   Then the LORD said to Noah, "Enter the ark, you and all your household; for you alone I have seen to be righteous before Me in this time" (NASB).

The Hebrew word translated *just* in Job 4:17 is translated *righteous* in Genesis 6:9 and 7:1. They are from the same root word.[14] The word means "to be righteous or just." Neither *just* nor *righteous* mean "sinless." To be righteous simply means that our sins are under sacrificial blood payment.

In Matthew Chapter 5 Jesus said,

5:44   But I say unto you, love your enemies, bless them that curse you, do good to them that hate you, and pray for them which despitefully use you, and persecute you;

5:45   That ye may be the children of your Father which is in heaven: for He maketh His sun to rise on the evil and on the good, and sendeth rain on the just and on the unjust (KJV).[15]

In Matthew 5:45, the New American Standard Bible uses the word *righteous* instead of "just." The word can be translated correctly either way.

Romans 4 gives us further insight into being righteous or just before God:

4:9   " . . . Faith was reckoned to Abraham as righteousness."

God reckoned Abraham righteous because of his faith. As believers we are declared the righteousness of God in Christ Jesus.[16] Now we can Scripturally answer the spirit's question to Eliphaz. Yes, a man *can* be just or righteous before God.

Then in Job 4:17 this spirit asked if a man can be pure before his Maker. The word *pure* means "cleansed, to be made purified, bright, shining; declared clean." Matthew gave answer to the question.

5:8   "Blessed are the pure in heart, for they shall see God."

David also revealed the answer in a Psalm.

24:3   Who may ascend into the hill of the LORD? And who may stand in His holy place?

24:4   He who has clean hands and a pure heart.

The Apostle Paul in Titus Chapter 2 says:

2:14   who gave Himself for us, that He might redeem us from every lawless deed and purify for Himself a people for His own possession, zealous for good deeds.

The question that the spirit is asking implies that the answer should be, "A man cannot be pure before God." According to Scripture, however, a man *can* be pure before God. Verse 18 of Job Chapter 4 gives us more of the spirit's thinking: "He puts no trust even in His servants; and against His angels He charges error."

The spirit's comment infers that God doesn't trust His servants and that He even charges His angels with error. What the spirit is saying is a partial truth. Since demons emulate their leader, they will also tell a bit of truth when it is to their advantage. Satan was God's top angel, until iniquity was found in him, then God charged that angel and his followers with error. Scripture further informs us that Satan disguises himself as an angel of light, in order to seem genuine.

This spirit pronounced that God didn't even trust His own servants. Is that true? Consider Noah and his situation. He was a righteous man, blameless in his time, who also walked with his Creator. God informed Noah how He felt about mankind: He was about ready to destroy them due to their violence. He then told Noah to build an ark and gave him specific instructions on how to go about that monumental task. God confided to Noah that He was going to bring a flood upon the entire earth and destroy every living thing. He disclosed to this newly enlisted ship-builder that He would establish a covenant with him. God further instructed Noah to take two of every kind of animal with him, making provision for them and his family. How did Noah respond to God's instruction? He did exactly as God had told him to do. Does that sound like God did not trust His servant, Noah? Not at all. This spirit was not simply misinformed; he was lying.

In Job Chapter 4 verse 19 the spirit continues, "How much more those who dwell in houses of clay, whose foundation is in the dust, who are crushed before the moth!" The whole idea conveyed here is this: What chance does a man have against a God that treats the higher angels unfairly? Demons want to cause us to feel hopeless and to question God's fairness. They want to make us think there would be no value in following God because we couldn't be righteous anyway. These inhibitors from the kingdom of darkness want us to feel like we can't win.

Verse 20 says, "Between morning and evening they are broken in pieces; unobserved, they perish forever." Are we really unobserved? No. Psalm

139:13 tells us that we are observed from our mother's womb. Jesus said we are greater than the sparrows; we are God's children and treated as such.

Demonic Method of Operation

Demons interject their thoughts into our mind. Think about that! A demon—something you can't normally see or discern with your senses—can interject his thoughts into your mind. If you are unaware of this, you may think the demon's thought is your own. When that demon puts his feelings into your emotions, you may think they are your own feelings. Then, if you exercise your will based upon the information you have mentally received and upon your emotional response, you will make a decision based on faulty information. Once that process starts, that demon will begin to build a stronghold in your life by manipulating your will and suggesting his own pernicious desires. In your confusion and uncertainty, the probability that you will find yourself accepting the demon's will as your own is greatly enhanced.

Review: How Satan and Demons Scheme
Old Testament

1. Demons come to us; they seek us out. We do not have to seek or provoke them (Job 4:12).

2. They stealthily put their thoughts into our minds. No bells sound, nor do bright lights come on as they insidiously do their work. Their activities are done in secret, purposefully, craftily trying to deceive us with their "revelations" (Job 4:12).

3. Between disquieting thoughts, they will project their feelings into a person's emotions (Job 4:13).

4. The demons' thoughts may cause anxiety or uneasiness. Their intent is to cause disturbance and fear (Job 4:13).

5. Not only do demons give people thoughts during their waking hours, they can do the same thing at night while they are sleeping (Job 4:13).

6. The thoughts they give can cause dread, great fear, or terror. Where does fear or terror register? It registers in the emotions. When a demon puts his thoughts into a person's mind, the demon triggers or manipulates the victim's emotions. The person will, at times, feel just like the demon wants him to feel, and may even tremble physically (Job 4:14).

7. A person may physically respond to the presence of the demon; the hair may bristle on a person's arm or on the back of his neck (Job 4:15).

8. The thoughts they give a person are generally lies. Their purpose for lying is to cause the person to doubt God in some way. When we doubt God, we begin to trust in something else. At that time we become rebellious and disobedient to God (Job 4:17).

9. Demons may even impart some particular truth if it serves their purpose in adding weight to their deceptions (Job 4:18).

Since demons emulate their leader, they can also tell the truth when it is to their advantage.

Part 2: Saul

Another Old Testament example of how Satan schemes can be found in 1 Samuel Chapter 16.

16:14   Now the Spirit of the LORD departed from Saul, and an evil spirit from the LORD terrorized him.

If God's Spirit left Saul and an evil spirit from God terrorized him, we need to find out why that occurred.[17]

Samuel's Instructions: Saul's Response

Saul had been made king. Samuel, a prophet of the LORD, had informed Saul that God was going to punish Amalek for what he had done to Israel. Samuel then instructed Saul to fight against Amalek and destroy everything he had: men, women, children, oxen, sheep, camels, and donkeys.

Saul had begun doing what Samuel had instructed him to do: fight against the Amalekites. According to 1 Samuel 15, however, Saul had not completely followed Samuel's instructions.

15:8   And he captured Agag the king of the Amalekites alive, and utterly destroyed all the people with the edge of the sword.

15:9   But Saul and the people spared Agag and the best of the sheep, the oxen, the fatlings, the lambs, and all that was good, and were not willing to destroy them utterly; but everything despised and worthless, that they utterly destroyed.

Saul had gone to war against Amalek. He had defeated the Amalekites and destroyed all the people with one exception: he had captured their king, Agag. Saul and his people, however, had kept the best of the sheep, the oxen, the fatlings, and the best of the lambs. They kept all that was good.

1 Samuel 15 tells us what God thought of Saul's "obedience."

15:10   Then the word of the Lord came to Samuel saying,

15:11   "I regret that I have made Saul king, for he has turned back from following Me, and has not carried out My commands."

When Samuel heard what God said, he was brokenhearted; the next day he set out to find Saul. When they met, Saul told Samuel he had carried out the word of the Lord. But Samuel responded by saying,

15:14   "What then is this bleating of the sheep in my ears, and the lowing of the oxen which I hear?"

In essence Samuel was saying, "Well, if you have done such a good job of following God's command to wipe out the Amalekites and all their possessions, why is it I hear sheep bleating and oxen lowing?" Notice Saul's response in verse 15.

15:15   And Saul said, "They have brought them from the Amalekites, for the people spared the best of the sheep and oxen, to sacrifice to the LORD your God; but the rest we have utterly destroyed."

Isn't it interesting that Saul said, "*They* have brought . . ." He did not include himself in this statement. They—the others—have brought them from the Amalekites; *the people* spared the best of the sheep and oxen. Then, as though to impress Samuel and God, Saul said, "The people spared the best of the sheep and oxen in order to sacrifice them to the LORD your God." Then Saul added, "But the rest *we* have utterly destroyed." Here Saul included himself, because he wanted Samuel to see how obedient *he* was to the Lord's command.

Samuel was apparently unimpressed with what he'd heard; in verse 16 he said to Saul, "Wait, and let me tell you what the LORD said to me last night."

Can't you imagine Saul thinking, "Wow, I haven't been king very long! God has already sent me on a mission, and I have followed His instructions. Now His servant, Samuel, is going to tell me all my rewards because I did this for God!"

Then Samuel said,

15:17   "Is it not true, though you were little in your own eyes, you were made the head of the tribes of Israel? And the LORD anointed you king over Israel,

15:18   and the LORD sent you on a mission, and said, 'Go and utterly destroy the sinners, the Amalekites, and fight against them until they are exterminated."

Surely as Saul listened to Samuel he felt very good, at least until Samuel spoke again. One can almost imagine Saul's blood running cold in his veins as Samuel continued,

15:19   "Why then did you not obey the voice of the LORD, but rushed upon the spoil and did what was evil in the sight of the LORD?"

15:22   "Has the LORD as much delight in burnt offerings and sacrifices as in obeying the voice of the LORD? Behold, to obey is better than sacrifice, and to heed than the fat of rams.

15:23   "For rebellion is as the sin of divination, and insubordination is as iniquity and idolatry. Because you have rejected the word of the LORD, He has also rejected you from being king."

It's clear from this that when God tells us to do something, He expects us to obey; to do exactly what He said. He does not expect us to deviate from His truth or instruction in any way. If we are only partially obedient, we are in rebellion against God!

God Sends an Evil Spirit

We are told in 1 Samuel 16:14 that the Spirit of the LORD had departed from Saul, and that an evil spirit from the LORD terrorized him. The reason the Spirit of the Lord departed from Saul was because of his partial obedience to God. We are also told that an evil spirit terrorized Saul. When terrorized, a person becomes extremely fearful.

Although King Saul had an entire army at his disposal to protect him, he was still terrorized by only one demon. We can be oppressed even in the presence of God's army, the church. The reason? It was not the job of Saul's army—neither is it the job of the church to deal with our oppression. That is our own personal responsibility. In Chapter 9 we will study how to do this in more detail so we may be better equipped.

Now let's consider Saul's servants' observations.

16:15   Saul's servants then said to him, "Behold now, an evil spirit from God is terrorizing you.

16:16   "Let our lord now command your servants who are before you. Let them seek a man who is a skillful player on the harp; and it shall come about when the evil spirit from God is on you, that he shall play the harp with his hand, and you will be well."

When Saul's servants said, "You will be well," they indicated that while the harp was played, Saul would not be terrorized. The harp music would make that demon leave. Verse 23 says,

16:23   So it came about whenever the evil spirit from God came to Saul, David would take the harp and play it with his hand; and Saul would be refreshed and be well, and the evil spirit would depart from him.

Demons and Flesh Work Together

The servants' system was true; but like all men's ways, it didn't work every time. Consider what we are told in 1 Samuel 18.

18:10   Now it came about on the next day that an evil spirit from God came mightily upon Saul, and he raved in the midst of the house, while David was playing the harp with his hand, as usual; and a spear was in Saul's hand.

18:11   And Saul hurled the spear for he thought, "I will pin David to the wall." But David escaped from his presence twice.

18:12   Now Saul was afraid of David, for the LORD was with him but had departed from Saul.

18:15   When Saul saw that he was prospering greatly, he dreaded him.

Verse 10 says, "Now it came about on the next day . . ." If something is to happen tomorrow because of something happening today, we need to discover what happened today that produces tomorrow's event. In Chapter 18, verses 5–9, we see David had gone wherever Saul had sent him and had prospered. We also see that Saul had put David in authority over his army. When David had returned from killing the Philistines, the women had come out of the cities of Israel, singing and dancing, to meet King Saul. They had met him with tambourines, with joy and with musical instruments. While singing and playing they harmonized, "Saul has slain his thousands . . ." Don't you imagine King Saul was very pleased with himself and quite proud of his accomplishments when he heard that? However, the women continued their singing, " . . . and David his ten thousands." David was now out-shining Saul, just as he had done in his youth when he stood alone against the giant, Goliath, before Saul's frightened army. How did Saul respond?

18:8   Then Saul became very angry, for this saying displeased him; and he said, "They have ascribed to David ten thousands, but to me they have ascribed thousands. Now what more can he have but the kingdom?"

18:9   And Saul looked at David with suspicion from that day on.

Verse 8 tells how Saul had become very angry after the women sang about David slaying his ten thousands. There is no mention made of Saul's repenting of that anger.

Operating After the Flesh Gives a Demon an Opportunity

Galatians Chapter 5 gives important information for us on God's way to avoid Saul's problem.

5:16   But I say, walk by the Spirit, and you will not carry out the desire of the flesh.

5:17   For the flesh sets its desire against the Spirit, and the Spirit against the flesh; for these are in opposition to one another, so that you may not do the things that you please.

5:19   Now the deeds of the flesh are evident, which are: immorality, impurity, sensuality,

5:20   idolatry, sorcery, enmities, strife, jealousy, outbursts of anger, disputes, dissensions, factions,

5:21   envying, drunkenness, carousing, and things like these.

There is a principle disclosed in these verses. Look at Ephesians Chapter 4.

4:26   Be angry, and yet do not sin; do not let the sun go down on your anger,

4:27   and do not give the devil an opportunity.

The word *opportunity* in the Greek means "a place, a spot or location." When we give a demon an opportunity, we are providing him with a dwelling place. We are giving him space in our territory! I like to think of it as "giving ground to the enemy." Hebrews 12:14, 15 say,

12:14   Pursue peace with all men, and the sanctification without which no one will see the Lord.

12:15   See to it that no one comes short of the grace of God; that no root of bitterness springing up causes trouble, and by it many be defiled;

A root of bitterness will spring forth from ground given because of improper responses to others.

Have we ever known anyone who has been angry with their spouse without settling the issue before nightfall? Are we aware of what happens in the spiritual realm when a person goes to bed angry and lets the sun go down on his anger?

The Scripture plainly teaches that if we allow this to happen, we give the devil an opportunity. We give him ground; we give him a spot from which to work. We give him a location or a place from which to build a stronghold. What is the principle involved? Not dealing with our anger gives a demon the legal right or authority to afflict or oppress us. That is a serious thought that Christians need to spend some serious time pondering.

1 Samuel Chapter 18 continues:

18:10 "Now it came about on the next day that an evil spirit from God came mightily upon Saul, and he raved in the midst of the house, while David was playing the harp with his hand, as usual; and a spear was in Saul's hand.

18:11 And Saul hurled the spear for he thought, 'I will pin David to the wall.' But David escaped from his presence twice."

We see that while David was playing the harp, Saul raved. While he raved, he had a spear in his hand which he hurled at David because of a "thought." Was this just Saul's thinking, or was he influenced by a demon? Scripture informs us in 1 Samuel 18:10 that "an evil spirit from God came mightily upon Saul, and he raved." Therefore, we *know* he was being influenced by a demon. This demon was putting thoughts into Saul's mind and manipulating his emotions. Saul then exercised his will in agreement with what the demon was saying: "and Saul hurled the spear for he thought, I will pin David to the wall." The word *pin* means "to strike, to kill, to slaughter, to murder, to slay, or to wound." When Saul sought to pin David to the wall, he was not playing the game *Pin the Tail on the Donkey*. He intended to kill David. Why was Saul no longer relieved from the demonic oppression as David played the harp? How was the demon able to drive him to such hatred that he desired to murder the one person who brought him national victories and personal comfort? This will be easier to understand as we look at the make-up of man.

The Make-up of Man

1 Thessalonians 5:23 tells us that man is made up of three parts: the spirit, the soul, and the body. Watchman Nee gives an excellent description of those parts and their various functions. The spirit has the functions of intuition, conscience, and communion; the soul carries the functions of the mind, emotions, and will. The body is the physical container in which these function.[18]

Here is what most likely happened to Saul: a demon had come mightily upon Saul and put thoughts into his mind. The demon then manipulated Saul's emotions. The demon continued by suggesting a response;

Saul chose to act in agreement with the demon rather than choosing the ways of God.

Just because a person gets a demonic thought in his mind and a demonic feeling in his emotions does not mean the person has sinned. The power of sin has continually waged war with our soul and won many skirmishes, developing strong desires of self-gratification and self-protection. Any time we accept a thought or response which is not in agreement with God's truth and ways, these strongholds of sin are built within our soul. Action is not necessary to establish sin. Putting demonic or worldly thoughts and emotions into action, however, accomplishes the enemy's scheme, and destruction is always his purpose.

When a person flips back and forth, trying to choose God's truth while yet hanging on to demonic lies and the world's deceptions, he becomes double-minded. A double-minded man has set himself up for strong oppression and is an easy target. The believer must choose to take his thoughts captive to the obedience of Christ.

The enemy knows terror affects our emotions and our thought processes. In counseling, I often find people in an emotional state of extreme fright. Many times a demon has either triggered these emotions or has expressed himself by utilizing the person's emotions. They think it is their own emotion they are not handling well, and can't figure out why they can't effectively deal with how they feel. They are terrorized because the demons have deceived them and exercised power over them by placing thoughts into their mind. When a person gets a thought in his mind, it's very easy for that person to think he produced the thought. Then when the demon adds or manipulates feelings, the person is sure he's condemned, and is easily convinced he is just a wicked person and God could never love such a scoundrel, etc., etc.

This type of demonic activity can be very subtle. Very often a person is not aware that the source of the thought is demonic and not from himself. If he doesn't learn how to take those thoughts—and the source of the thoughts—captive, he may be in for a very rough time spiritually.

1 Samuel 18:12 tells us that Saul was afraid of David because the LORD was with him but had departed from Saul. The demon had incited suspicion of David but the young hero had escaped Saul's anger twice.

"Now Saul was afraid." Once the demon had gained a foothold, Saul became fearful. Any time a demon gains a foothold in a person's life, some kind of fear can usually be found as strong evidence.

Verse 15 tells us that Saul saw David prospering greatly and dreaded him. To *dread* means "to be in extreme apprehension; great fear." When a person is fearful, he gathers together his defenses. Saul had already been told by Samuel that God had rejected him as king because of his rebellion. He knew he was on the way out. He saw that God's hand was on David and he needed to regroup in order to hang onto power as long as possible.

How Demons Place Their Thoughts

I met a man one Sunday morning in a large Sunday School class I was attending with my wife. In our greeting we shook hands, but never had any other association other than an occasional salutation on Sunday mornings.

Several years later, this man sensed a call on his life to enter the ministry. Before he left town to enter seminary, he called me and scheduled an appointment. He had heard I had some knowledge and experience dealing with demonic issues. He thought that once he became a pastor there was a slight possibility he might encounter someone during his ministry that could be affected by a demonic spirit. He came to see me in order to learn a little more about how demons work. As we interacted, we discovered there were demonic spirits influencing him. Then he revealed something I found quite interesting.

He said, "When we met that first Sunday morning and shook hands, something told me not to come close to you. My thoughts warned me to avoid you. Now I know what that was. At the time, I thought it was probably God's Spirit speaking to me. I know now that the information which came into my mind was not from the Holy Spirit. That information was from a demonic spirit that saw the Lord Jesus Christ in you and knew of your ministry. That tormenting spirit knew that if I had much association with you, the chances of the demon being exposed would be much greater. Therefore, he warned me to avoid you."

A Spiritual Process

As we have looked at 1 Samuel, we see there is a process at work. Saul had rebelled against God by not obeying what He had told him through Samuel. As a result, God rejected Saul as king. We saw that God had sent a demon to Saul. Though He sent it and allowed it to terrorize him, He also provided a way for Saul to get rid of this demon. That way was for Saul to repent and confess his sins of rebellion and anger.

How does this apply to believers today? 1 Corinthians 10 tells us that . . .

10:13   No temptation has overtaken you but such as is common to man; and God is faithful, who will not allow you to be tempted beyond what you are able, but with the temptation will provide the way of escape also, that you may be able to endure it.

Although there are demons trying to find a way to oppress us, God has provided a way of escape. Therefore, we don't need to be apprehensive about demons. Yes, they definitely are around, but God has given us a way to deal with them effectively so that they will have to leave our presence when appropriately commanded. James tells us that we are to submit ourselves to God. Then, when we resist the devil, he will flee from us. In Chapter 9 we will study in more detail about submitting to God and resisting the devil and his cohorts. We need to clearly understand our part in resisting the devil if we expect him to obediently flee from us.

We can easily recognize that man's flesh is ineffective against spiritual enemies. Saul's anger gave the demon immunity from the harp music. Man's system of ridding his problems is often as effective as aspirin for a headache. The pain may go away, but the cause is still there. This demon had built a stronghold in Saul's life. He had legally gained ground and exercised power over Saul. Bear in mind that the demon's legal right was given by Saul himself; he had never repented. He just tried to justify his actions.

The same is true for each of us. In our own life, we are the one that gives the demon the legal right, or ground, to oppress us.[19]

Saul's time as being king over God's people was soon to end. Saul pursued David and persisted in trying to kill him until just before his own death. God did not talk to Saul during his time of rebellion. When Saul sensed a need for counsel, he consulted a medium. Afterward, when Saul was in battle against the Philistines and badly wounded, he realized that he could not get away without being captured and losing face completely; he fell on his own sword and died rather than turning to God.

Scriptural Warning

There is a warning in these Scriptures. We must deal with our flesh and our anger before it settles into vulnerable ground yielded to the enemy. We must not give the devil or demons any opportunity to oppress us.

Review: How Satan and Demons Scheme
Old Testament

1. Demons gain authority to oppress a person because of their rebellion against God (1 Samuel 15:1–23).

2. Demons can approach a believer under the authority or direction of God (1 Samuel 16:14).

3. Demons can terrorize an individual (1 Samuel 16:15).

4. Even when we are obedient, demons don't vanish forever—they wait in the sidelines for an opportunity (or ground) to be yielded. Once that ground is given to them, they may come mightily upon a person in order to oppress (1 Samuel 16:23–18:10).

5. Demons gain ground to oppress when we operate after the flesh (1 Samuel 18:8–10).

6. Demons counterfeit the work of God. Compare Saul under the influence of the Holy Spirit (1 Samuel 10:10) with Saul under the influence of an evil spirit (1 Samuel 18:10).

7. Demons attempt to get us to break our vows to God (1 Samuel 19:6, 9, 11).

8. When demons oppress an individual, those who are around them may become a demonic target for destruction (1 Samuel 19:9, 10).

9. Demons work in conjunction with the flesh. Once their overtures are accepted, the flesh is programmed; a stronghold system comprised of thoughts and responses is then developed and cultivated (1 Samuel 20:30).

10. Demons find easy ground when anger is not dealt with quickly (Ephesians 4:26, 27).

11. Though man's plans may occasionally seem to ward off demonic attack, their effectiveness is partial and temporary at best (1 Samuel 16:23 & 18:10, 11).

It is not the job of the church to deal with our oppression—that is our personal responsibility.

Part 3: David

We can see another of Satan's schemes in 1 Chronicles Chapter 21.

21:1 Then Satan stood up against Israel and moved David to number Israel.

21:2 So David said to Joab and to the princes of the people, "Go, number Israel from Beersheba even to Dan, and bring me word that I may know their number."

21:3 And Joab said, "May the LORD add to His people a hundred times as many as they are! But, my lord the king, are they not all my lord's servants? Why does my lord seek this thing? Why should he be a cause of guilt to Israel?"

21:4 Nevertheless, the king's word prevailed against Joab. Therefore, Joab departed and went throughout all Israel, and came to Jerusalem.

21:5 And Joab gave the number of the census of all the people to David. And all Israel were 1,100,000 men who drew the sword; and Judah was 470,000 men who drew the sword.

21:6 But he did not number Levi and Benjamin among them, for the king's command was abhorrent to Joab.

21:7 And God was displeased with this thing, so He struck Israel.

21:8 And David said to God, "I have sinned greatly, in that I have done this thing. But now, please take away the iniquity of Thy servant, for I have done very foolishly."

Verse 1 says, "Then Satan stood up against Israel . . ." Remember, Israel is God's chosen people. We, too, are God's chosen people, and Satan stands the same way against us today. "Then Satan stood up against Israel and moved David to number Israel." The word *moved* means "to provoke, to stimulate, to bring out of inactivity, to persuade, and to entice." Satan enticed David to number Israel; he wanted David to find out how many soldiers he had in his army. What was so wrong with David numbering Israel? He was king. He answered to no other man. Why shouldn't he know how many soldiers he had in his army?

The book of Isaiah, Chapter 31, will help us answer these questions.

31:1   Woe to those who go down to Egypt for help, and rely on horses, and trust in chariots because they are many, and in horsemen because they are very strong, but they do not look to the Holy One of Israel, nor seek the LORD!

What was David's sin? Did Satan's provocation reveal pride and David's reliance on the number of warriors, horses, chariots, and horsemen he had instead of delighting and trusting in God's protection of his kingdom? What had happened to the simple young man of faith who had defeated Goliath with a stone and a slingshot? He had become a statistic of a satanic plot.

Satan wants the same for us. He wants us to learn to delight and trust in our paycheck, our church, our spouse, our job, our marriage, our expertise, our natural ability, or in our accrued savings. It doesn't matter what we idolize. From the enemy's standpoint, anything will work as long as we do not trust in God. Something had happened to David; he had begun looking to numbers rather than God.

Verse 2 tells us that David spoke to Joab and to the princes of the people saying, "Go number Israel from Beersheba even to Dan, and bring me word that I may know their number." Satan may have accomplished this move by either suggesting a good idea that appealed to David's pride—pride in all the victorious battles with extraordinary enemies—or by provoking some fear deep within him. Fear, perhaps, that his army might not be able to win over the next enemy. The previous chapter in Chronicles talks about a giant of great stature with six-fingered hands and feet with six toes. Did he fear finding greater enemies? Regardless of the strategy Satan used, David exercised his will in favor of what Satan wanted him to do.

In verse 3, Joab makes this comment: "May the LORD add to His people a hundred times as many as they are! But, my lord the king, are they not all my lord's servants? Why does my lord seek this thing? Why should he be a cause of guilt to Israel?"

Joab was trying to talk David out of numbering Israel. Verse 4 shows us Satan's ability to convince. "Nevertheless, the king's word prevailed against Joab." Joab's advice was spiritually sound, but David would not listen. Bear in mind that Joab was not some fly-by-night character who was trying to sell David a used chariot. Joab was David's commander-in-chief. Even so, David listened to what Satan had planted in his mind, choosing to ignore the advice of his five-star General.

Verses 5 and 6 tell us that Joab obeyed David and took the census. Verses 7 and 8 tell us that God was displeased and struck Israel. David responded with repentance and said to God, "I have sinned greatly in that I have done this thing." David became aware that he had fallen into sin; he had been listening to Satan instead of trusting in God. "But now, please take away the iniquity of Thy servant, for I have done very foolishly." The word *iniquity* refers to one's natural propensity to sin through a deceived system of flesh. David was confessing and acknowledged his wrongdoing.

God's Discipline

Now let's look a little deeper into 1 Chronicles Chapter 21.

21:9   And the LORD spoke to Gad, David's seer, saying,

21:10   "Go and speak to David, saying, 'Thus says the LORD, "I offer you three things; choose for yourself one of them, that I may do it to you."

21:11   So Gad came to David and said to him, "Thus says the LORD, 'Take for yourself

21:12   either three years of famine, or three months to be swept away before your foes, while the sword of your enemies overtakes you, or else three days of the sword of the LORD, even pestilence in the land, and the angel of the LORD destroying throughout all the territory of Israel.' Now, therefore, consider what answer I shall return to Him who sent me."

21:13　And David said to Gad, "I am in great distress; please let me fall into the hand of the LORD, for His mercies are very great. But do not let me fall into the hand of man."

21:14　So the LORD sent a pestilence on Israel; 70,000 men of Israel fell.

It took David about ten months to recognize his sin.[20] David had been trusting in his 1,570,000 men and lost a part of the focus of his faith: 70,000 lives. The Lord was not only dealing with a wrong focus in David, He was also angry with Israel, who bore the brunt of His discipline. If we are trusting in things, God may take a percentage of what we are trusting in. He shows us the total absurdity of trusting in such unreliable resources in the first place.

Sometimes God's discipline seems very harsh—and perhaps at times it is. God teaches believers to trust Him and to obey Him. We take our need to be obedient to God too lightly. We cannot be disobedient to God and expect to have His full protection. When a person is disobedient to God, His hedge of protection is lowered from around the person, which allows the enemy to get to him. When that hedge is down, demons will come to oppress that person and will do as much damage as they are allowed to do. Demons will put thoughts into a person's mind, and manipulate the person's emotions. They will attack every area in which the will is weak. Once the enemy has gained ground, he will start building a stronghold. As he builds thought patterns and systems of incorrect responses, that demon can literally destroy him, according to John 10:10, if he does not take his thoughts captive to the obedience of Christ. Thankfully, we have been given the weapons of warfare needed to accomplish that task.

A grizzly bear will not usually attack unless you are in his territory, threatening its young, or its lunch. But Satan is the god of this world, and we *are* in his territory. God's people are prime targets for his attacks. We cannot presume upon God to protect us when we allow areas of sin to remain in our lives. If we do not take precautions, we may become a spiritual statistic.

Remember what we are told in Hebrews Chapter 12?

12:5 "My son, do not regard lightly the discipline of the LORD, nor faint when you are reproved by Him;

12:6 for those whom the LORD loves He disciplines, and He scourges every son whom He receives."

12:7 It is for discipline that you endure; God deals with you as with sons; for what son is there whom his father does not discipline?

12:8 But if you are without discipline, of which all have become partakers, then you are illegitimate children and not sons.

12:9 Furthermore, we had earthly fathers to discipline us, and we respected them; shall we not much rather be subject to the Father of spirits, and live?

12:10 For they disciplined us for a short time as seemed best to them, but He disciplines us for our good, that we may share His holiness.

12:11 All discipline for the moment seems not to be joyful, but sorrowful; yet to those who have been trained by it, afterwards it yields the peaceful fruit of righteousness.

Before we were born again, Satan and his hosts had a field day with us. But once we become a child of God, He will discipline us when we are disobedient. The word *discipline* means "the whole training and education of children which relates to the cultivation of mind and morals, and employs for this purpose now commands and admonitions, now reproof and punishment."[21] Satan wants to tempt us to sin. God knows the areas in our souls that need to be transformed in order for us to better image Christ. Satan tries to discourage us and get us mad at God. Then we will find it even harder to trust and believe in Him and may revert to the ways the enemy suggests. If Satan or demons can accomplish that in our lives, they know God cannot use us as effectively as He wants and has planned. It will also remove the threat of our tearing down the works of the kingdom of darkness in some way. God will then have to raise up someone else, and that will give the enemy more time to steal, kill, and destroy.

Review: How Satan and Demons Scheme
Old Testament

1.   Satan is goal oriented. He is not distracted and never forgets his purpose. He is very aggressive in looking for ways to implement his ill-favored goal in our lives (1 Chronicles 21:1).

2.   Satan attempts to persuade us to do what he suggests. He tries to stimulate us to action on his behalf (1 Chronicles 21:1).

3.   Satan is so convincing that advice from qualified counselors can fall on deaf ears (1 Chronicles 21:4).

4.   Satan knows that if we accept his lies, God will discipline us (1 Chronicles 21:9–14). During the chastening, Satan will be right there prompting us to distrust God and to become angry with Him.

We cannot presume upon God to protect us
if we allow areas of sin to remain in our lives.

Part 4: Ahab

Once there was a man named Naboth who owned a vineyard. Naboth's vineyard was beside the palace of King Ahab, who wanted the vineyard for a vegetable garden. When King Ahab talked to Naboth about purchasing or trading vineyards, Naboth refused to negotiate because he had inherited the property from his ancestors.

When Naboth turned King Ahab down, the king became depressed. He went to bed, faced the wall, and refused to eat. His wife, Jezebel, noticed he was despondent and questioned him concerning the matter. He then related to her what had happened during his conversation with Naboth.

When Jezebel heard Ahab's story, she reminded him that he was the king and that he should get up, eat, and snap out of his depression. Jezebel promptly informed King Ahab she was going to get Naboth's vineyard for him. She then wrote letters to the elders and nobles that lived in the city in which Naboth lived. In those letters she told them to proclaim a fast and to have Naboth attend. They were instructed to seat two worthless men near him and have them openly accuse Naboth of cursing God and the king; afterward, they were to take Naboth and stone him to death. Jezebel then sealed the letters with the king's personal seal.

The elders and nobles read their mail and did exactly as the wicked Jezebel had ordered. After complying with the queen's instructions, they sent word telling her that Naboth was dead.

When Jezebel received the news, she relayed the message to King Ahab. Once the king knew Naboth was dead, he took his queen's advice and took possession of Naboth's vineyard.

God, however, was not unaware of what had transpired. Therefore, He called upon Elijah to give King Ahab the message we find in 1 Kings 21.

21:17 Then the word of the LORD came to Elijah the Tishbite, saying,

21:18 "Arise, go down to meet Ahab king of Israel, who is in Samaria; behold, he is in the vineyard of Naboth where he has gone down to take possession of it.

21:19 "And you shall speak to him, saying, 'Thus says the LORD, "Have you murdered, and also taken possession?"' And you shall speak to him, saying, 'Thus says the LORD, "In the place where the dogs licked up the blood of Naboth the dogs shall lick up your blood, even yours."'"

God's Judgment

Peace followed Elijah's prophecy for three years in Israel. During the third year, King Jehoshaphat from Judah visited with King Ahab. King Ahab reminded his servants that Ramoth-gilead belonged to Israel and asked King Jehoshaphat if he would be willing to help his people get the city back. The visiting king made one requirement: before they did anything, he wanted King Ahab to make an inquiry as to what God might have to say about their upcoming plans.

Therefore, King Ahab gathered about four hundred of his prophets and asked their advice about engaging Ramoth-gilead in battle. They all gave a resounding "yea" to the king's question and assured him the Lord would ensure Ahab's victory.

Apparently King Jehoshaphat was not as convinced by their message as was King Ahab. The king of Judah was interested in questioning a different prophet of the LORD. Ahab recalled one prophet who could inquire of the Lord, but he hated the man. Ahab's aversion toward this prophet, Micaiah, was based on the fact that he never gave the king any good prophesies. But King Jehoshaphat insisted that Micaiah get involved in the decision, so Ahab sent for him.

The two kings sat on their thrones dressed in their royal robes and waited for Micaiah to arrive on the scene. In the intervening time, Ahab's prophets were busily predicting that the Syrians were going to be consumed and that the Lord would make the king prosperous.

At the same time, Ahab's messenger talked to Micaiah and asked him to prophesy favorably toward King Ahab, as all the other prophets had done. Micaiah was not moved by the messenger's request; he would tell it like it was. He would speak only what God wanted the king to hear.

When Micaiah came to the king, Ahab asked him whether they should go up and fight against Ramoth-gilead. Micaiah painted a verbal picture of all Israel being scattered in the mountains like a bunch of sheep without a shepherd; since there was no master, they could all return home. Micaiah was indirectly saying that Ahab would be killed and his army scattered.[22]

In essence, King Ahab then looked at King Jehoshaphat and said, "I told you so! This guy never prophesies any good concerning me; his prophesies are always evil!"

But Micaiah was not finished. There was more to the message for Ahab. Look at what he had to say and observe how the king and another of the king's prophets, Zedekiah, respond to what they hear. It's recorded in 1 Kings Chapter 22:

22:19 And Micaiah said, "Therefore, hear the word of the LORD. I saw the LORD sitting on His throne, and all the host of heaven standing by Him on His right and on His left.

22:20 "And the LORD said, 'Who will entice Ahab to go up and fall at Ramoth-gilead?' And one said this while another said that.

22:21 "Then a spirit came forward and stood before the LORD and said, 'I will entice him.'

22:22 "And the LORD said to him, 'How?' And he said, 'I will go out and be a deceiving spirit in the mouth of all his prophets.' Then He said, 'You are to entice him and also prevail. Go and do so.'

22:23 "Now therefore, behold, the LORD has put a deceiving spirit in the mouth of all these your prophets; and the LORD has proclaimed disaster against you."

22:24   Then Zedekiah the son of Chenaanah came near and struck Micaiah on the cheek and said, "How did the Spirit of the LORD pass from me to speak to you?"

22:26   Then the king of Israel said, "Take Micaiah and return him to Amon the governor of the city and to Joash the king's son;

22:27   and say, 'Thus says the king, "Put this man in prison, and feed him sparingly with bread and water until I return safely."

In verse 20 we read, "Who will *entice* Ahab to go?" The King James Version uses the word "persuade." The Hebrew word means "to open up one's mind as a child, to delude or mislead the mind; to deceive." This verse could be read: "Who will go to delude and deceive King Ahab? Who will open up his mind, and mislead him away from the truth? Who will persuade him to go into battle against Ramoth-gilead so that he will fall wounded and die?"

Does that question sound harsh? Yet look at who asked the question: it was the LORD who sought a deceiver for Ahab!

Notice something else. The passage states a spirit volunteered to be a lying spirit in the prophets' mouths. It is interesting to note that Zedekiah described it as "the Spirit of the Lord."

We have seen in the previous studies of this chapter how the Lord had been in authority over Satan's attack on Job, and He ordered an evil spirit's oppression of Saul. He also instigated Satan's provocation of David.[23] Again we see a sovereign God using a spirit-messenger to accomplish His will. He is righteous and does not tempt anyone to sin. However, He knows the ground within each soul that is vulnerable to the enemy. In order to accomplish His justice with all people and to conform believers to the image they were created to reflect, He uses messengers from the spirit realm to do whatever is necessary to achieve His purpose. All creatures in heaven or on earth, whether belonging to the kingdom of darkness or the kingdom of light are, in the final analysis, under His authority to accomplish His will.

The newly-commissioned spirit set off toward Ahab's prophets with the intention and God-given mission to purposely delude the king's mind. Demons utilize the same approach today. They come to a person with their nefarious intent, but with the qualified permission of God. Their intention is to open one's mind to their delusion, misleading that person's mind away from the truth of God. God's higher intention, however, works for the good of the believer.

In verse 22 the spirit revealed how he would accomplish God's mission: he would go to Ahab's prophets and deceive them. In this way Ahab would believe his prophets, act on their faulty advice, and be killed. But why would God want a spirit to go on such a mission? God remembered what Ahab had done to Naboth. Though Ahab had not done anything directly against the land owner, he knew Jezebel purposed to obtain Naboth's garden property for him. By not stopping her, he affirmed her actions, was a part of the whole thing, and gladly received the spoil. Through Elijah, God told Ahab that he had sold himself to do evil in the sight of the Lord; he had also provoked the Lord to anger because he had made Israel sin (1 Kings 21:20, 22).

In verse 23 Micaiah told King Ahab that God had put a deceiving spirit in the mouth of his prophets, and that He had proclaimed disaster against him. It is interesting to note in verse 24 that Zedekiah—one of Ahab's leading prophets—struck Micaiah on the cheek and said, "How did the Spirit of the LORD pass from me to speak to you?"

God had put this deceiving spirit in the mouth of all Ahab's prophets, including Zedekiah. So Zedekiah had a deceiving spirit speaking through him, but he thought it was the Spirit of the Lord. Since Zedekiah thought this, he must have thought that the Spirit of the Lord could not have been speaking through Micaiah. Although Zedekiah was the deceived one, he thought Micaiah was deceived. Isn't it interesting—the one who is deceived doesn't know it and accuses another of deception!

Then Zedekiah displayed his sentiment: he walked up and hit Micaiah in the face. Don't you suspect he did it in anger—a self-righteous indignation?

The fact that Zedekiah and all the other prophets of Ahab could be deceived should convince us that demonic forces are extremely crafty and effective in their deceptions.

How did King Ahab respond to Micaiah's prophesy? He had him thrown in jail! Verse 27, loosely translated, tells us he gave Micaiah a private room with a high carbohydrate, low-calorie diet.

Was the spirit that had been sent by God effective in enticing Ahab? The next few verses of 1 Kings 22 give the answer.

22:28   And Micaiah said, "If you indeed return safely the LORD has not spoken by me" And he said, "Listen, all you people."

22:29   So the king of Israel and Jehoshaphat king of Judah went up against Ramoth-gilead.

22:30   And the king of Israel said to Jehoshaphat, "I will disguise myself and go into the battle, but you put on your robes." So the king of Israel disguised himself and went into the battle.

22:34   Now a certain man drew his bow at random and struck the king of Israel in a joint of the armor. So he said to the driver of his chariot, "Turn around, and take me out of the fight; for I am severely wounded."

22:37   So the king died and was brought to Samaria, and they buried the king in Samaria.

22:38   And they washed the chariot by the pool of Samaria, and the dogs licked up his blood . . . according to the word of the LORD which He spoke.[24]

God's Use of Demonic Forces

This story shows very clearly that God sometimes uses demons as agents of discipline. The Apostle Paul had no problem believing God used Satan and his kingdom to discipline those who had gone astray. Read what Paul said in his first letter to Timothy.

1:18   This command I entrust to you, Timothy, my son, in accordance with the prophesies previously made concerning you, that by them you may fight the good fight,

1:19   keeping faith and a good conscience, which some have rejected and suffered shipwreck in regard to their faith.

1:20   Among these are Hymenaeus and Alexander, whom I have delivered over to Satan, so that they may be taught not to blaspheme.

Paul directed Timothy to fight the good fight, to keep faith, and a good conscience. He also told Timothy that there were two people who had not followed that advice and, as a result, their faith had been ship-wrecked. Because these two had not held fast in faith or conscience, Paul had delivered them over to Satan. His purpose was that they might learn not to treat God or His word with contempt.

God will send demons to rebellious believers today with the purpose of getting them back on track with Him. It is one way He disciplines His children. Because He loves them, He aspires to correct their wayward path and direct them into His ways of righteousness.

Review: How Satan and Demons Scheme
Old Testament

1. Demons understand and submit to the Lordship of God. All the host of heaven stood before Him on His throne (1 Kings 22:19).

2. Demons still answer to God and listen when He speaks (1 Kings 22:20).

3. Demons comply and help bring about the wishes of God (1 Kings 22:20, 21).

4. Demons are deceptive and try to entice us to believe their lies (1 Kings 22:21, 22).

5. Demons obey God and operate under His limitations (1 Kings 22:22).

6. Demons are sometimes used to execute God's discipline (1 Kings 22:23).

7. Demons deceive so thoroughly, the oppressed do not recognize the deception. (1 Kings 22:24).

Why do I go mourning because of the oppression of the enemy?

Psalm 42:9

Chapter 4

How Satan and Demons Scheme: New Testament

Part 1: Peter

As Jesus spoke to His disciples, He asked them who people thought He, the Son of Man, really was. They reported that some thought He was John the Baptist; some thought He was Elijah. Still others believed He was Jeremiah, or one of the prophets. Then Jesus asked the same question of His disciples. He wanted to know who they thought He was. It was Simon Peter who answered by saying, "Thou art the Christ, the Son of the living God" (Matthew 16:16).

Matthew reports on Jesus' response in the next verse:

16:17 "Blessed are you, Simon Barjona, because flesh and blood did not reveal this to you, but my Father who is in heaven."

Jesus told Peter he was blessed because he had not received his information from flesh and blood, but from God. Flesh and blood can refer to your brain, or to another person. Jesus was saying that Peter had not gotten his information from his own reasoning power, nor had he received it from his neighbor. Simon Peter had received it from the God of the universe.

Then Jesus said something very interesting in verse 18: "You are Peter . . ." In the Greek language, the word for Peter is *Petros* which means "a detached stone; a stone that might be thrown or easily moved." When we—as a detached stone—lean unto our own understanding and use what we have received from flesh and blood, we can be thrown, easily moved, or persuaded.

Jesus continued by saying, " . . . and upon this rock . . ." The Greek word for rock is *petra* which means "a large rock; bedrock." In other words, *petra* is a solid foundation. Was Jesus saying that Peter was a large, solid foundation? That seems very unlikely because in just five verses down the road, the Son of God informed Peter he was a stumbling block!

Jesus told Peter that he was Petros—a detached stone that might be thrown or easily moved. Then He said, "Upon this petra—upon this large bedrock or upon this solid foundation—I will build My church." What is this petra, bedrock, or solid foundation upon which the Lord promised to build His church?

This solid foundation, or rock, is the truth which had been revealed intuitively to Peter by God. The Lord Jesus Christ builds His church upon truth. When we get in on God's revelation and stand on His truth, even the gates of Hades shall not overpower us. God's revelation truth is the bedrock.

Then Jesus told His disciples that He was going to give them the keys to the kingdom of heaven. He began to reveal to His disciples that He would go to Jerusalem and suffer considerably at the hands of the elders, the chief priests, and the scribes. He informed His disciples He would be killed, but would also be raised from the dead on the third day.

Peter's Rebuke

Matthew informs us that Peter listened as Jesus spoke and responded immediately by taking Jesus off by Himself to rebuke Him. To *rebuke* means "to express sharp, stern disapproval of; reprove; reprimand." Listen to Peter's rebuke:

16:22 "God forbid it, Lord! This shall never happen to you."

Look a little closer at what Peter said. He spoke only ten words, but began by invoking the name of God. To *invoke* means "to call for with earnest desire; make supplication or pray for; to appeal to, as for confirmation." Peter wanted God's support; he wanted God to agree with him to make sure this thing would not be! Peter did not know it, but he was asking God, the Father of the Lord Jesus Christ, to oppose His own plan for the redemption of mankind. In essence Peter said, "God must forbid that this happen to you, Lord."

Remember, Peter rebuked what Jesus revealed was going to happen to Him. Jesus had just shared the will of God. He had come to earth for that specific purpose. However, Peter sharply disapproved of His plan. By invoking the name of God, Peter tried to persuade God to go along with him and rebuke Jesus, too.

Then, trying to put Jesus' mind at ease, he said, "This shall never happen to You." Can you imagine Jesus saying, "Well, Peter, I am really grateful you feel that way. I saw you sharpening your sword the other day—I'd imagine it's sharp enough to cut off a person's ear. I'm very thankful you are so protective of Me. You don't realize what a sense of security that gives Me!" However, that is not what Jesus said. When Peter took Him aside and said, "Lord, this shall never happen to You," look at Jesus' response in verse 23.

Jesus Recognized Satanic Oppression

16:23   But He turned and said to Peter, "Get behind Me, Satan! You are a stumbling block to Me; for you are not setting your mind on God's interests, but man's."

"Get behind Me, Satan?" Can you imagine that! Peter had just told Jesus not to worry because He was not going to suffer as He had thought. The idea of Jesus having to die was not acceptable to Peter; but Jesus looked at him and said, "Get behind me, Satan!"

Peter probably looked all around and said, "To whom are you speaking? Why are You looking at *me* when You say that? What do you mean, 'Get behind Me, Satan'? Jesus, this is me—PETER!"

Was Jesus saying in this Scripture, "Peter, you don't know it, but you are satanically possessed!" We know that Peter was not just walking after the flesh. If that were true, Jesus would not have addressed Satan. He would have said, "Peter, if you will walk by the Spirit, you will not carry out the desires of the flesh." Jesus did not infer either.

A Closer Look at Oppression

Was Peter oppressed? Yes. Remember the definition for oppress? *Oppress* means "to exercise power over; to exercise dominion against." It means "to exercise the power or right to govern or control; to burden with cruel or unjust burdens, obligations or restraints; to subject to a burdensome or harsh exercise of authority or power." Simon Peter was oppressed. How was he oppressed? Look at the definition of "oppress" one more time.

'Oppress' Defined

To *oppress* means "to exercise power over." Satan had exercised power over Peter and influenced his thinking process. And he did it without Peter ever being aware of what had happened.

Another meaning of the word *oppress* is "to exercise dominion against; it is the power or right to govern or control." Satan governed or controlled what Peter was thinking. The evil one had placed thoughts into Peter's mind. Peter accepted those thoughts as though they had originated in his own mind and were true. He did not stop and rationally think about what he was about to say. He did not take his thoughts captive, although he had just heard Jesus reveal truth to him. The ruler of the demons took advantage of Peter by stirring up his emotions. Peter had become a victim and simply acted on what he was thinking and feeling. In no way does that excuse Peter. We are all responsible for taking our thoughts captive, or for allowing them to captivate us. Peter, unfortunately, did the latter.

We've seen that the word *oppress* also means "to burden with cruel or unjust burdens, obligations or restraints." Satan had placed thoughts into Peter's mind, wanting to accomplish his own culpable desires. That was a cruel and unjust burden that had been placed on Peter by Satan.

What is Scripture Saying to Us?

We know that Satan planted thoughts into Peter's mind. He may have triggered Peter's emotions, but Peter was not aware of what was going on in the spiritual realm. He thought he was just interested in defending his Lord. Instead, he unknowingly exercised his will in favor of what Satan wanted him to do. Then Peter used his own physical body to take Jesus aside to rebuke Him.

However, Jesus *did* recognize what Satan was doing in the spiritual realm. He knew that Satan was scheming against Him by using Peter's mind, emotions, will, and body. Bear in mind, Peter is the one who had earlier received a revelation from God—Jesus is the Christ, the Son of the living God.

Jesus did not reject Peter. He demonstrated to him how to respond to an emotional blow—check the source of your information. If it is from God, accept it. If it is from the enemy, resist him with truth from God's Word. Then Jesus taught Peter why he had not recognized the source of his information.

Peter is a Stumbling Block

Peter had received a revelation from God Himself! Yet right after that, verse 23 says, " . . . you are a stumbling block to Me; for you are not setting your mind on God's interests, but man's." Although Peter had just received revelation knowledge from the Father of the Lord Jesus Christ, he had also been used by Satan as a stumbling block to his Lord!

What is a stumbling block? A stumbling block is a snare; it's an occasion to fall, stumble, or to sin. If we are not setting our mind on God's interests, we can be easily tripped up and used to cause others to stumble. That is one scheme Satan and demons readily utilize. They want us to set our mind on other things with the hope that we will become a stumbling block to those around us.

Jesus recognized Satan's devices and countered with a very effective measure. He resisted the devil by saying, "Get behind Me, Satan!"

How do Satan and Demons Scheme?

The inhabitants of the kingdom of darkness want to oppress believers by deceiving them into working against the plans of God. It is not God's desire for believers to be under the oppression of Satan or his demonic forces. Satan and his demonic hordes talk to pastors and church leaders.

They talk to church people in any kind of authority role. Demons are not past talking to seminary and college professors. The hosts of Hades talk to Sunday School teachers and to those who fill the church pews saying things like, "Satan? Demons? Where do you think we are, Africa? There are no demons around here! What do we have to worry about? We are God's children; we are filled with the Holy Spirit." Such are the kind of thoughts they give.

I'm afraid there are many Christians that are falling into the same trap as Peter. They are being used to express thoughts directed by satanic forces. In doing so, they are stumbling blocks to the work of God.

Review: How Satan and Demons Scheme
New Testament

1. Satan wants to exercise power over us. He influenced Peter in much the same manner as he had provoked David to number Israel (Matthew 16:22).

2. Satan wants to govern, control, or manipulate our thinking (Matthew 16:22).

3. Satan wants to manipulate and use our emotions against God's plans (Matthew 16:22).

4. Satan wants to cause us to set our mind on the interests of man instead of on God's interests (Matthew 16:23).

5. Satan uses believers to try to keep others from accomplishing the will of God, thus becoming stumbling blocks (Matthew 16:23).

...and upon this rock I will build My church; and the gates of Hades shall not overpower it.

Jesus Christ
Matthew 16:18

Part 2: Ananias and Sapphira

Do you recall the time that Peter and John had been arrested for teaching about Jesus and the resurrection from the dead? They had been warned and commanded not to teach in the name of Jesus any longer. They had been released and had gone to their friends. The entire group had prayed and had been filled with the Holy Spirit. The congregation was of one heart and soul; they were in unity.

Satan and demons do not want churches in unity. All you need to stir up disunity in the body of Christ is to talk about the reality of demonic activity against Christians. Whenever you address that subject, Satan and his hordes will attempt to cause disunity. They do that because they do not want any believer to understand what they are doing. They do not want a body of believers to become aware of their presence and that they are actively working in the lives of *Christians.*

The flock found in Acts 4 was of one heart and soul, but it was young and inexperienced with Satan's ways.

4:34   For there was not a needy person among them, for all who were owners of land or houses would sell them and bring the proceeds of the sales,

4:35   and lay them at the apostles' feet; and they would be distributed to each, as any had need.

Let's look in on a couple from the same congregation. Ananias and Sapphira had witnessed what had gone on and wanted to get in on the action. The story unfolds in Acts Chapter 5.

5:1   But a certain man named Ananias, with his wife Sapphira, sold a piece of property,

5:2   and kept back some of the price for himself, with his wife's full knowledge, and bringing a portion of it, he laid it at the apostles' feet.

5:3   But Peter said, "Ananias, why has Satan filled your heart to lie to the Holy Spirit, and to keep back some of the price of the land?

5:4   "While it remained unsold did it not remain your own? And after it was sold, was it not under your control? Why is it you have conceived this deed in your heart? You have not lied to men, but to God."

5:5   And as he heard these words, Ananias fell down and breathed his last; and great fear came upon all who heard of it.

Ananias and Sapphira had sold a piece of property. They took the money and agreed together to give only a part of it, giving the impression that what they had given was everything. However, we see in verse 3 that Peter knew what they were doing and said, "Ananias, why has Satan filled your heart . . ." Peter had learned well that Satan is the father of lies; he had also filled Ananias' heart. Ananias had been victimized, and Peter declared that Satan had initiated the whole thing.

Intuitive Knowledge

Look at Ephesians Chapter 5.

5:18   And do not get drunk with wine, for that is dissipation, but be filled with the Spirit.

The word *filled* in Ephesians 5:18 is the same Greek word that is used in Acts 5:3. The command in Ephesians 5:18, however, is to be filled with the Holy Spirit.

Satan had filled Ananias' heart. The heart refers to the soul in its relationship with the spirit. Ananias' spirit had been so grieved and its power over his soul so quenched that Satan had full opportunity to work. When our spirit is not grieved and the power of the Holy Spirit is fully at work within our soul, Satan has no ground to work. That is why Ephesians 5:18 commands us to be filled with the Holy Spirit. As long as this is our true state, the Spirit of God works in our spiritual intuition and we are able to perceive the purposes of God and of Satan.

When God reveals truth to us intuitively, we know something we did not know before. Though people may argue that we have not heard from God, we can thank them for their opinion, but know what God has revealed. God does speak truth to believers intuitively and they hear His voice. People may present their fleshly evidence to convince us of their particular viewpoint, which contradicts what we have received from God. Look at 1 John 5:

5:13   These things I have written to you who believe in the name of the Son of God, in order that you may *know* that you have eternal life.

Now look at Romans 15:

15:14   And concerning you, my brethren, I myself also am convinced that you yourselves are full of goodness, filled with all knowledge, and able also to admonish one another.

God-given "knowing" cannot be refuted; it *can* be disobeyed. When the Holy Spirit fills us, He gives us gifts of knowledge and wisdom. We take the truth God has given us in our spirit and process that information through our mind. The enemy may trigger our emotions, especially if God shows us something we don't want to do. Then we will either exercise our will, choosing to be obedient to what God has shown us, or we will choose to act upon what our emotions are demanding. If we do the latter, we will be disobeying God.

When God revealed to me intuitively to become involved in the area of the demonic, my emotions didn't always respond as positively as you might think. But our emotions are not to control us. By the power of the Spirit, we must exercise our will based upon the information God has provided. We must learn to reject information demons place into our minds. As believers, we have to use our own will. God will not allow us to bypass our responsibility; it is part of His process to grow us to spiritual maturity. We must take the knowledge God has given our spirit and apply that truth to our soul, which governs the behavior of the body. The Spirit-filled life then reflects the life of the Lord Jesus Christ outwardly toward other people.

Counterfeiting the Work of God

Scripture describes Satan as a counterfeiter. In 1 Samuel 10:10 we saw how the Spirit of God came upon Saul mightily and he prophesied. In 1 Samuel 18:10 we saw how an evil spirit came upon Saul and did the same thing. The demon counterfeited the work of the Holy Spirit.

In Acts 5:4 Peter said, "While it remained unsold, did it not remain your own? And after it was sold, was it not under your control? Why is it that you have conceived this deed in your heart? You have not lied to men, but to God."

Notice that in verse 3 Peter said, "Why has Satan filled your heart?" In verse 4 he said, "Why is it that *you* have conceived?" You, Ananias, not Satan; *you* have conceived. We see again that Ananias has exercised his will. He had received information in his mind, had become emotionally involved, and made his decision. The Greek reads: "Why was put in the heart of thee this action." Ananias is the receiver of this action. He is a victim, but a willing victim.

The word *conceived* is defined by Webster as "forming a notion or idea of, to imagine; to hold as an opinion." Thayer defines the Greek word as "to fix in one's mind; to place for the execution of one's purpose; to lay a thing up in one's heart to be remembered and pondered."[25] So Peter was asking Ananias, "Why is it you have formed this notion or this idea? Why did you imagine this in your mind? Why do you hold the opinion that it is all right to hold back part of the price of the land?"

The word *conceived* has another meaning. It means "to become pregnant." The mind is like a womb and a thought is like a seed. Demons will put a thought into our mind; if we don't take that thought captive and eject it, we give it life and power to accomplish its destruction. When that thought is conceived—when we accept that thought and nurture it as our own opinion—it gives birth to sin. Listen to James Chapter 1.

1:13   Let no one say when he is tempted, "I am being tempted by God"; for God cannot be tempted by evil, and He Himself does not tempt anyone.

1:14   But each one is tempted when he is carried away and enticed by his own lust.

1:15   Then when lust has conceived, it gives birth to sin; and when sin is accomplished, it brings forth death.

A demon will not only plant thoughts into a person's mind, but will plant feelings into a person's emotions. When he does, that person is tempted to accept those thoughts and feelings as though they were his own; sin is then crouching at the door of his heart. When he receives those thoughts and feelings as his own, he is carried away and enticed by his own lust (undisciplined desire). When lust conceives, it gives birth to sin, which then carries out those thoughts and feelings. Sin breaks or damages a person's fellowship, not only with God, but with others.

Colossians 3 says,

3:2   Set your mind on the things above, not on the things that are on earth.

When Scripture refers to the mind, in the Greek language, it often denotes the way one thinks, referring to the thoughts. When Scripture says "set your mind," it means to direct your thoughts. We are to control what we think. According to God's Word, we are to think on things above. We are not to focus primarily on earthly matters. Those are the things that fill a natural man's interests.

In our previous study of Matthew 16:23, we saw a negative example of how Peter's mind was set. A positive example would be Jesus in the Garden of Gethsemane in Matthew 26:39. In that verse, Jesus prayed, "My Father, if it is possible, let this cup pass from Me; yet not as I will, but as Thou wilt." Jesus set His mind on the interests of God. He did not concentrate on his own physical situation, although that would have been much easier, considering the circumstances occurring in His life.

Satan Uses the Same Tactics Today

Satan wields the same schemes today that he used with Ananias; he fills our heart. He fills our mind and emotions with ideas that promise to gratify the desire of our hearts, hoping we exercise our will in his favor.

Ananias said, "I will keep back some of what I claim to give to God." Demons want us to keep back proclaimed forgiveness. Matthew Chapter 18 teaches that unforgiveness will cause a person to be turned over to the torturers. These tormentors revel at the thought of stirring up strife and suggesting adultery and divorce to hardening hearts.

We may think, "I will keep back some of my employer's goods as my own." Consider Titus Chapter 2 verses 9 and 10.

2:9   Urge bondslaves to be subject to their own masters in every-
        thing, to be well-pleasing, not argumentative,

2:10   not pilfering, but showing all good faith that they may adorn the
        doctrine of God our Savior in every respect.

The Greek word translated *pilfering* in verse 10 is the same word translated in Acts 5:3 as *keep back*, which means "to appoint for one's use." When we take something that belongs to our employer—or anyone else for that matter—and apportion it for our own use without the other party's knowledge and consent, we give the enemy a right to afflict us.

We might say, "I will keep back some longstanding habit or some sin I've claimed to overcome." What is the result of an individual say-ing, "I will keep back?" That individual is acting as though he believes he can deceive God. Therefore that person is walking in darkness. The individual is speaking death toward his finances, marriage, or spiritual maturity. When a person lies to God by trying to hold something back from Him, that person has no fellowship with God according to 1 John.

1:6   If we say that we have fellowship with Him and yet walk in the
        darkness, we lie and do not practice the truth;

Review: How Satan and Demons Scheme
New Testament

1. Satan doesn't mind if we give to the church as long as our motives are impure (Acts 5:1, 2).

2. Satan doesn't mind if a husband and wife are in agreement as long as their consensus is based on a lie (Acts 5:1, 2).

3. Satan counterfeits the work of God; he will fill our hearts if allowed (Acts 5:3).

4. Satan wants us to lie to God (Acts 5:3, 4).

5. Satan wants us to hold back on our claims and promises (Acts 5:3, 4).

6. Satan wants us to lie to cover our sin (Acts 5:4).

As believers, we must exercise our own will; God will not ignore our responsibility. It is part of His process to grow us to spiritual maturity.

Part 3: Jesus Christ

We will now consider how Satan tempted Jesus. The account is given in Matthew Chapter 4.

4:1   Then Jesus was led up by the Spirit into the wilderness to be tempted by the devil.

4:2   And after He had fasted forty days and forty nights, He then became hungry.

4:3   And the tempter came and said to Him, "If You are the Son of God, command that these stones become bread."

4:4   But He answered and said, "It is written, 'Man shall not live on bread alone, but on every word that proceeds out of the mouth of God.'"

4:5   Then the devil took Him into the holy city; and he had Him stand on the pinnacle of the temple,

4:6   and said to Him, "If You are the Son of God throw Yourself down; for it is written, 'He will give His angels charge concerning You'; and 'On their hands they will bear You up, lest You strike Your foot against a stone.'"

4:7   Jesus said to him, "On the other hand, it is written, 'You shall not put the LORD your God to the test.'"

4:8   Again, the devil took Him to a very high mountain, and showed Him all the kingdoms of the world, and their glory;

4:9 and he said to Him, "All these things will I give You, if You fall down and worship me."

4:10 Then Jesus said to him, "Begone, Satan! For it is written, 'You shall worship the LORD your God, and serve Him only.'"

4:11 Then the devil left him; and behold, angels came and began to minister to Him.

Jesus was Led by the Spirit of God

Verse 1 informs us that it was the Spirit of God that had led Jesus into the wilderness to be tempted by the devil. Why would the Spirit of God want to do such a thing? Ryrie's comment will shed some light on the subject:

> Satan's intention in the temptation was to make Christ sin so as to thwart God's plan for man's redemption by disqualifying the Savior. God's purpose (note that the Spirit led Jesus to the test) was to prove His Son to be sinless and thus a worthy Savior. It is clear that He was actually tempted; it is equally clear that He was sinless (2 Corinthians 5:21).[26]

Hebrews Chapter 4 gives us further insight:

4:15 For we do not have a high priest who cannot sympathize with our weaknesses, but one who has been tempted in all things as we are, yet without sin.

Ryrie also comments on the last phrase:

> Not that Christ experienced every temptation man does, but rather that He was tempted in all areas in which man is tempted (the lust of the flesh, the lust of the eyes, and the pride of life, 1 John 2:16), and with particular temptations specially suited to Him. This testing was possible only because He took the likeness of sinful flesh (Rom. 8:3), for had there not been an incarnation, Jesus could not have been tempted (cf. Jas. 1:13). Yet our Lord was distinct from all other men in that He was without sin. . . . Because He endured and successfully

passed his tests, He can now offer us mercy and grace to help in time of need, for He knows what we are going through.[27]

The First Temptation of Jesus

The first words that Satan spoke to Jesus at this time were, "If You are the Son of God . . ." Satan was saying, "If you really are who God says You are, then command these stones to become bread." Jesus did not question nor have to prove who He was. He did not even respond to that issue. The Lord Jesus Christ, as our example, demonstrated the importance of knowing our true identity.

The Son of God had just engaged in a forty-day and forty-night fast. The Scripture records that afterward He became hungry. Satan tried to capitalize on Christ's hunger, bringing a temptation that would fulfill a strong desire; he tempted Him with turning stones into bread to prove His identity.

Jesus had the ability, and the stones were available. What would be so wrong with turning stones into bread? Jesus would have had to use His God-given power in order to do something He had not heard the Father instruct Him to do. He would have been walking after the flesh.

Jesus did not consider His physical needs as He was presented with the tempter's suggestion. Jesus was not ruled by His body. Instead, He found His answer in a portion of the third verse of Deuteronomy Chapter 8:

8:3 . . . Man does not live by bread alone, but man lives by everything that proceeds out of the mouth of the LORD.

It is important to note that after Christ quoted Scripture, Satan did not argue with Him. Why? Because the Son of God knew the Scripture was true. Satan also knew what Jesus had quoted was true. The prince of the power of the air was unable to dispute the truth with Jesus, because He *knew* the truth.

The Second Temptation

The devil removed Jesus from one physical location and moved Him to a different place. If given the chance, he would do the same thing with us mentally or emotionally. The enemy of our souls will attempt to deceive us into believing how much better things are from his perspective. If we buy into his program, we will find ourselves in a different place than where God wants us.

Taking Jesus to the top of the temple's pinnacle in the holy city, Satan told Jesus if He were the Son of God, He could safely jump. The tempter used the same weaponry that Jesus had employed; God's archenemy quoted Scripture and reminded the Lord that angels would protect Him from harm. In Psalm 91:11, 12 God had promised this very angelic protection. For the second time, Satan tried to provoke Jesus to try to prove He was the Son of God, then provided a plan that would prove "the theory." What might have happened if Jesus had taken a flying leap off the top of the pinnacle? What a spectacular way to gain recognition as the One sent by God! The event would also serve to provide affirmation to "sign-seeking" Jews. Would angels from on high swoop down and cushion his fall? Jesus' response was, "'You shall not put the LORD your God to the test.'" This is a quotation from verse 16 of Deuteronomy Chapter 6.

6:16   "You shall not put the LORD your God to the test, as you tested Him at Massah."

The children of Israel had camped at Rephidim, but found no drinking water. Exodus Chapter 17 provides the details:

17:2   Therefore the people quarreled with Moses and said, "Give us water that we may drink." And Moses said to them, "Why do you quarrel with me? Why do you test the LORD?"

17:3   But the people thirsted there for water; and they grumbled against Moses and said, "Why, now, have you brought us up from Egypt, to kill us and our children and our livestock with thirst?"

17:4   So Moses cried out to the LORD, saying, "What shall I do to this people? A little more and they will stone me."

The Lord then instructed Moses to meet Him at the rock at Horeb. By striking the rock with his staff, water would be provided for the people. Moses obeyed, but listen to the Scripture's comment.

17:7   And he named the place Massah and Meribah because of the quarrel of the sons of Israel, and because they tested the LORD, saying, "Is the LORD among us, or not?"

The word *Massah* means "tempting." Moses named the place *Meribah* because of the striving of the children of Israel, and because they tempted Jehovah.[28]

By putting the Lord to the test, we are saying, "Is the Lord among us or not?" When we test Him, we doubt God's provision and try to force Him to prove Himself.

Satan wanted Jesus to test whether or not God would back Him up if He did something the Father had not instructed Him to do. How often do we question our mental activities? Are we concerned that what comes into our mind is our own idea, the enemy's, or one that is directed by God?

The Third Temptation

The devil then took Jesus to a very high mountain and showed Him the world in all its glory and offered to give it all to Him if only He would worship Satan. Jesus did not argue that it was not his to give; He just told him to go. He then spoke from Deuteronomy 6:13:

6:13   "You shall fear only the LORD your God; and you shall worship Him, and swear by His name."

The second chapter of Hebrews tells us something about Jesus Christ in His humanity:

2:18   For since He Himself was tempted in that which He has suffered, He is able to come to the aid of those who are tempted.

Satan's temptations must have been real to the Son of God or they would have been meaningless. The devil was aware of what Scripture says in Colossians 1:

1:16   For by Him all things were created, both in the heavens and on earth, visible and invisible, whether thrones or dominions or rulers or authorities—all things have been created by Him and for Him.

Satan may have been hoping Jesus would be reminded of His power and authority, which He had been accustomed to in heaven. Was the tempter offering all the kingdoms of the world to Jesus as a better way— as a shortcut to accomplish His rule over all peoples?

Jesus, however, was not interested in doing things man's way or Satan's way. He wanted to do things according to His Father's wishes. Philippians 2 tells us about Jesus' decision.

2:7 but emptied Himself, taking the form of a bondservant, and being made in the likeness of men.

2:8 And being found in appearance as a man, He humbled Himself by becoming obedient to the point of death, even death on a cross.

The Lord Jesus Christ had stripped Himself of His right to exercise His power and authority as God. He even called Himself "the Son of Man" (Matthew 16:13).

How did Jesus respond to the suggestion given by the His archenemy? For each of Satan's lures, Jesus utilized a Scripture. He countered the tempter's enticements with truth. He *knew* the value of God's Word.

Review: How Satan and Demons Scheme
New Testament

1. They will try to afflict us after a time of heavy spiritual activity. Jesus had fasted for forty days and forty nights (Matthew 4:2).

2. They will afflict us during a time of physical need and vulnerability; Jesus was hungry (Matthew 4:2).

3. They come to us with their temptations and will speak directly into our mind. Satan *spoke* to Jesus (Matthew 4:3, 6, 9).

4. They don't want us, as children of God, to believe by faith our true identity in Christ. Satan tried to cause Jesus to question God's Word about His deity—"If You are the Son of God. . . ." (Matthew 4:3, 6).

5. They want us to use our gifts for selfish reasons. Satan tried to convince the Lord to use His supernatural power to meet His own natural needs (Matthew 4:3).

6. They want to lure us away physically, mentally, or emotionally to other places. Satan took Jesus with him to "another place" (Matthew 4:5).

7. Satan and demons want us to act with unwarranted boldness. Satan tried to get Jesus to act presumptuously instead of in obedience (Matthew 4:6).

8. The forces of darkness may come as angels of light giving us a convincing Scripture. Satan used God's Word to try to prove his point to the Lord (Matthew 4:6).

9. They allure us with the world and the things of the world in an attempt to gain our devotion. Satan showed Jesus the kingdoms of the world and their glory—offering to give them to Him in exchange for His worship. He may offer us idols of food, possessions, security, fame, etc., but his goal is to distract us from God (Matthew 4:8, 9).

> The Lord Jesus Christ, as our example,
> demonstrated the importance of knowing our true identity.

Chapter 5

More Ways the Enemy Afflicts Us

Part 1: Examples from Scripture

Satan and Demons Tempt Us to
Depend Upon Human Strength and Wisdom

Asa had become king and had done well in God's sight. He had removed the idolatrous altars and had commanded the nation Judah to seek the Lord and to observe the law and the commandments. Scripture records that Asa's kingdom was undisturbed because the LORD had given him rest. Peace, however, came to an end all too soon, and a disturbance arose in the land. Zera, the Ethiopian, had come against Asa's kingdom with an army of one million men and 300 chariots. Asa's army, consisting of 580,000 valiant warriors, was grossly outnumbered. Second Chronicles Chapter 14 records the events when Asa and his men went out to meet Zera and his army:

14:11   Then Asa called to the LORD his God, and said, "LORD, there is no one besides Thee to help in the battle between the powerful and those who have no strength; so help us, O LORD our God, for we trust in Thee, and in Thy name have come against this multitude. O LORD, Thou art our God; let not man prevail against Thee."

14:12   So the LORD routed the Ethiopians before Asa and before Judah, and the Ethiopians fled.

14:13   And Asa and the people who were with him pursued them as far as Gerar; and so many Ethiopians fell that they could not recover, for they were shattered before the LORD, and before His army. And they carried away very much plunder.

14:14   . . . the dread of the Lord had fallen on them. . . .

Why does Satan tempt us to use our own human wisdom and strength instead of relying upon God? It's because Satan *knows* that when people follow God, the enemy will be routed. If he can cause us to depend upon our own human strength and wisdom—or that which comes from others—he has nothing to worry about from us. He knows the flesh profits nothing in a spiritual battle. God's Word warns us that there is a way that seems right to a man, yet leads to death. It is, therefore, very important to Satan's kingdom to try to persuade us to live our lives independently of God and His ways.

Satan and Demons Cause Physical and Emotional Pain

Mark Chapter 9 informs us that Jesus had been with Peter, James, and John on a high mountain. While there, Jesus had been transfigured. Returning to the rest of His disciples, He found a large crowd gathered and inquired into the subject of their discussion. A concerned parent answered the Lord. Listen to his account of what a demon was doing to his son.

9:17   And one of the crowd answered Him, "Teacher, I brought You my son, possessed with a spirit which makes him mute;

9:18   and whenever it seizes him, it dashes him to the ground and he foams at the mouth, and grinds his teeth, and stiffens out.

This demon afflicted the father's son by making him mute; that is, he kept the boy from speaking. The King James Version tells us the boy had a "dumb spirit," which does not mean the spirit was stupid. Rather, he afflicted the boy by not allowing him to talk. Verse 18 says, "And whenever it seizes him, it dashes him to the ground and he foams at the mouth, and grinds his teeth, and stiffens out." The dashing, foaming, grinding, and stiffening were not continuous. That only occurred when the demon seized him, although the demon apparently always made him mute. To *seize* means "to apprehend, to lay hold of so as to possess as one's own."[29] When this demon seized the boy, it took him as though he were his own. What did the spirit then do with the child? The demon dashed him to the ground. The boy would then foam at the mouth, grind his teeth, and become rigid. The boy was brought to Jesus; verse 20 begins recording the event.

9:20   And they brought the boy to Him. And when he saw Him, immediately the spirit threw him into a convulsion, and falling to the ground, he began rolling about and foaming at the mouth.

The father told Jesus that this had been going on since childhood. "Since childhood" can refer to anything from a child just born to a more advanced child.[30] The father also informed Jesus that the demon had thrown the boy into both fire and water in an attempt to destroy him. What might have happened had there been no one to pull him out of the fire or out of the water? The activities of a demon can be very harmful and frightening in the physical and spiritual realms.

Try to put yourself in the shoes of this father for just a moment. Imagine how you might have felt as you watched a demon throw your child into a burning campfire, or into deep water. Wouldn't you be in extreme emotional pain? Demons have the ability to inflict physical and emotional pain in those attacked, and in those who may be watching.

Satan and Demons Hinder Answers to Prayer

Daniel 10:1–13 demonstrates how demons hindered Daniel's prayer. On the day Daniel prayed for his countrymen, God sent an angel with Daniel's answer, but it was 3 weeks before the angel could deliver his message. Why the delay? The Prince of Persia had fought against God's messenger. So God sent Michael, an angel of higher rank, to provide assistance. The angel was then able to get through the demonic blockade and deliver the message.

Can you imagine that? When Daniel prayed, a demon hindered God's messenger from delivering His answer to Daniel's prayer. It is astounding to think that a demon could prevent an answer to prayer that God had sent! If we could physically see into the spirit realm, we would be amazed at what goes on.

Satan and Demons Will Tempt
A Believing Spouse with Immorality

Consider Paul's advice in 1 Corinthians Chapter 7:

7:1   Now concerning the things about which you wrote, it is good for a man not to touch a woman.

7:2   But because of immoralities, let each man have his own wife, and let each woman have her own husband.

7:3   Let the husband fulfill his duty to his wife, and likewise also the wife to her husband.

7:4   The wife does not have authority over her own body, but the husband does; and likewise also the husband does not have authority over his own body, but the wife does.

7:5   Stop depriving one another, except by agreement for a time that you may devote yourselves to prayer, and come together again lest Satan tempt you because of your lack of self-control.

This is one area the enemy uses greatly to gain a foothold. During counseling, I've heard men say their wives occasionally use sex as a weapon. When a spouse withdraws, the couple can not meet each other's needs sexually. By withholding from each other, they give Satan an opportunity. They give him legal ground to afflict and tempt them through lust, which could easily lead to either mental or physical immorality.

Verse 5 says, "Stop depriving one another, except by agreement for a time that you may devote yourselves to prayer." In the years I have been counseling, I've not yet had any couple tell me that they had agreed not to have a sexual union because they had devoted themselves to prayer! I have counseled many of them that have not been in sexual union and have heard many reasons for their abstinence; devoting themselves to prayer has not been one of them. Isn't it strange? That is the only reason given in Scripture for sexual abstinence in marriage.

If you are physically capable, yet abstain from sexual union with your spouse for any reason other than devoting yourself to prayer, you are giving the enemy opportunity to oppress and tempt you or your spouse with immorality.

Satan and Demons Tempt
Believers to Harbor Unforgiveness

Consider what the Apostle Paul says as he addresses the importance of forgiveness in 2 Corinthians Chapter 2.

2:10   But whom you forgive anything, I forgive also; for indeed what I have forgiven, if I have forgiven anything, I did it for your sakes in the presence of Christ.

2:11   in order that no advantage be taken of us by Satan; for we are not ignorant of his schemes.

Paul in effect is saying, "I have forgiven so that Satan will not take advantage of us; we know how he plans to work with unforgiveness and bitterness."

The word *scheme* reminds me of playing chess. Before a chess player makes a move, he first scrutinizes his opponent's men, and begins to plan his strategy. As he plays the game, he has full intention of maneuvering his adversary's king into checkmate. To do so, he cannot play haphazardly. A plan must be formed deciding which men he is to move and where they are to be moved. Sacrificing various pieces is considered in an attempt to lure the opponent into a costly move and provide a later advantage. A conspiracy is created to place his rival's king in checkmate. During the process, some of the opponent's key men must be taken out of the game. If this is done, the objective is more easily reached. By crippling the opposing forces, the chance for winning increases.

Bear in mind chess is only a game. Think about how much more viciously the forces of darkness scheme against believers. We have an opponent in life that is scheming against us, trying to gain the advantage through the strategy of unforgiveness.

It is doubtful when we first awaken each morning that we see a huge, ugly demon looking at us. If we did, it would get our immediate attention. I have personally never seen a demon. Nonetheless, they are real, and they are watching us. They are scheming against us and are continually looking for ways to take advantage of us. They want to maneuver us into spiritual checkmate.

Satan and Demons Block Our Witness
By Blinding the Minds of Unbelievers

Paul, in 2 Corinthians, tells us more of how Satan and his demons work.

4:3   And even if our gospel is veiled, it is veiled to those who are perishing,

4:4   in whose case the god of this world has blinded the minds of the unbelieving, that they might not see the light of the gospel of the glory of Christ, who is the image of God.

Demons affect our witness by blinding the minds of those to whom we witness. It is amazing how they accomplish this blindness; I have no physical explanation. Yet demons can prevent a person from hearing what is being read, or can prevent them from seeing the words on a page.

When we witness to the unsaved, it is very beneficial to do warfare praying for that person before we ever begin to talk with them. We must bind any demons that are either in or around those unsaved people and forbid them to blind their minds prior to, or during, our witnessing. Even if demons are afflicting those people, once the demons are bound they are unable to prevent a person from hearing about and receiving Christ as their personal Savior. Once an oppressed individual does receive the Lord Jesus Christ, we can expect the demons to be very angry with him and the one who witnessed to him because they have lost a great deal of ground in that person's life.

The Scripture declares that the god of this world blinds the minds of the unbelieving. That can also refer to a child of God who does not believe God at some point. When someone is blinded, he cannot see. The kingdom of darkness wants to prevent the unsaved person from understanding the gospel as it is being presented. In like manner, demons can snatch the Word from a believer's mind if he does not understand and receive what he has read. Demons can do the same with our words of witness, negating our efforts.

Do not presume that unsaved friends will necessarily be saved if demonic spirits are bound. That may be true. However, they must of their own free volition choose to reject or to receive Christ, apart from any binding work you have done. By doing warfare for your unsaved friends, you are only preventing demonic forces from blinding their minds to the truth as you share the gospel. Then the person will be able to make a decision by God's grace without interference from demons.

Satan and Demons Lure
A Believer's Mind from Pure Devotion to Christ

In 2 Corinthians 11, Paul voices a concern . . .

11:3   But I am afraid, lest as the serpent deceived Eve by his crafti-ness, your minds should be led astray from the simplicity and purity of devotion to Christ.

Keep in mind that this verse is written to believers. Paul tells us that Satan and his demonic forces are so crafty they would deceive our minds and lead us astray from the truth. They want to corrupt and pervert our thoughts, leading us astray morally. They want to turn our thinking to things other than honest, single-minded devotion to the Lord Jesus Christ.

When people with demonic problems are being counseled, it is com-mon for their mind to wander as the Scriptures are being read. People may also have lustful or other unwanted thoughts contrary to their desire and nature as a Christian. I am not referring to what the Scripture calls *flesh*. Oppressed people are being harassed and tormented with a thought life they do not want but cannot seem to overcome, regardless of any determined action they take.

One man reported the battle had become so severe and had lasted so long that he was tired of fighting it. He said, "I don't know what my problem is. When I pick up my Bible to read, it's like something just hits my mind. I have just about given up."

A Fish Story

Fishermen will take a lure, fasten it to their fishing line and throw it out into the lake by a log or a rock. Then they slowly drag it back, trying to make the lure appear natural. They are trying to deceive a fish, causing it to be attracted to something artificial that a fish would not normally think of eating.

If you were to smell that lure or taste it, you'd find nothing that would make it desirable to eat. Based on those two factors, neither would a fish. But a fish sees that lure spinning in the water; reflected light catches its attention. The fish thinks it could be good to eat, so it hits the lure. The next thing the fish knows—if fish know anything—is the lure's capacity for stick-to-it-iveness. If he cannot overcome it, the fish will find himself a victim of his own carelessness or lack of knowledge.

That is what Satan and demons want to do with us. They lure us. They will put something in front of us in such a light that we think it's attractive. Or they will lure us with something that makes us feel good. The demon's intention is to deceive us away from the Lord Jesus Christ.

Satan Disguises Himself as an Angel of Light

Paul, in 2 Corinthians Chapter 11, exposes one of Satan's disguises.

11:14   And no wonder, for even Satan disguises himself as an angel of light.

11:15   Therefore it is not surprising if his servants also disguise themselves as servants of righteousness; whose end shall be according to their deeds.

We would expect Satan to tell us a lie any chance he gets. Never forget, however, that Satan and his kingdom will also tell us a truth if it is to their advantage. If they can get us to focus on the kingdom of darkness as a source of truth, it is easier for them to slip in a lie later. One example of this is given in Genesis Chapter 3.

3:4   And the serpent said to the woman, "You surely shall not die!

3:5   For God knows that in the day you eat from it your eyes will be opened, and you will be like God, knowing good and evil."

3:22   Then the LORD God said, "Behold, the man has become like one of Us, knowing good and evil; and now lest he stretch out his hand, and take also from the tree of life, and eat, and live forever."

In verse 4 the serpent told the woman she would not die if she ate from the tree of the knowledge of good and evil. In a sense that was true. Let's look at Genesis 2 for further insight.

2:16   And the Lord God commanded the man, saying, "From any tree of the garden you may eat freely;

2:17   but from the tree of the knowledge of good and evil you shall not eat, for in the day that you eat from it you shall surely die."

God's words were spoken from three different perspectives: God spoke to them from a spiritual, a temporal, and a physical point of view. The serpent suspected that if Adam and Eve ate from the tree, they would not die physically that day, but some time later. Secondly, he knew that they would die spiritually that very day. Thirdly, he knew that the very day they ate of the forbidden tree, the process of death would be established in every area of their lives and relationships.

So in a sense, the serpent told Eve the truth, but it was only a partial truth. In verse 4 he was telling her that eating from the tree of the knowledge of good and evil would not cause death that very day. We know that was true because Eve did not die physically on the day she ate of the tree. What the serpent failed to tell her was that on the day she ate of the tree she would die spiritually, just as God had said. He also did not mention to her that the wages of sin is death; the process of death begins in any area sin touches.

The serpent informed Eve that if she ate from the tree of the knowledge of good and evil, she would be like God; she would know good and evil. According to Genesis Chapter 3 verse 22, the serpent spoke the truth. In that verse God said, "Behold the man has become like one of Us, knowing good and evil."

That is what eating from the fruit of that tree produced. We know the serpent told them the truth because of the narrative from Genesis 3:7–11:

3:7   Then the eyes of both of them were opened, and they knew that they were naked; and they sewed fig leaves together and made themselves loin coverings.

3:8   And they heard the sound of the Lord God walking in the garden in the cool of the day, and the man and his wife hid themselves from the presence of the Lord God among the trees of the garden.

3:9   Then the LORD God called to the man, and said to him, "Where are you?"

3:10   And he said, "I heard the sound of Thee in the garden, and I was afraid because I was naked; so I hid myself."

3:11   And He said, "Who told you that you were naked? Have you eaten from the tree of which I commanded you not to eat?"

The moment Adam and Eve had eaten from the proscribed tree, their eyes were opened and they knew of their nakedness. Yet the knowledge produced fear and they hid themselves from God. Never before had they experienced fear, especially fear of God. Why were they afraid? Because they knew their nakedness made them vulnerable. Now they knew what it was like to separate themselves from God's fellowship. God had come to them; it was they who avoided fellowship with God.

Neither God nor the serpent informed them of their nakedness. They *knew* because they had eaten from the tree of the knowledge of good and evil. Genesis 3 continues the narrative.

3:21   And the LORD God made garments of skin for Adam and his wife, and clothed them.

Garments of skin cannot be made without first taking the skin from a sacrificial animal. Supposing Adam and Eve witnessed the death of an animal, they would have to realize that sin brought death. One of the animals that Adam had named—that probably lived in the Garden with them—had been sacrificed because of their sin.

Although Adam and Eve had disobeyed God, Genesis 3:22 shows how much God loved them by preparing a way for all of mankind's salvation. How? He drove them from the Garden of Eden. At first glance, we might think God was harsh and unforgiving, but examine the second half of verse 22 again.

3:22   " . . . and now, lest he stretch out his hand, and take also from the tree of life, and eat, and live forever"—

If they had also eaten from the tree of life, they would have been forever saddled with the power of sin in their flesh. Had they eaten from the tree of life, neither they nor their offspring would ever have been free from the compounding effects of sin's destructiveness. Therefore,

He drove them out of the Garden of Eden and set the cherubim and the flaming sword at the east of the Garden so that would not happen.

Satan is still telling man partial truth; to this truth he adds a lie. The sad part is this: many Christians believe a partial truth without question. Here is one of the things he tells believers in our time that is only partially true: "The Lord Jesus Christ defeated Satan at the cross, therefore we do not have to deal with Satan and his demonic forces today."

The truth is: The Lord Jesus Christ did defeat Satan at the cross. The lie is: We do not have to deal with Satan and demonic forces today. If the aforementioned lie was true, there would be no need for believers to put on the full armor of God or to be on the alert to resist the devil.

Listen to what Scripture tells us in Colossians 2:15:

2:15   When He had disarmed the rulers and authorities, He made a public display of them, having triumphed over them through Him.

In verse 15, Scripture tells us Jesus had publicly disgraced His enemies and had triumphed over them. But the Lord did not triumph over them in His own strength! He triumphed over them through *Him*—through the Father. Later, when Jesus commissioned his disciples, he said in Matthew Chapter 28:

28:18   "All authority has been given to Me in heaven and on earth.

28:19   "Go therefore and make disciples of all the nations, baptizing them in the name of the Father and the Son and the Holy Spirit,

28:20   teaching them to observe all that I commanded you; and lo, I am with you always, even to the end of the age."

One thing Jesus said—among the many included in this Scripture—is sometimes overlooked: "teaching them to observe *all* that I commanded you." In Matthew 10, the Lord Jesus Christ made this command:

10:7   "And as you go, preach, saying, 'The kingdom of heaven is at hand.'

10:8   "Heal the sick, raise the dead, cleanse the lepers, cast out demons; freely you received, freely give."

In verse 8, one of the things Jesus commanded was to cast out demons; we are to deal with them in our day. When Jesus was crucified and resurrected, no one saw him physically fighting with Satan or demons, but Colossians 2:15 says that He disarmed the rulers and authorities and made a public display of them. Being crucified and resurrected in Him, we are to do the same thing as we triumph over them through Him.

Satan and Demons Look for Opportunities to Afflict Us

Ephesians Chapter 4 gives us further insight.

4:26   Be angry, and yet do not sin; do not let the sun go down on your anger,

4:27   and do not give the devil an opportunity.

If you are provoked to anger and do not deal with that anger, Scripture says your anger will give the enemy an opportunity to afflict you. We see an example of this in the parable given in Matthew 18:21–35. One who had been forgiven much seized and tried to choke his slave because of a small debt. As a result, the one who could not deal with his anger and forgive was turned over to the torturers.

An Illustration from Your Radio

Demons seek every opportunity to afflict us. On my car radio I have a button labeled *scan*. When I push the button, the radio will play for 3–5 seconds on each consecutive station it receives. It will continue to do this until I push the button again to stop on the desired station.

Demons push our *scan* button. They will bring various temptations our way until they find an area of vulnerability. Then they hone in on that spot. You control whether they push the button that second time by your response to their various temptations. They are cunning and continually search for weak points. They know our history and, by our response to their temptations, are aware of what to do to activate our flesh. These are the areas they return to most often.

Satan and Demons Hinder the Work of Christians

In 1 Thessalonians Chapter 2, Paul discloses his heart's desire:

2:18   For we wanted to come to you—I, Paul, more than once—and yet Satan thwarted us.

Demons will do anything they can to discourage or keep us from accomplishing God's work. Throughout the book of Nehemiah, we see the delaying tactics of the enemy to hinder the rebuilding of Jerusalem's wall. The enemies mocked Nehemiah and his fellow workers in Chapters 2 and 4; they conspired to disturb the group with fights in Chapter 4, and kept a continuing interruption of messengers arriving to draw them into negotiations in Chapter 6.

How well demons understand that "Hope deferred makes the heart sick . . ." Proverbs 13:12 continues . . ."But desire fulfilled is a tree of life." We must learn to resist the enemy and faithfully expect the fulfillment of God's work in our lives, trusting in Him to accomplish that work according to His will and power.

Satan and Demons Catch Believers in a Snare

Second Timothy 2:26 provides us with a caution:

2:26   and they may come to their senses and escape from the snare of the devil, having been held captive by him to do his will.

Snared Rabbit

A rabbit has been caught by its hind leg in a trap set in a lush, green, grassy spot. A 3-foot chain is attached from the trap to a metal stake in the ground, yet the rabbit is still very much alive. The rabbit can eat a circle around the stake until it depletes its food supply and can die with his nose only one inch away from nutritious, life-giving grass simply because he cannot reach it.

In the same way, a person taken captive—or caught in a snare—has limited freedom to make and carry out his own choices. He can go only as far as the chain attached to the trap will allow. That is how Satan works with us. He tries to entrap us, to tie us up with any bondage we allow him to use. You may think this principle applies only to unbelievers; look at 1 Timothy Chapter 3.

3:7   And he must have a good reputation with those outside the church, so that he may not fall into reproach and the snare of the devil.

Here the Scripture is talking about overseers and deacons and gives their qualifications. Paul is saying that a believer—one who is being considered as a leader in the church—may be caught in a snare of the devil if he does not keep his character above reproach. If he does not, the enemy can use his failures as chains which hold him back from the ministry God intends for him.

Satan and Demons Deceive by Promoting False Doctrine

First Timothy 4:1 issues a grim fact:

4:1 But the Spirit explicitly says that in later times some will fall away from the faith, paying attention to deceitful spirits and doctrines of demons.

Satan's ploy to divide the church has probably been most successful with false doctrine. Man has always desired to have religion codified for him; it makes thinking unnecessary. Even in the wilderness, Israel requested a set of laws so they might know what they must do to please God. We seem to have a desire to avoid walking with Him in intimate fellowship and to learn His ways in quiet submission. Instead we prefer a list of do's and don'ts, a system of explanations to avoid His grace and stand on our works.

Demons are more than happy to focus on this propensity and to distort God's ways with their doctrines. Throughout church history, demonic forces have attempted to implant their ideas into the minds of men. From their efforts we have divided into judgmental denominations, sects, and even cults. Traditions of men, the philosophies of the world, and the deceptions of the latest psychological fad—each seems more interesting and workable than the "old-fashioned" ways of God.

We swallow the lies of demons, while denying the existence of the demons themselves. If we do acknowledge their existence, we deny their power, believing they won't bother us—especially if we don't bother them.

The reason demons promote false doctrine is because they know the truth sets us free; a lie believed puts us in bondage.

Satan and Demons Seek to Devour Us

Listen to Peter's frequently quoted but seldom obeyed admonition in the fifth chapter of 1 Peter.

5:8   Be of sober spirit, be on the alert. Your adversary, the devil, prowls about like a roaring lion, seeking someone to devour.

In the Old Testament we find two men who experienced the enemies' pursuit of their destruction. In Psalm 7:1, 2, David sought refuge in God to save him from those who pursued to tear his soul like a lion. In Psalm 10 he described what it is like being pursued by the wicked. Verses 9, 10 liken their methods to an old lion lurking to catch the afflicted, drawing them in, crouching; the afflicted fall by his young mighty ones.

One such person who fell under this prowling enemy is found in Genesis Chapter 4. When Cain grew angry in response to the refusal of his offering, his focus was upon his brother. Though the Lord warned him that sin was crouching at the door desiring him and that he must master it, Cain was consumed by the enemy's hatred of righteousness and murdered his brother.

David's response was right. He knew the principle of James 4:7, 8. When we draw near to God in submission, He will draw near to us. Under these conditions, it is no wonder the devil will flee from us as we resist him; we are in pretty awesome company!

Satan and Demons Entice with
Worldly Values, Possessions, and Pursuits

James shows us why demons can entice us in this manner.

1:14   But each one is tempted when he is carried away and enticed by his own lust.

Over and over throughout Scripture we are admonished to fix our eyes on eternal things. In the Old Testament, Joshua was promised a prosperous way of success, conditioned upon meditating on God's Word so that he might be obedient to all that was written in it (Joshua 1:8). Yet once the victories had been won and they had settled into God's Promised Land, Israel turned to the wicked ways of the world around them—even after undergoing repeated discipline. Finally, God gave them over to their own stubbornness.

In the New Testament, Paul reviews this same propensity for men to deny God and walk in the wicked ways of the world until He turns them over to depraved minds (Romans 1). But the believer is admonished not to continue walking according to the course of this world, according to the prince of this world who works in the sons of disobedience. We are now His children, and our attitude toward the world is outlined in 1 John 2:15, 16; 5:19.

2:15   Do not love the world, nor the things in the world. If anyone loves the world, the love of the Father is not in him.

2:16   For all that is in the world, the lust of the flesh and the lust of the eyes and the boastful pride of life, is not from the Father, but is from the world.

5:19   We know that we are of God, and the whole world lies in the power of the evil one.

Satan and Demons Test Us with Tribulation

Observe what John said in Revelation Chapter 2:

2:10   'Do not fear what you are about to suffer. Behold, the devil is about to cast some of you into prison, that you may be tested, and you will have tribulation ten days. Be faithful until death, and I will give you the crown of life.'

Probably more than any New Testament person apart from Christ, Paul understood the imprisoning, testing, and tribulation brought on by Satan and demonic forces. In 2 Corinthians he shared a long list of afflictions: imprisonment, beatings, whippings, being stoned, shipwrecks, thefts, sleeplessness, hunger, cold, exposure, and a thorn in the flesh—whatever that might have involved. He had been troubled but not distressed, bewildered but not at a loss, hunted but never abandoned, knocked down but never overcome. He was exposed to the very suffering of Christ, and in this way Jesus' life could be expressed through him.

Satan and Demons Accuse Believers before God

Consider Revelation Chapter 12.

12:10 And I heard a loud voice in heaven, saying, "Now the salvation, and the power, and the kingdom of our God and the authority of His Christ have come, for the accuser of our brethren has been thrown down, who accuses them before our God day and night."

The Greek word translated *accuse* is from a root meaning "to harangue." This well describes the enemy's attack against believers. He not only accuses us before God, he hammers these accusations into our minds, battering us with a barrage of guilt.

Revelation 12:10 tells us what God did with this prosecutor: He cast him down. The hour of God's victory was established when all authority was placed in the Lord Jesus Christ, the rightful ruler. Satan and his recriminations were overcome by the blood of the Lamb and by every word of their testimony in verse 11 of the same chapter.

When he comes with his taunts and reproaches, heaping guilt upon our heads, we must keep in mind there is no condemnation for those united with Christ (Romans 8:1). We are not saying that we have no sin. We are saying that our sin is forgiven, and through confession we are set free and cleansed from our sins by a faithful and righteous God (1 John 1:8, 9).

A Need for Awareness

These are some of the ways that Satan and his demonic forces afflict God's people. We need to be aware of what they do. Only then can we be more effective in protecting ourselves against the onslaught of the enemy.

Review: More Ways the Enemy Afflicts Us

1. They tempt us to depend upon our own human strength and wisdom—and that of others.

2. They cause physical and emotional pain.

3. They hinder answers to prayer.

4. They use our negligence to tempt a believing spouse with lust or immorality.

5. They tempt believers to harbor unforgiveness.

6. They block our witness by blinding the minds of unbelievers.

7. They lure a believer's mind from pure devotion to the Lord Jesus Christ.

8. They disguise themselves as angels of light.

9. They watch for opportunities to afflict us.

10. They hinder the work of Christians.

11. They catch believers in a snare.

12. They deceive by promoting false doctrine.

13. They seek to devour us.

14. They entice us with worldly values, possessions, and pursuits.

15. They test us with tribulation.

16. They accuse believers before God and harangue them with guilt.

The truth sets us free; a lie believed puts us in bondage.

Part 2: Examples from the Present

Satan and Demons Accuse God's People

Zechariah shows us how Satan is more than ready to accuse us before God.

3:1   Then he showed me Joshua the high priest standing before the angel of the LORD, and Satan standing at his right hand to accuse him.

Let me illustrate this with a situation in which a man's wife was used by a demon to accuse him falsely.

False Accusations

The man was in a worship service with his wife; their teenage son planned to come later. The man knew where his son normally sat, so he occasionally glanced in that general vicinity to see if he had arrived. Once, after he had looked to locate his son, his wife whispered to him, wanting to know which woman he was observing. He told her what he was doing and thought no more about it.

The next day he was eating lunch with his wife. At the end of the meal she again wanted to know what woman had held his attention during church service the day before. Again he told her what he had been doing.

Then he remembered that he had been around a man the previous week who was extremely jealous. Every time this man's wife would look at any man for any reason, he would accuse her of flirting, even if it was a passing waiter or the postman.

Armed with this reminder, the man did spiritual warfare on behalf of his wife, and together they took authority over what had come to oppress her, making the oppressing demon leave. That was the end of the false accusations from his wife.

Demons love to accuse. If we fall in with them and walk after the flesh, these false accusations can begin to build walls in our relationships, eventually destroying them.

Satan and Demons Steal the Word from Our Hearts

In giving the Parable of the Sower in Matthew 13, Jesus said . . .

13:19 "When anyone hears the word of the kingdom, and does not understand it, the evil one comes and snatches away what has been sown in his heart."

When we hear the Word and do not understand it, *then* the evil one comes and snatches away what was sown. If we understand the Word and receive it, the enemy can't do that.

It is hard to understand how a demon can take away a thought and prevent its penetrating a person's mind, but it occurs frequently with people I counsel. I will be reading or giving instructions concerning prayers I want them to read. As I am doing this, some have stopped me. They have told me they can see my lips moving, but they want to know why I am not discussing or reading the prayer aloud so they can hear what I'm saying. The truth is, I am reading audibly, but due to the demonic activity going on they are unable to hear me. They can see my lips move, but hear nothing. When I command the demons to stop what they are doing, the person can hear normally again.

If a demon can prevent a person from hearing something as it is being read, why couldn't that same demon steal the Scripture out of that person's mind after they have read it? According to the Scripture, they can do just that.

Satan and Demons are Liars

Take note of what the Apostle John, speaking to the Scribes and Pharisees, says about Satan:

8:44   "You are of your father the devil, and you want to do the desires of your father. He was a murderer from the beginning, and does not stand in the truth, because there is no truth in him. Whenever he speaks a lie, he speaks from his own nature; for he is a liar, and the father of lies."

Demons will lie to everyone—believers and unbelievers—endeavoring to tempt them to receive lies for themselves or to lie to others. The following example will bear that out.

Rachel

Rachel accepted the truth about the Lord Jesus Christ at the age of eight. By age ten she had grown in her relationship with Christ and wanted to serve Him. As a teenager she was involved with a youth group that had gone overseas for a year to work with an indigenous church. While there, the group was exposed to people allegedly practicing witchcraft. One evening as the girls were praying, two of them physically collapsed. Another ran from the group and was found convulsing in her room. Rachel blacked out. When she regained consciousness, she was told she also had been convulsing, though she could not remember it. The pastor and the youth leader proceeded to cast out demons, but she said she was not aware of any difference either during or after the experience.

When Rachel returned to the United States, she stayed with people who were concerned for her. They brought her for counseling due to her depression and feelings of spiritual deadness. Prior to going overseas, Rachel had a vibrant faith. At the time she came for counseling, she wasn't sure God even existed.

Rachel's Christian hosts suspected something demonic occurring in her life and asked me to help determine the validity of their suspicions. Because Rachel was not sure God existed, she was not sure if demons existed either. Based only on her friends' recommendation and her trust in them, she decided to explore the possibility, even though her mind and emotions were not in agreement.

During counseling it was found that Rachel's friends had been quite accurate in their assessment: Rachel was being demonically oppressed. The demons lied to her and tempted her to doubt the very existence of God. As we worked that day, we removed the demons' ground to remain around Rachel and made them leave. The demons had been lying to her, and she had believed their lies. The more she believed, the stronger the demons' hold on her became. Before leaving the office, Rachel told us she was feeling spiritually normal again. She no longer doubted the existence of God—or of demons.

The following day I saw Rachel's friends and they reported an immediate change in her. They said, "It is nice to have Rachel back again!"

This may seem to be an amazing phenomenon. A demon that cannot normally be smelled, tasted, touched, heard, or seen with the physical senses can come alongside a person and plant thoughts into that person's mind or trigger feelings in that person's emotions without that person having a clue as to what is happening. Though amazing, it is also a very sobering thought.

Satan and Demons Lead a Believer's Mind Astray

Paul, in 2 Corinthians 11, tells us what the kingdom of darkness can do to our minds.

11:3   But I am afraid, lest as the serpent deceived Eve by his craftiness, your minds should be led astray from the simplicity and purity of devotion to Christ.

I once counseled a woman whom demons just would not leave alone. They would plant negative thoughts about her or others, and she would be distracted as she attempted to read the Word or tried to pray. As we worked together, we found there was an area of sin in her life she had not confessed before God. It was pointed out that the area of unconfessed sin could be giving demonic forces the right to oppress her. I asked if she thought it would be a good idea to confess her sin.

She readily admitted that she needed to take care of it as soon as possible. I suggested she do so right then and not put it off. She agreed. We bowed our heads. After a few moments of silence, I suggested she pray aloud, and she agreed. We bowed our heads again. After even longer moments of silence, I asked if she was ready to pray. She said she was ready, so we bowed our heads the third time. The silence over the next few moments was deafening. I wondered if I had made myself clear, or if she was confused. Again I told her I wanted her to pray aloud right then, confessing her sin to God, taking away the legal right the demons had to oppress her. She seemed to be in complete agreement, understanding what I was saying. We bowed our heads again—only silence came to my ears. I asked, "Is there some reason you're not praying?"

She replied, "When I bow my head to pray, it is as though something begins choking me. I can't get the words to come out."

I took authority over the demon doing the choking and preventing her from praying, commanding it to stop. I then gave the lady another opportunity to pray. We bowed our heads once more and she broke the silence, confessing her sin to God and receiving His forgiveness.

She could not pray audibly until the demons were stopped, no matter how hard she tried. The demons had been leading her mind astray as she read her Bible and prayed. They also had not wanted her to confess her sin. They knew if she did, they would lose their right to remain and to continue afflicting her; and they were right.

Demons Buffet God's Servants

Paul becomes transparent in 2 Corinthians 12:7:

12:7   And because of the surpassing greatness of the revelations, for this reason, to keep me from exalting myself, there was given me a thorn in the flesh, a messenger of Satan to buffet me—to keep me from exalting myself!

Red, Yellow, or Green

I have a Christian friend who told me something unusual. He told me his problem would surface while he would be driving to work. If the traffic light changed to yellow as he went through the intersection, he would think and feel that he was about to lose his salvation. If the light turned red while he was in the intersection, he thought and felt like he had definitely lost his salvation. If the light stayed green through the intersection, he had no thoughts or problems in this area at all. It was only when the light turned yellow or red that the battle would begin.

He came to me and asked if I'd help him work through his predicament. As it turned out, there was an oppressing demon that would come alongside and give him those thoughts and feelings. We took authority over the antagonizing demon and sent it away.

My friend told me he is no longer bothered by those thoughts or feelings as he drives through intersections.

We think demons are in Africa. They are, but they are also here in the United States of America. If given the opportunity, they will buffet God's servants.

Keeping Things in Perspective

We can be thankful that God expects us to live in victory and that He has provided all we need to do so. Remember, as you read this book, we are taking a microscopic view of only one area of the Christian life. What has been written in this book is not what Christians usually read or hear. However, the fact remains that demons are present and can affect our lives, causing great calamity if we don't know how to stop them. We do not have to be paranoid about demons. We do not get up each morning fearing our day might be ruined because some demon lurking in the bushes might bushwhack us when least expected. It is true, however, that we do need to be on the alert and be aware that demons are around. We also need to know what to do when they aspire to afflict us.

We need not be preoccupied with demons any more than with germs. Keeping our homes relatively free of harmful bacteria does not take all of our time, but it is a necessary part of living in a healthy home. If it is not done, the occupants will soon be jeopardized. Though we need to be aware of germs and of demons, we need not be fearful of either.

Review: More Ways the Enemy Afflicts Us

1. They accuse God's people.

2. They steal the Word from our hearts.

3. They lie to believers.

4. They lead a believer's mind astray.

5. They buffet God's servants.

Satan's Game Plan
Satan attempted to disqualify the Lord Jesus Christ from providing salvation and other blessings.
Satan and demons want to disqualify believers from receiving the blessings of God that are rightfully ours.

Chapter 6

Dynamics of Oppression

Part 1: How Ground is Yielded

Disobedience

Paul is careful in Romans Chapter 2 to tell us about those who are not obedient. God . . .

2:6   who will render to every man according to his deeds:

2:7   to those who by perseverance in doing good seek for glory and honor and immortality, eternal life;

2:8   but to those who are selfishly ambitious and do not obey the truth, but obey unrighteousness, wrath and indignation.

2:9   There will be tribulation and distress for every soul of man who does evil, of the Jew first and also of the Greek.

Because believers are no longer under condemnation—being in Christ Jesus, who took our curse and its payment upon Himself—we often don't apply this Scripture to ourselves. But we overlook that His predetermined plan for every believer is to conform us to the image of Christ. We must not deceive ourselves; God will not be slighted with disrespect. We will reap what we sow. He will use the very seeds of our disobedience, whatever form or intensity it might take, to bring about His discipline in our lives.

We are told that God starts enforcing His righteousness within His own household and that our salvation will be worked out with great difficulty (1 Peter 4:17, 18). Because He is holy, we, too, have been made holy in Christ (2 Corinthians 5:21). Now He, as a good Father, must teach us to live out that holiness.

Paul delivered over to Satan some in the churches who persisted in treating God with contempt; and He recommended leaders in the church do the same so the spirits of the rebellious would be saved and their flesh destroyed.[31]

Lack of Knowledge

Hosea 4 says,

4:6   My people are destroyed for lack of knowledge.

4:14   People without understanding are ruined.

If we don't know the truth, it is easy for someone to lead us astray. Satan continues to use the same ploy he used with Eve: "Has God said . . ." When we do not know what God has said, Satan can say what he likes. Isaiah 5 says,

5:13   Therefore My people go into exile for their lack of knowledge . . .

What happens when a person is exiled? Does he not live under the authority of a foreign or unfriendly power? Remember the story of the lady with all the physical problems who attended a spiritual warfare seminar?[32] Her oppression occurred because she lacked knowledge. She was not aware that demons could oppress her in such a way. Because of her lack of knowledge, for more than a year she was oppressed by demonic forces that attacked her physically. Not only did she suffer much pain, her finances also suffered.

Ancestral Sins

Exodus 20 says,

20:5   "I, the LORD your God, am a jealous God, visiting the iniquity of the fathers on the children, on the third and the fourth generations of those who hate Me."

If there are unconfessed areas of sin in our family—even in past generations—demons have been given access to involve us in the same sin. Our areas of unrepentance open future generations to the same demonic oppression.

You are not guilty or accountable for any sin your ancestors may have committed. Because of their sin, however, demonic forces may have gained access to oppress you.

Many believe God is inflicting condemnation upon children for the fathers' sins. But His law established that no son was to pay for his father, or father for his son (Deuteronomy 24:16). The *visiting* in this reference in the Hebrew language not only denotes "going in order to search or inspect, to look after as a shepherd his flock," it also connotes God's faithful desire to be in the presence of His people though He may find them sowing to the wind and reaping the whirlwind of multiplied generations. As each follows the model of the preceding, the result increases in scope and intensity. The devil and his demons then seem to enjoy unrestricted freedom in their strongholds.

Believers Residing Among Unbelievers

Isaiah 52 says,

52:4   For thus says the LORD God, "My people went down at the first into Egypt to reside there, then the Assyrian oppressed them without cause.

52:5   "Now therefore, what do I have here," declares the LORD, "seeing that My people have been taken away without cause."

Though these verses are talking about the children of Israel in Egypt, there is a spiritual parallel for us in regard to demonic oppression. Demons will oppress us without cause, without our yielding ground for them to work. It is their purpose to gain a legal foothold in our lives; then they can legally control us with their oppression.

Lot's life among the Sodomites is a good illustration of this undeserved distress. In 2 Peter 2:7, 8 Lot is declared righteous but oppressed through the immoral conduct of unprincipled men. As he lived among them, his soul was greatly vexed with what he saw and heard. But when he stood against them in protection of his angelic guests, they resented his actions as an alien's judgment upon them and tried to break into his home and take his visitors.

The gospel of John says,

10:10 "The thief comes only to steal, and kill, and destroy . . ."

The enemy wants to do this to us because he hates believers and all upon which we Scripturally stand. Demons look for ways to steal from us. Apart from God's protective hedge, they would kill us. When they can't do that, they do all they can to destroy us. They normally do their work without our even realizing their presence. As believers reside among those who are not born-again, demons will utilize any advantage to try to demonstrate that the believer is no better off than the unsaved.

Snared by the Enemy

1 Timothy 3 says,

3:7 And he must have a good reputation with those outside the church, so that he may not fall into reproach and the snare of the devil.

A young college man had gotten involved with some fellow students in the area of homosexuality. By the time I talked with him, he knew he had taken a wrong path. As we worked together, he confessed his sin, wanting to be rid of all that was oppressing him. When we dealt with the legal aspects of why the demon was there, we were able to force the demon to leave.

The young man saw that demons were dedicated to his destruction and that they tried to prevent his being what God wanted him to be. He had fallen into the snare of the devil, but learned God's way of deliverance.

Association with Others Who are Oppressed

1 Peter 5 says,

5:8 Be of sober spirit, be on the alert. Your adversary, the devil, prowls about like a roaring lion, seeking someone to devour.

We have an enemy. He is looking about, seeking for a way to capti-vate us, trying to find our weak spots. Peter describes this enemy as a roaring lion. The purpose of the "roaring" is to induce fear; the old, slow lion goes upwind and roars, frightening the prey into running into the jaws of the waiting young lions of the pride.

Demons love to "roar in our ear," suggesting thoughts which will induce negative responses. For example, if we are around someone who has a demon afflicting them, that demon may put a negative thought about us into the other person's mind, or put a negative thought into our mind about the other person. By this "roaring," he can trigger emotions such as anger or rejection. If those thoughts and feelings are not taken captive, the demon gains ground to work. The forces of darkness can do this very quickly, even though our contact with an oppressed person may be minimal—a phone call, a letter, or some other indirect contact.

Belief of Lies

Genesis 3 says,

3:1   Now the serpent was more crafty than any beast of the field which the LORD God had made. And he said to the woman, "Indeed, has God said, 'You shall not eat from any tree of the garden'?"

3:2   And the woman said to the serpent, "From the fruit of the trees of the garden we may eat;

3:3   but from the fruit of the tree which is in the middle of the garden, God has said, 'You shall not eat from it or touch it, lest you die.'"

3:4   And the serpent said to the woman, "You surely shall not die!

3:5   "For God knows that in the day you eat from it your eyes will be opened, and you will be like God, knowing good and evil."

In this Scripture we see the serpent delivering a lie to Eve: she would not die if she ate of the fruit of the tree of the knowledge of good and evil. Because she was deceived by the serpent's word, and because Adam took no action against the lie-teller or his lie, the fall of man was not far behind.

Though we might fault Adam and Eve, are we aware that believers continue to fall into the same trap today in the same way? Satan and his multitude of demons use the same tactics today. They lie to us. When we believe their lie, the result is still the destruction of man.

When a person believes a demon's lie, that demon gains access to his mind and begins to build a stronghold of thought patterns. The demon has the right to oppress because the individual has passively—or actively—allowed them passage to his mind.

Unforgiveness

Matthew 18 addresses the issue of unforgiveness.

18:21 Then Peter came and said to Him, "Lord, how often shall my brother sin against me and I forgive him? Up to seven times?"

18:22 Jesus said to him, "I do not say to you, up to seven times, but up to seventy times seven.

18:23 "For this reason the kingdom of heaven may be compared to a certain king who wished to settle accounts with his slaves.

18:24 "And when he had begun to settle them, there was brought to him one who owed him ten thousand talents.

18:25 "But since he did not have the means to repay, his lord commanded him to be sold, along with his wife and children and all that he had, and repayment to be made.

18:26 "The slave therefore falling down, prostrated himself before him saying, 'Have patience with me, and I will repay you everything.'

18:27 "And the lord of that slave felt compassion and released him and forgave him the debt.

18:28 "But that slave went out and found one of his fellow slaves who owed him a hundred denarii; and he seized him and began to choke him saying, 'Pay back what you owe.'

18:29 "So his fellow slave fell down and began to entreat him, saying, 'Have patience with me and I will repay you.'

18:30 "He was unwilling however, but went and threw him in prison until he should pay back what was owed.

18:31 "So when his fellow slaves saw what had happened, they were deeply grieved and came and reported to their lord all that had happened.

18:32   "Then summoning him, his lord said to him, 'You wicked slave, I forgave you all that debt because you entreated me.

18:33   'Should you not also have had mercy on your fellow slave, even as I had mercy on you?'

18:34   "And his lord, moved with anger, handed him over to the torturers until he should repay all that was owed him.

18:35   "So shall my heavenly Father also do to you, if each of you does not forgive his brother from your heart."

Verse 34 tells us that his lord, moved with anger, handed him over to the torturers. The torturers in this Scripture can refer to demonic spirits. God lowers His hedge of protection and allows demons to come to afflict or torment us for a purpose. Is God cruel? No! God is concerned with our spiritual well-being. Therefore, He will allow demons to afflict us in order to show us the result of sin and to draw us back to Him and His ways of righteousness. The repayment owed by the one turned over to the tormentors in this parable was forgiveness. Based on His payment for sin, Jesus taught that we owe forgiveness in the same way we have been forgiven.

Giving the Devil a Place

Ephesians 4 speaks about anger:

4:26   Be angry, and yet do not sin; do not let the sun go down on your anger,

4:27   and do not give the devil an opportunity.

We must not let the sun go down without dealing with our anger. To do so gives the devil or demons a place, a spot, or a location in our minds from which to work. Letting the day end without having resolved our anger will give demonic forces the legal right to oppress us.

Performance-Based Self-Righteousness

Consider again the book of Job:

1:22   Through all this Job did not sin nor did he blame God.

2:10   In all this Job did not sin with his lips.

3:1   Afterward Job opened his mouth and cursed the day of his birth.

Although he had gone through much adversity, isn't it interesting that in verse 22 God declares that Job did not sin or blame God—period. In verse 10 of the second chapter, however, God says, "In all this Job did not sin with his lips." In other words, Job did not sin in his response *verbally*.

What happened between Chapter 1 verse 22, where his response is declared sinless, and Chapter 3 verse 1, where anger is expressed? God was aware of self-righteousness in Job and desired the axe to be laid to the root. Therefore, God lowered His protective hedge. God wanted Job to experience freedom from the rigors of performance because He saw something that Job hadn't seen in himself as he busily upheld his grown children's position before God, as well as his own. As a result of his suffering, Job for the first time saw God as He really is. Before, he had been unable to see God accurately because of the beam in his own eye—the beam of self-righteousness.

A Cracked Hitch

This illustration might facilitate a better understanding of God's process. You have a truck equipped with a heavy-duty trailer hitch that you are about to take on a trip. You don't know it, but your trailer hitch is cracked. You can't see the crack because it is microscopic. If you pull your heavy trailer with a cracked hitch, you can be headed for disaster, especially if the hitch breaks and your trailer comes loose as you drive up a steep mountain road.

Assume you have a friend who knows about trailer hitches and knows they can fail. He suggests checking your hitch and you agree. When he puts a special dye on the hitch, the dye enters the microscopic crack. Once he wipes off the excess dye, he shines a special light on the hitch. The once invisible crack is now visible.

This is how God uses demons with us. He looses them into the crack, so to speak. When the light of His Word shines on the crack, our flaw shows up and we can deal with it. When we confess our flaws, He is faithful to forgive and cleanse. We can then purge ourselves from the oppressive demonic spirits and live the kind of life God wants us to live apart from their destructive influence.

Review: Dynamics of Oppression
How Ground is Yielded

Ground is yielded to the enemy through . . .

1. Disobedience

2. Lack of knowledge

3. Ancestral sins

4. Believers residing among unbelievers

5. Being snared by the enemy

6. Association with others who are oppressed

7. Belief of lies

8. Unforgiveness

9. Giving the devil a place

10. Performance-based self-righteousness

We can be thankful that God expects us to live in victory and that
He has provided all we need to do so.

Part 2: True Symptoms of Oppression

The following list is a compilation of symptoms that people experiencing demonic oppression have commonly reported operating in their lives.

Sudden Mental Confusion

A lady once told me of a time she was driving her car to a familiar area downtown, knowing exactly where she was going. On the way to her destination, she became confused—so confused she was unable to get there before the business closed. She attempted to return home. In her confusion, she began driving in circles, unable to find her way or to remember where she was.

Finally, she stopped driving and began to question the reason for her confusion. Because she could not remember which way to turn to return home, she wondered if her confusion was due to some kind of demonic oppression and immediately undertook warfare she had learned. Her mind cleared; she looked around and knew where she was. She then proceeded to drive home with no further confusion.

Icy Chills and Internal Shakiness

If you are outside in 20° below zero temperatures with thirty mile per hour winds blowing and get an icy chill, it is not due to demonic oppression. You can put on a heavy coat and you will warm up. If you get an icy chill when the temperature is comfortably warm, you probably are experiencing demonic oppression.

I remember talking on the phone to a pastor who had called. We did not know each other, but as he spoke I began experiencing icy chills to the extent of feeling shaky internally. I looked at my hand held in front of me, but it was not visibly shaking. I felt like I was in a freezer; my voice even felt shaky. After hanging up the phone, I did warfare against anything that might have been influencing the pastor or his church and the cold sensation and the shakiness stopped, as though nothing had ever happened.

The next day a man came in for counseling and mentioned the name of the pastor with whom I'd talked on the phone. He knew this pastor. Because of the chills I had experienced the previous day, I listened with much interest. He told me this pastor was suspected of practicing homosexuality and was therefore in trouble with his church. The only thing I know for a fact is that I had icy chills when I talked to that pastor on the phone. I highly suspect a correlation.

If you experience this type of icy chill, there may be a demon involved, doing what he can to try to gain the right to oppress you.

Sudden Depression

It seems that demons enjoy causing depression in a person even after they've had a great victory in some area. They plant such thoughts as, "What is the use? Why go on?" They introduce all kinds of thoughts that will produce discouragement. If a person listens to them, they will easily become depressed.

Flying to Oklahoma to do a seminar on spiritual warfare, I experienced this kind of attack. I had thoughts such as, "Why should I present this seminar? Why does it have to be me? God, why don't you send someone else?" I found myself becoming increasingly depressed as those thoughts continued. Shortly thereafter I recognized their origin and took them captive to the obedience of Christ. They ceased as quickly as they had begun.

Demons continually watch for opportunities to oppress us. We need to be constantly on the alert to the possibility, as well as to the probability, of that happening.

Feeling Hopeless

Right after God had begun showing me how to deal with demonic oppression, I made a discovery. While I was in my home I was not bothered with any kind of depression. But when I would go to church, I would begin to feel dejected. As long as I was in church, the depression would build and I would find myself growing more critical of everyone and every thing. At the time, I thought it was caused by circumstances, or by the leaders in the church not doing things right. One Sunday I reached the point of feeling so hopeless I didn't care if I lived or died.

When I went home, that hopeless depression remained in full swing. It hadn't lifted as I left church. That afternoon as I looked at a newspaper, I read a short article about a man who had suffered a heart attack and thought, "Oh, why couldn't that have been me? I could have had that fatal heart attack and be gone. My family wouldn't have to worry about any financial pressure; they'd have the insurance. My wife could remarry someone who could supply her needs financially better than I. It would be better for everyone involved."

My wife, Carol, had prepared lunch and as I picked through it, trying to look and act normal, I was feeling miserable.

Carol looked at me and said, "Areon, I started feeling that way in church, too, but I did some spiritual warfare and all my depression lifted."

That made me angry! But not at Carol! Every week I deal with this kind of thing. I earn my living working in this area. I warn people, "Watch out! The enemy is shrewd. He is sly. He will slip up on your blind side." Well, he had successfully slipped up on my blind side. It was hard to believe I had not suspected that I was experiencing a demonic oppression. I thought it was just because of circumstances, or because of what some-one in the Sunday School class had said, or because of what the preacher had said, or had not said, that he should have said. While I was in this depressed state, I felt hopeless and had an I-don't-care attitude. I felt like giving up. I thought, "What's the use? Why should I even try to go on?"

I got up from the table, went into the bedroom, and did some warfare praying. By the time I sat at the table again to finish lunch, I was back to normal. I felt fine; the depression had lifted. I felt as though I'd never been depressed at all.

In reality, my feeling hopelessly depressed had been a demonic oppression; it had come from an outside source. Demons had been around me placing thoughts into my mind and triggering my emotions. I had naively accepted them as my own and responded accordingly. As I agreed with their lies, demons gained the legal right to continue to pro-duce feelings of criticism and discouragement within me.

Reoccurring Areas of Temptation

Do you repeatedly experience the same temptation without encountering lasting relief? Perhaps you are battling against some sin that seems to encircle and overwhelm you, taxing your strength.

I'm not referring here to a problem produced by a fleshly weakness. I'm talking about a continuing harassment, which nearly drives you to commit sin. You have worked diligently against the temptation, desperately trying to conquer it. You have confessed everything to God. You have no desire to yield to the temptation, but it will not go away. The problem continues to exist, becoming commonplace in your actions or your thought-life when your desire is to please God. It may be demonically induced; if so, you must focus warfare against the source of harassment, taking authority by making use of the tools provided by the Son of God.

Unexplainable or Irrational Fears

A lady whom I had taught spiritual warfare once came to me with this account. She had taken some kids from her church to a roller skating rink for a social outing. On the way to the rink, she had felt just fine, happy to be with the kids. All that had changed once she walked through the doors of the rink. As she had entered, it was as though confusion had come over her. Fear welled up and she had wanted to cry for no apparent reason; she had felt like life was not worth living. As she began to consider what was happening, she wondered if some sort of demonic force was oppressing her. Since she had learned how to do spiritual warfare, she applied what she had assimilated and took authority over whatever demonic forces were around her. Her countenance had changed immediately. She had been fine the rest of the evening and had enjoyed her time with the kids at the skating rink.

She experienced no further negative feelings like those at the skating rink. She excitedly reported that she knew she had authority over any oppressing demons that might come to afflict her in the future.

Inconsistent Attitudes or Feelings

A number of people have reported that during their expression of anger, it is like watching themselves fly into a rage. They knew they needed to gain control of their emotions. At the same time, there was a sense of enjoying their anger. However, once the anger was spent, they were very sorrowful and could not imagine why they had ever gotten so angry in the first place.

When a person has been expressing fleshly anger, he has usually justified his action in his own mind. He has normally insisted he had the right to be angry and would become angry again under the same circumstances, and might insist you would do the same thing in a similar situation.

Under demonic oppression, a person commonly feels out of control in some way; controlled by *something* else. If this oppression is not stopped with proper warfare, demons will program the flesh with strongholds, increasing their grasp.

Visual Distractions and Distortions

While editing a book about demon activity, a woman began experiencing visual distortions. These went away completely when she exercised warfare with authoritative prayer. She was able to continue working on the manuscript without further problems.

Some people report catching movement in the corner of their eye. When they look to see what was there, nothing unusual is visible. This should not be confused with a "floater" within one's vision, which nearly everyone sees; these are opaque particles detectable by an ophthalmologist's examination and are not of serious import.[33]

Scary Dreams or Nightmares

It is very common for demons to cause nightmares or to interject troubling situations through dreams. It is also common for people to experience goose bumps, cold chills, or fear after they awaken from these dreams. The disturbances and fright may continue to be projected even after the dreams are over, unless warfare is conducted.

Unsolvable Problem

Are you doing everything you know to do Scripturally, but nothing seems to work? Does it seem you are unable to overcome some particular problem in your life? Are you doing your best to be victorious in all honesty before God, but still cannot move past your problem area or find peace in it? Perhaps your perspective should be broadened to consider the possibility of demons at work in this area. If true, you must engage in warfare, resisting the enemy's spiritual forces, captivating all thoughts in obedience to the Lord Jesus Christ.

Irrational Thinking

When my wife used to sell jewelry, she would have parties in homes of people she didn't know; some were in unfamiliar areas of town she didn't care to know. At times, while she was at one of these parties, thoughts would come to my mind: "Well, it's 9:00 P.M. and Carol is late. I wonder if she had a flat tire or car trouble? What if it happened in an undesirable neighborhood? What if some sleazy character comes up pretending to want to help her? What if . . ." and my imagination was off and running. Before long, I was ready to call the police and ask them to rescue my wife from eminent danger. I would begin to worry, to fret, and to imagine all kinds of illogical things.

Once I learned to do spiritual warfare against demonic forces bringing those thoughts, I could relax and go about my business. Shortly after doing warfare, my wife would return safely with no horror stories about any close encounters of any kind.

Demons love to put their thoughts into our minds. If we accept those thoughts, we give a demon the legal right to begin building a stronghold.

Discussions about Demons Cause Fear

A lady once told me about riding down the freeway with her father-in-law who had mentioned something about demonic activity. She became so frightened that she felt like jumping out of the car to avoid what he was saying. The reason for her fear was later discovered. Demons were afflicting her and did not want her hearing such talk.

When we do not understand the victory of the Lord Jesus Christ and the authority He has given us in His name, we can easily become fearful. Knowing and believing that His salvation includes freedom from demonic powers is a necessary part of being released from their fear.

Review: Dynamics of Oppression
True Symptoms of Oppression

1. Sudden mental confusion

2. Icy chills and internal shakiness

3. Sudden depression

4. Feeling hopeless

5. Reoccurring areas of temptation

6. Unexplainable or irrational fears

7. Inconsistent attitudes or feelings

8. Visual distractions and distortions

9. Scary dreams or nightmares

10. Unsolvable problem

11. Irrational thinking

12. Discussions about demons cause fear

For God hath not given us the spirit of fear;
but of power, and love, and of a sound mind.

2 Timothy 1:7 (KJV)

Part 3: False Symptoms of Oppression

There are "symptoms" people sometimes experience that cause them to believe they are being harassed by demonic forces, when in reality a demon had nothing to do with the symptom. We need to consider some of this false symptomology.

Sugar Demon

When you are around cakes, pies, cookies, or other sweets and find yourself having a difficult time refraining from savoring them, you probably need not look for a "sugar demon."

Low blood sugar as well as PMS, hormonal, and other chemical deficiencies are not caused by demons. These can be diagnosed by qualified physicians and corrected with proper diet or prescribed medication.

A pastor called me once. He told me his son had demons and wanted me to help him. I drove to his little town and did everything I knew to do. I could not find any evidence of a demon involved in his son's life. The pastor told me his son would be sitting in church or at home feeling fine. Then suddenly, in the middle of the afternoon, he would begin to shake. The pastor and his wife were certain that a demon had grabbed him. They had vigorously rebuked the demons, all to no avail.

I suspected there were some physical problems and had them look over a list of symptoms associated with low blood sugar; their son had many of the symptoms. They followed my suggestion to take their youngster to a physician to find out if hypoglycemia was a factor. After testing, the doctor suggested taking their son off all refined sugar products. He also recommended they change his diet; they followed his advice.

The pastor called me a few weeks later and told me he could not believe the changes in his son. He no longer had the symptoms he had previously experienced. There had been no demonic forces involved at all, though the symptoms seemed to suggest the presence of demons.

Hearing Nonsense Words or Phrases

I once talked to a man who told me demons were terrorizing him. When asked what they were doing, he said they were speaking words to him. When questioned about the contents of those words, he said, "They say the words 'up, up, up, up' repeatedly."

In this writer's opinion, demons don't give someone nonsensical words. Demons speak things that belittle you, give contrary thoughts about God, or the Bible. Their intention is to pull you away from your fellowship with God in some way. However, if the words are meaningless, that is normally not demonic. Other factors are involved.

"I Know I Have Demons Bothering Me!"

There are times when the Spirit of God will reveal to a person that demonic forces are at work in his life. He may reveal it directly, or through the agency of another person. It is typical, however, that if God does not reveal the presence of demons or if another person with a knowledge of demons doesn't talk to the oppressed about it, the individual usually does not recognize the source of the irritation.

The forces of darkness have a purpose: to steal, kill, and destroy. In order to remain hidden and to facilitate their task, demons are not usually going to let a person know they are afflicting them.

Some people use this phrase as an excuse or as a method of placing the blame on demons rather than on their own flesh. One man I once saw informed me he was being demonically harassed. I could find no evidence in support of his claim, however. I concluded that he should learn to deal more effectively with his flesh. He informed me I simply did not have authority over demons and then explained his reasoning: I had not yelled, screamed, pounded the desk or made any other forceful exhibitions necessary to get their attention.

I responded by saying, "If one had authority over demons, it appears to me he would not need to engage in that type of activity."

Walking After the Flesh

If someone could figure a way to cast out the *flesh* to dry waterless places, they would provide us all a real service. The flesh, however, cannot be treated in the same manner that is used with demons.

If your car is riding rough because you have a flat tire and you change a spark plug instead of the tire, you are not solving the problem. You will have to change the flat tire if you want the car to function properly. Different tools are needed to change a flat tire than are needed to change a spark plug.

That is why it is important to diagnose the difference between the work of the flesh and that of demons. You have to use the right tools and deal with the right problem. Getting rid of demonic oppression does not deal with your flesh. Neither will dealing with your flesh overcome demonic oppression; at best it will give demons less opportunity to afflict you.[34]

Review: Dynamics of Oppression
False Symptoms of Oppression

We have looked at the following which are not symptomatic of demonic oppression:

1.   Sugar demon

2.   Hearing nonsense words or phrases

3.   "I know I have demons bothering me!"

4.   Walking after the flesh

...knowledge is easy to him who has understanding.

Proverbs 14:6

Part 4:

Why God Permits Oppression

To Test Our Obedience to God's Commandments and Ways

Judges 2:21–3:1–4

2:21   "I also will no longer drive out before them any of the nations which Joshua left when he died,

2:22   in order to test Israel by them, whether they will keep the way of the LORD to walk in it as their fathers did, or not."

2:23   So the LORD allowed those nations to remain, not driving them out quickly; and He did not give them into the hand of Joshua.

3:1   Now these are the nations which the LORD left, to test Israel by them (that is, all who had not experienced any of the wars of Canaan;

3:2   only in order that the generations of the sons of Israel might be taught war, those who had not experienced it formerly).

3:4   And they were for testing Israel, to find out if they would obey the commandments of the LORD, which He had commanded their fathers through Moses.

One reason God allows oppression is to test us. God wants us to find out if we will obey His commandments and follow His ways. Therefore, He will allow demonic forces around us and will permit them to put thoughts into our minds, and to manipulate our emotions. He knows—

and we should know—these thoughts and feelings are contrary to His Word. In this way we will give evidence as to whether we believe God's Word, or whether we believe what Satan and his demonic forces say.

Does God not already know our hearts? Is not the test a part of His discipline process? Remember there is a positive side to discipline: to instruct, educate, train children; to cause to learn!

In earthly classrooms, teachers give tests as well. Part of their reasoning (which we easily can see) is for the teacher to discern whether we have learned enough to pass the course. Another reason is so that the students can see how much they have learned and are able to apply.

Since God is omniscient and knows the thoughts and intents of the heart, is testing done for His benefit or ours? In chemistry we did lab tests on elements to prove the truth of an element. Does not God use us to prove out His ways as right to all those who see us in the test (as well as the spiritual "watchers"—the angels and demonic forces whom He teaches about His grace through us)?

God was doing the same thing with Adam and Eve in the Garden of Eden. He commanded them not to eat from the tree of the knowledge of good and evil; it would produce death. The serpent told them the fruit would give them knowledge so they would be like God, knowing good and evil. God gave them the ability to choose—they had to decide what to believe.

God is doing the same thing today. He allows Satan and his hordes to test us with information contrary to what is available to us in His Word. We must choose which will be our source of information. Will we choose, believe, and live by His commandments and ways?

To Show Angelic and Demonic Forces God's Wisdom

In Ephesians 3, Paul states the following:

3:8   To me, the very least of all saints, this grace was given, to preach to the Gentiles the unfathomable riches of Christ,

3:9   and to bring to light what is the administration of the mystery which for ages has been hidden in God, who created all things;

3:10　in order that the manifold wisdom of God might now be made known through the church to the rulers and the authorities in the heavenly places.

Grace was given to Paul to reveal the manifold wisdom of God to the church. In turn, His wisdom was to be exhibited before the rulers and authorities in the heavenly places, which included Satan and his demons. From the beginning, God chose to display His manifold wisdom to these rulers and authorities through the church, the body of Christ, which includes all believers.

We are on stage, so to speak. The angels of God are watching; throughout the Scriptures they are presented as watchers. Satan and his demons are also watching us when we go through a trial, or some kind of tribulation, or problem. We may want to give up, but by standing firm on the Word of God and continuing to obey Him, our trust and obedience reveal the glory of His grace.

The forces of darkness don't like seeing us stand firm on God's Word; they cannot deny the manifold wisdom of God as it is revealed in our lives. His wisdom is shown through us, the church, in an infinite number of ways as we go through every kind of situation. We may not understand why we are going through a particular trial, but we need to seek God's Word, believe Him, and stick with Him. We need to determine that we will be obedient, no matter what the situation brings, and no matter what the cost. When we do, that will glorify God. It will shine forth to the demonic forces the manifold wisdom of God.

To Cleanse Us

Jesus speaks to Peter in Luke 22:31, 32:

22:31　"Simon, Simon, behold Satan has demanded permission to sift you like wheat;

22:32　but I have prayed for you, that your faith may not fail; and you, when once you have turned again, strengthen your brothers."

God has a purpose for our lives as believers. If any of us decide to follow God and do exactly what He says, Satan may demand permission to sift us like wheat.

If we are doing something that is somehow side-tracking Satan's activities, the god of this world desires to throw us off track or derail us in some way. God permits him to sift us in order to reveal and remove our false faith and dead works. When these things are removed, we are better able to do the works He's gifted and empowered us to do. He uses Satan to shake all that is shakable in us, so only the unshakable remains (Hebrews 12:26, 27.)

A Powerful Locomotive

Before Satan and his hordes next try to derail you, consider a train's locomotive. It can pull many railroad cars carrying tons of cargo to the marketplace to be used for various purposes. If that locomotive was placed *beside* the track instead of *on* the track, it would be powerless to get itself or the cargo to its destination. The power would be there all right, but all that power would be useless unless the locomotive were in full, proper contact with the railroad tracks.

God has prepared works for us to accomplish (Eph. 2:10). Satan and his demonic forces want to derail us, and get us just a little "off track." Then we will be unable to carry out what God has entrusted to us and those who need what we have will suffer loss as well. Whatever we would have accomplished of God's design, would not be done by us; we would lose the joy of fulfillment and the Lord's reward. God would have to raise up another person to do the work. Until then, Satan's kingdom would continue to be effective in that area. We are sent by the Lord Jesus Christ in the same way as the Father sent Him (John 17:18); He came for the purpose of destroying the devil's works (1 John 3:8).

To Give Us Our Heart's Desire

As we saw in the first and second chapters of Job, it was God who had called Satan's attention to Job, whom He proclaimed as righteous. It was as though He had waved a red flag in front of a charging bull; when the flag was jerked down, there stood innocent Job. Did God have a purpose not readily seen? Does He have the same purpose for us today?

In the thirty-seventh Psalm we find both a command and a promise.

37:4   Delight yourself in the LORD; and He will give you the desires of your heart.

When we delight ourselves in the Lord and He becomes our chief desire, He gives us the desire of our heart. He will not fill our petitions if we are harboring wrong motives or if we desire to appease our own lusts or pleasure. However, as we delight ourselves in the Lord, He will place His desire into our hearts.

Psalm 139 reveals how thoroughly God knows our thoughts and is acquainted with all our ways. God knew us in the womb. He knows the words we speak before they are spoken. David assures us that no matter where we go, the hand of God will lead us. He has many precious thoughts toward us. David pronounced that he hated those who hated God and that they were his enemies as well. No wonder God called him a man after his own heart. That is delight.

The Hebrew word *delight* means "to be soft or pliable." When we choose to be soft or pliable, like clay in the hands of the Master Potter, He can then give us the desire of our heart; His desire and ours melted together brings us real fulfillment. Read and consider David's request in Psalm 139.

139:23   Search me, O God, and know my heart; try me and know my anxious thoughts,

139:24   And see if there be any hurtful way in me, and lead me in the everlasting way.

God requires that we be holy, as He is holy; He places that desire within us. He searches us, putting us to the test to reveal any way that would be hurtful to His desire for us. When the enemy is permitted to oppress us, those ways are revealed. When they are dealt with, we—like David—will desire God to guide us into doing things the everlasting way; God's way. Satan's way is hurtful and leads to death.

Now read David's response in Psalm 119.

119:67 Before I was afflicted I went astray, but now I keep Thy word.

119:68 Thou art good and doest good; teach me Thy statutes.

To Expose the Ways of the Flesh

When we cannot discern the false ways the enemy has programmed in our flesh, it is difficult to obey Paul's admonition we find in Galatians Chapter 5.

5:16   But I say, walk by the Spirit, and you will not carry out the desire of the flesh.

5:17   For the flesh sets its desire against the Spirit, and the Spirit against the flesh; for these are in opposition to one another, so that you may not do the things that you please.

Then, in this same chapter, Paul tells us how the flesh operates.

5:19   Now the deeds of the flesh are evident, which are: immorality, impurity, sensuality,

5:20   idolatry, sorcery, enmities, strife, jealousy, outbursts of anger, disputes, dissensions, factions,

5:21   envying, drunkenness, carousing, and things like these . . .

These are produced by the flesh in all its glory. Scripture never accuses Job of anything in this list. But as you read the book of Job, you find his defense expressed in outbursts of anger and a dispute with God Himself! The word *dissention* mentioned in verse 20 means a "strong disagreement; discord; a contention or quarrel."

Next in our list, *factions*, we see "ambition, self-seeking, rivalry; self-will being an underlying idea in the word. It also has the meaning of seeking to win followers."[35] Job willfully justified himself and tried to convince his friends he was right! He may not have been guilty of what Christians sometimes refer to as "gross flesh." His flesh would more likely fall under the category called "good flesh." But in God's eyes, all our righteousness is as filthy rags (Isaiah 64:6).

We begin to see how self-righteousness was deeply rooted in Job when we realize there is no more declaring of Job as sinless after Chapter 2. God knew that Job's flesh, like ours, was in opposition to the will of God. Only the greatest of refining fire would bring it to the surface to be cleansed through confession and forgiveness. God had to allow everything to be shaken in Job's life so that only the unshakable would remain.

Is this not why God brought Job to the attention of Satan in the first place? He allowed Satan to test Job in order that his flesh might be exposed for what it really was. Only then could Job see himself as God had seen him; then Job could respond in a manner that would restore fellowship with his God.

To Call Believers to Righteousness

Because of Saul's rebellion, God sent a demon to terrorize him. Why couldn't Saul get rid of the oppressing demon? He had not dealt with the issue of repentance. If an oppressed person wants to rid himself of an oppressive spirit, he *must* deal with the issue of repentance. One may argue that "God's provision" of harp music didn't always work for Saul. But was that God's provision? Or was it the provision of Saul's servants? When God provides, His provision *always* works. "Good flesh" doesn't always work. When Saul's flesh got involved, his disobedience gave the demon ground to intensify the affliction. David's playing the harp was only a temporary method to make the demon leave. The demon had ground to return because Saul had not repented. God does not haphazardly send demons to someone. He sends demons for the same purpose He raised up nations against the children of Israel: to discipline them and draw them back to Himself.

God sent a demon to Saul to terrorize him; the terror was but a tool of discipline. The terror should have been an incentive to drive him back to God through repentance. Once the cause was discovered and dealt with, there would have been no reason for the demon to remain.

Satan's goal is to keep us operating after the flesh and in disobedience to God. When we operate in that manner, Satan's kingdom is not threatened by our warfare. Satan and his kingdom of darkness then have more opportunity to terrorize their victims.

Had Saul been openly seeking the purpose of God in his life, God would have used this situation as a springboard for training in righteousness.

To Reprove the People of God

In Chapter 3 we studied the Scripture in 1 Chronicles 21 about Satan moving David to sin by numbering Israel. Now looking at 2 Samuel 24, we see that the Lord was very much involved as well:

24:1   Now again the anger of the LORD burned against Israel, and it incited David against them to say, "Go number Israel and Judah."

We can now see that the Lord's agenda was two-fold. First He was dealing with a flesh problem in David. His second purpose involved His people as a whole. We often forget that circumstances involving us are rarely limited to us alone. When God is at work in the life of a man, we can be certain that his wife and children will be affected as well.

For a New Testament perspective on David and Israel's experience, we can read two statements in Peter's letters written to Christians who were scattered throughout the world. First Peter Chapter 2 tells us . . .

2:9   But you are a chosen race, a royal priesthood, a holy nation, a people for God's own possession, that you may proclaim the excellencies of Him who has called you out of darkness into His marvelous light.

Peter declared that God's people are chosen to be a holy nation for God's own possession. In Chapter 4 of Peter's first letter, he warns that no one in the church is to suffer as a murderer, thief, evildoer, or meddler. He continues in verse 17.

4:17   For it is time for judgment to begin with the household of God; and if it begins with us first, what will be the outcome for those who do not obey the gospel of God?

The judgment Peter addresses is not condemnation, though it may often seem that severe. Throughout Scripture God deals severely with the whole of His people and often inflicts sickness, captivity, and even death. It is truly a fearful thing to fall into the hands of a living God who is holy and demands His people be holy in reflection of Him.

But as with the reproof of Israel through David's sin in 1 Chronicles 21 and 2 Samuel 24, the mercy of God endures and He uses His anger to lay bare our sin, showing us its consequences. When we agree with Him that His way is right, He raises us up to walk with Him from darkness to light.

To Teach Us Submission to His Word

In Matthew 16:16 Peter had received a revelation of Christ's identity. Jesus had informed His disciples He would build His church upon the bedrock of that revelation knowledge. He also promised that the gates of Hades would not be able to overpower the church built on that truth.

Afterward, the Lord began to show his disciple what would happen to Him in Jerusalem; He would be killed, yet in 3 days, He would be resurrected.

Then Satan got in on the act. He influenced Peter to try to persuade the Lord that such a thing need not happen. However, the disciple was unsuccessful. Jesus was aware that Satan was behind Peter's logic and Peter found himself rebuked as a stumbling block to Christ's ministry.

What did Jesus want Peter—and believers today—to learn? Even though a person may have received a revelation of God's truth, he is not immune from being deceived and becoming a stumbling block to the work of Christ on this earth.

Before we implement any plan, we need to be certain that plan does not oppose any truth already given in God's Word. Just because we start out in truth, we cannot assume all that follows is true; it must be tested.

God will take Satan's schemes and utilize them as a means to teach His people submission to His Word.

To Provide an Example for Others

In Acts 5 Ananias and Sapphira had seen what was happening in the church. They had seen landowners selling their houses and land, giving the proceeds to the apostles. Wanting to be a part of it all, they also had sold a piece of property. At some point, Satan had gotten involved: he had filled Ananias' heart to lie to the Holy Spirit. Satan had given him an idea, which he shared with his wife, who agreed: "Let's sell a piece of property, give only part of it to the apostles, but claim we gave it all. That way we can help those in need, gain a good reputation, and still keep some of the money for ourselves." Ananias and Sapphira had devised a plan, but little did they realize the plan was not their own.

Satan must have rejoiced when Ananias, taking only part of the income from the sale, implemented the plan he had been given. The plan seemed like a good idea to the couple until it was executed. When Ananias took his money to Peter, the apostle exposed all that Ananias had done. Ananias' response to Peter's revelation shocked everyone present: he died! Can you imagine what kind of message that gave to those who were witnesses? Scripture tells us they were filled with great fear.

About three hours later Sapphira arrived on the scene, unaware of what had happened. Peter questioned her and she stuck to the story the couple had concocted. Then Peter informed her that her husband had been buried and she would join him; she immediately fell at his feet and was also taken out and buried. All those present had an indelible message written in their minds: lying to God does not pay! He *knows* the truth.

Review: Dynamics of Oppression
Why God Permits Oppression

1.   To test our obedience to God's commandments and ways

2.   To show angelic and demonic forces God's wisdom

3.   To cleanse us

4.   To give us our heart's desire

5.   To expose the ways of the flesh

6.   To call believers to righteousness

7.   To reprove the people of God

8.   To teach submission to His Word

9.   To provide an example for others

The forces of darkness don't like seeing us stand firm on God's
Word; they cannot deny the manifold wisdom of God
as it is revealed in our lives.

Chapter 7

Essentials of Warfare

This chapter may be rather weighty; several theological points are covered that may seem wearisome. It is essential, however, to understand them thoroughly. Once you do, you will be able to better understand how to war efficiently in the full armor of God. You won't want to read this chapter like you would a novel; in fact, you may need to go through it more than once to become more effective in your spiritual warfare.

Part 1: The Lord's Strength

This foundational truth of warfare is found throughout Scripture. We will start in Ephesians 6, which says,

6:10   Finally, be strong in the Lord, and in the strength of His might.

Be Strong in the Lord

Why should we as Christians have to be strong in the Lord? As we have already seen, Satan and demons want to tempt us and deceive us. They want to infiltrate our minds and emotions. They try to manipulate us. Demonic forces want to lure, deceive, agitate, and afflict us. They are at war against us, scheming to hinder us; they want to ensnare, oppress, and devour us. We are not strong enough in ourselves to resist attacks like that!

The command to be strong means to be empowered with the ability to be effective in our endeavors. Without His ability working through us, we would not be able to survive spiritually.

In the Strength of His Might

Verse 10 continues by telling us to be strong in the Lord, and in the strength of His might. The word *might* refers to inherent physical strength, as in a strong man's muscles. *Strength* is the manifestation of that might; it is might in action. In this context, it is Christ's might put into effect through the believer. We are merely weak vessels, but the Lord Jesus Christ wants His might to be expressed through us.

We must be strong in the Lord because, even as Christians, the battle set before us is as awesome as that which Judah faced in 2 Chronicles 20:

20:14   Then in the midst of the assembly the Spirit of the Lord came upon Jahaziel . . .

20:15   and he said, "Listen all Judah and the inhabitants of Jerusalem and King Jehoshaphat: thus says the Lord to you, 'Do not fear or be dismayed because of this great multitude, for the battle is not yours but God's.'"

Does that mean that the battle is God's alone? Does it mean that we are to be simply passive and just let go and let God? Are we to sit by like a bump on a log and consider it God's problem if something negative happens? If a problem confronts us, are we to just ignore it because the battle is not ours anyway? No. If that were true, there would be no need for the instruction to be strong in the Lord and in the strength of His might. We, like Israel, must stand in His victory.

Philippians 4 confirms that this is a possibility in the life of every believer.

4:13   I can do all things through Him who strengthens me.

The word *strengthens* comes from the same root word that is used in Ephesians 6:10. It means "to be empowered." What each of us accomplishes of spiritual value cannot be done in our own strength; whatever we do of any spiritual significance, we do by being empowered by the

Lord. The verse might be paraphrased like this: "I can do anything through Him because He is my source of power and strength."

Requirements for Being Strong in the Lord: The Believer Must Be Weak

2 Corinthians 12 says,

12:9   And He has said to me, "My grace is sufficient for you, for power is perfected in weakness . . ."

This is the first requirement for being strong in the Lord. Any believer who wants to become strong must first become weak. Becoming weak is not our job. It is God's job to expose our weaknesses. Our tendency is to try proving just the opposite. When we have a problem, what do we attempt to do? We try to show we are strong in that area. If we succeed in our objective and overcome our problem, we begin to believe we don't need God. We have proven we are strong enough to conquer the problem ourselves. So the training process of God is to provide His children with a situation they can't handle on their own, which isn't very difficult. Then they have the opportunity to learn to depend upon Him instead of upon themselves.

The Lord Jesus Christ Must Be Lord

A Christian cannot be strong in the Lord if the Lord Jesus Christ is not acknowledged to be his Lord. After the defeat of Joshua's army at Ai, Scripture records an interesting fact in the seventh chapter of Joshua.

7:6   Then Joshua tore his clothes and fell to the earth on his face before the ark of the LORD until the evening, both he and the elders of Israel; and they put dust on their heads.

7:7   And Joshua said, "Alas, O Lord GOD, why didst Thou ever bring this people over the Jordan . . ."

In verse 6 it says, "Then Joshua tore his clothes and fell to the earth on his face before the ark of the LORD." Notice that the word LORD is written in capital letters. Verse 7 says, "Alas, O Lord, GOD . . ." This time the word *Lord* is written with a capital "L" but the rest of the word is in lower-case letters: L-o-r-d.

Do you suppose the publishers of these Bibles have made a mistake? Is this a typographical error, or could there be some meaning intended? When each letter of the word LORD is capitalized, it means "Jehovah." The word Lord, with only the "L" capitalized, means "Adonai."

The name Adonai is a Hebrew name for God. It means "Lord or Master; the One who must be obeyed." It implies that all those who come to know Him as Master can enter into Christ's perfect rest and expect to receive from Him God's direction, supervision, and provision. The name Jehovah implies "I am the source of all things especially to my people."

Israel relied on the Lord's victory without obeying the Lord's orders. If we desire to be strong in the Lord and the strength of His might, we must submit to His Lordship.

The Believer Must Be Obedient

Another requirement to be strong in the Lord is obedience. Luke 6 records the words of the Lord Jesus Christ when He said,

6:46   "And why do you call Me, 'Lord, Lord,' and do not do what I say?"

If Jesus Christ is Lord of a believer's life, that person will have the desire and the willingness to obey what God says. If a believer is not willing to obey Him, Jesus Christ is not "Lord" in that believer's life. Romans 6 tells us how obedience and Lordship go together.

6:16   Do you not know that when you present yourselves to someone as slaves for obedience, you are slaves of the one whom you obey, either of sin resulting in death, or of obedience resulting in righteousness?

So if we yield ourselves to sin, we are a slave to sin. As such, we will be producing death. If we yield ourselves to Christ's obedience—as indicated in 2 Corinthians 10:5—we are His slave and will thus produce righteousness. We are free to choose, but obedience is the only way to outwardly display the righteousness of God. We are not discussing returning to obedience to the Law for salvation because the believer, born-again of God, is under grace, as Paul's letter to Galatians plainly reveals. However, Paul explains that our freedom from the Law is not freedom to sin; it is freedom to serve God in a new spirit. In Romans Chapters 6–8 the apostle says:

6:6 Knowing this, that our old self was crucified with Him, that our body of sin might be done away with, that we should no longer be slaves to sin;

6:7 for he who has died is freed from sin.

7:5 For while we were in the flesh, the sinful passions, which were aroused by the Law, were at work in the members of our body to bear fruit for death.

7:6 But now we have been released from the Law, having died to that by which we were bound, so that we serve in newness of the Spirit and not in oldness of the letter.

8:1 There is therefore now no condemnation for those who are in Christ Jesus.

8:2 For the law of the Spirit of life in Christ Jesus has set you free from the law of sin and of death.

8:12 So then, brethren, we are under obligation, not to the flesh, to live according to the flesh—

8:13 for if you are living according to the flesh, you must die; but if by the Spirit you are putting to death the deeds of the body, you will live.

We see from these verses that while believers are exempt from the curse of the Law, we are not exempt from the consequences of sin. Paul has stated that death comes as the result of choosing to exercise our freedom to walk after the flesh. The decision to walk after the flesh could introduce death to our relationships with people through broken friendships or divorce. It could bring death to our fulfillment in not achieving our purpose of glorifying God. It also brings death, not to our relationship with God, but to our fellowship with Him. And if we persist in using our freedom as license to sin, death may come physically. We can see, therefore, that all these products of death are Satan's goal of oppression. He seeks to destroy all that God has provided for our lives: joy, peace, rest, and all the fruit of righteousness in the Spirit.

As we consider winning the battles and enjoying the fruit of God's promises to His children, we must understand the importance of obedience. In Romans 16 the Apostle Paul continues,

16:19   For the report of your obedience has reached to all; therefore I am rejoicing over you, but I want you to be wise in what is good, and innocent in what is evil.

16:20   And the God of peace will soon crush Satan under your feet.

It is God who is at work in us. He has given us the mind of Christ, and He has given us His Spirit. He is using every circumstance to train us to first desire and then to do His will. At the same time, Satan and his demons—through these same circumstances—seek to deceive, steal, kill, and destroy with their oppression.

God in us is greater than our opposition, but we must not allow the enemy to deceive us. The kingdom of darkness will try to lure us into bondage, making us think we need to prove God's love, patience, or forgiveness. They will provide us with a distorted view of freedom. We must not fall for their lies; our liberty in Christ is the freedom of obedience to the Spirit of God.

God has given us this new spirit so we might live life without fear of the enemy, his power, or his cunning. In 2 Timothy Chapter 1 Paul wrote,

1:7   For God has not given us a spirit of timidity, but of power and love and discipline.

The exercise of these in obedience to our Lord in the Spirit will build strength in our new spirit and glorify God.

Not following God's order in the spiritual realm looses Satan's hosts. They are given an opening to go to the disobedient one with deception in order to destroy his faith and fellowship with God. Once again, the person finds himself in spiritual bondage. Cooperating and agreeing with the enemy always brings bondage. Freedom and liberty accompany the Spirit of the Lord. This does not mean that because the Holy Spirit is present, freedom and liberty will automatically follow. But when the Holy Spirit is the authority being obeyed, the obedient ones will experience freedom. No believer automatically experiences freedom and liberty simply because the Spirit of the Lord lives within him.

The Result of Disobedience

Since believers desiring to be strong in the Lord must obey, what happens if we don't? Joshua 7 answers the question for us.

7:7   And Joshua said, "Alas, O Lord GOD, why didst Thou ever bring this people over the Jordan, only to deliver us into the hand of the Amorites, to destroy us? If only we had been willing to dwell beyond the Jordan!

7:8   "O Lord, what can I say since Israel has turned their back before their enemies?

7:9   "For the Canaanites and all the inhabitants of the land will hear of it, and they will surround us and cut off our name from the earth. And what wilt Thou do for Thy great name?"

7:10   So the LORD said to Joshua, "Rise up! Why is it that you have fallen on your face?

7:11   "Israel has sinned, and they have also transgressed My covenant which I commanded them. And they have even taken some of the things under the ban and have both stolen and deceived. Moreover, they have also put them among their own things.

7:12   "Therefore the sons of Israel cannot stand before their enemies; they turn their backs before their enemies, for they have become accursed. I will not be with you anymore unless you destroy the things under the ban from your midst.

7:13   "Rise up! Consecrate the people and say, 'Consecrate yourselves for tomorrow, for thus the LORD, the God of Israel, has said, "There are things under the ban in your midst, O Israel. You cannot stand before your enemies until you have removed the things under the ban from your midst.""'

What had the children of Israel done so terribly wrong that would allow God to permit their enemy to defeat them so thoroughly? It was He who had sent them into the land where the enemy lived! But they had been deceptive and they had stolen. They had not lived up to their part of their covenant with God.

After Moses died, Joshua became the leader of the Lord's people. God had promised to give Joshua and His people the land of Canaan. He promised that He would never fail them nor forsake them and that He would be with them wherever they went. Then He told Joshua to be strong and courageous and to follow carefully all His instruction. As we have seen, they did not obey His instructions. As a result, they found themselves being run over by the enemy.

The same principle is true today. We cannot stand against our spiritual enemies and keep them from oppressing us unless we are obedient to God. James 4 says,

4:7   Submit therefore to God. Resist the devil and he will flee from you.

If we are not obedient to God, we cannot expect God to bless us or allow us to keep the enemy at arm's length, even if we are practicing other spiritual battle tactics. It just doesn't work that way. Galatians 6 tells us why.

6:7   Do not be deceived, God is not mocked; for whatever a man sows, this he will also reap.

If we sow disobedience, we will reap the consequences, just like the children of Israel did. When we repent and sow obedience, we will reap God's blessings. This is the disciplinary training of our heavenly Father. He does not spoil His children.

Some of God's children that Joshua led were up and down spiritually. Their good days and their bad days seemed to be governed by the circumstances of life. They obeyed if it seemed advantageous. They disobeyed when the profit seemed greater. Joshua gave them some sound advice in Joshua 24.

24:14   "Now, therefore, fear the Lord and serve Him in sincerity and truth . . .

24:15   " . . . choose for yourselves today whom you will serve: . . . as for me and my house, we will serve the Lord."

Christians need to make the same decision. As true children of God, we have already made the decision to accept the Lord Jesus Christ as Savior. We also need to follow Him as Lord. His children must listen for His leadership and obey Him. We must not obey Him like King Saul, whose obedience was partial; God called it rebellion. We need to understand the importance of being obedient to the Lord Jesus Christ. We need to commit completely and wholeheartedly to obey God's will. When we do, we can expect His direction, supervision, and provision.

A Believer Needs Spiritual Sustenance

Another requirement for being strong in the Lord is taking in proper food and drink. In John 6 Jesus said,

6:35   "I am the bread of life; he who comes to Me shall not hunger, and he who believes in Me shall never thirst."

He is our spiritual food and we need to eat heartily. John 6:35 says, "He who comes to Me shall not hunger." Watching the actions of some believers, an observer might think Christians have no hunger for Him personally once they have come to Christ for salvation. Those believers often find themselves spiritually malnourished. Any true nourishment they receive comes from the spoon-feeding of more mature Christians.

When we come to a table for a meal, we don't appear one time only. We come daily and usually several times a day. The Lord Jesus Christ is our life-giving bread. If we do not want to suffer spiritual malnutrition, we need to come to Him frequently to receive spiritual food.

Babies are fed milk and easily digested baby food by their parents. As a child grows, his needs change and he must start eating some solid food, including meat. He also becomes more independent in eating that food. At an early age he begins to rebel against being fed by others and wants to feed himself. We look at that and see it as a healthy, natural growth process.

That same process of maturity is also important in the life of a believer. Listen to Paul in 1 Corinthians 3.

3:1   And I, brethren, could not speak to you as to spiritual men, but as to men of flesh, as to babes in Christ.

3:2   I gave you milk to drink, not solid food; for you were not yet able to receive it. Indeed, even now you are not yet able,

3:3　　for you are still fleshly. For since there is jealousy and strife among you, are you not fleshly, and are you not walking like mere men?

Paul speaks of jealousy and strife; he makes reference to the flesh. That is how the flesh works. Walking after the flesh is equated with being a spiritual baby. In Hebrews 5 we are told:

5:12　　For though by this time you ought to be teachers, you have need again for someone to teach you the elementary principles of the oracles of God, and you have come to need milk and not solid food.

5:13　　For everyone who partakes only of milk is not accustomed to the word of righteousness, for he is a babe.

5:14　　But solid food is for the mature, who because of practice have their senses trained to discern good and evil.

Here we see that the mature Christian has his senses trained to discern good and evil through disciplined practice. How does the mature Christian train? He daily practices obedience. It is inconsistent to think that any believer can have his senses trained to discern good and evil unless he unfailingly and emphatically practices obedience as a way of life.

The Scripture says we cannot grow strong on milk. This book provides you with some Scriptural teaching upon which to meditate. Your responsibility is to chew on the Word, pondering it in your mind until what He says becomes your way of thinking. Then determine to be obedient to whatever God shows you in any given situation. Search the Scripture and learn God's ways.

When the church first started, Scripture tells us that the Jews of Berea didn't naively accept everything they heard. They searched the Scripture to find out if what was being said was true. Believers in Christ need to do the same thing today. We need to search out truth as revealed by God's Spirit and not just accept any wind of doctrine. If we would do that, we would know far more about spiritual warfare than we know now.

A Believer Needs to Communicate with God

Prayer is another requirement to be strong in the Lord. In 1 Thessalonians 5:17 we are told to "pray without ceasing." Prayer is taught throughout the Scripture as a necessary ingredient. Jesus taught his disciples that prayer was important. There are volumes of excellent books that have been written on the subject of prayer. We would do well to utilize some of those resources.

There are several Greek words translated "pray" in the New Testament, indicating there are many types of prayers. What we are considering is the requirement of intimate communication; worshipful conversation with the God we are to love with all our heart, soul, mind, and strength. If we cannot pour out our innermost thoughts, desires, and struggles to Him and listen to His still, small voice of response, we will never learn to recognize His voice when He speaks encouragement and direction during our battle with the enemy.

A Believer Needs Spiritual Exercise

Another requirement to be strong in the Lord is exercise; not physical exercise, but spiritual exercise. We need to know the Scriptures. We need to read them, study them, ponder them, and memorize them. Each of us needs to personally know what the Scripture says and what God is saying to us through it. It is important to ask the Holy Spirit to reveal the truth of Scripture and make it alive as we read the Word. If truth does not take root, what we read may be snatched away.

Another thing we need to exercise and probably don't think about very often is the will. It is important to choose to put what we have learned from Scripture into practice. Learning what God says is not enough; choosing to be obedient to the Word and the will of God is the essential ingredient of true faith, without which it is impossible to please God. To know it in our head cannot substitute for living it out in our life just because we believe it. To do so brings dire consequences.

Review: Essentials of Warfare: The Lord's Strength
Prerequisites to be Strong in the Lord

1. The believer must be weak.

2. The Lord Jesus Christ must be Lord.

3. The believer must be obedient.

4. A believer needs spiritual sustenance.

5. A believer needs to communicate with God.

6. A believer needs spiritual exercise.

As for God, His way is blameless; The word of the LORD is tried;
He is a shield to all who take refuge in Him.

Psalm 18:30

Part 2: The Firm Stand

It does not do much good to be strong or to put on the full armor of God if we are unable to stand firm in obedience. An example of that is given in the opening chapter of Deuteronomy. Moses recounts the children of Israel's history and how they responded to God's wishes.

The Result of Standing Firm on Our Own

You will remember that God wanted the children of Israel in the land of Canaan. They had already spied out the Promised Land and had found it to be a land flowing with milk and honey; but they had also found giants. Due to that discovery, they refused to go in and take possession of the land. As a result, God gave the land of Canaan to their children and told Moses to take his group into the wilderness.

Read Moses' and the children of Israel's discussion of their current situation logged in Deuteronomy Chapter 1:

1:41 "Then you answered and said to me, 'We have sinned against the LORD; we will indeed go up and fight, just as the LORD our God commanded us.' And every man of you girded on his weapons of war, and regarded it as easy to go up into the hill country.

1:42 "And the LORD said to me, 'Say to them, "Do not go up, nor fight, for I am not among you; lest you be defeated before your enemies."'"

1:43   "So I spoke to you, but you would not listen. Instead you rebelled against the command of the LORD, and acted presumptuously and went up into the hill country.

1:44   "And the Amorites who lived in that hill country came out against you, and chased you as bees do, and crushed you from Seir to Hormah.

1:45   "Then you returned and wept before the LORD; but the LORD did not listen to your voice, nor give ear to you."

God did not listen because they were disobedient and rebellious. They were trying to do things in their own way, with their own strength, and on their own timetable. God is neither impressed nor cooperative with that kind of effort. His purpose is to reveal His way, His strength, and His timing through His people. We must listen to what He says to us and obey.

Standing Firm on God's Promises

We need not only to learn God's promises, but how to stand firm on these promises that God has given us. Many are conditional, not automatic. For example, Luke 6:38 tells us to "Give, and it will be given to you. . ." We must first give, and then more will be given to us.

God has given to us first; all we have has been given to us—life, talents, time, and everything it takes to survive and contribute in this world. And this is only in the natural realm. In the spiritual realm, salvation and eternal life have been given through the Lord Jesus Christ.

Once we learn to give, we recognize Him as our endless resource. Our faith in His provision grows as we stand on His Word. Our giving is based on His having given first and trusting Him to keep His word to provide for us. Our resistance to give is to refuse to believe Him as our sufficiency. Our unbelief blocks the flow of His provision.

A Principle for Standing Firm

A principle given in Matthew 8 shows the importance of standing firm on the promises that God gives.

8:18   Now when Jesus saw a crowd around Him, He gave orders to depart to the other side.

8:19   And a certain scribe came and said to Him, "Teacher, I will follow You wherever You go."

8:20   And Jesus said to him, "The foxes have holes, and the birds of the air have nests; but the Son of Man has nowhere to lay His head."

8:21   And another of the disciples said to Him, "Lord, permit me first to go and bury my father."

8:22   But Jesus said to him, "Follow me; and allow the dead to bury their own dead."

8:23   And when He got into the boat, His disciples followed Him.

8:24   And behold there arose a great storm in the sea, so that the boat was covered with the waves; but He Himself was asleep.

8:25   And they came to Him, and awoke Him, saying, "Save us, Lord; we are perishing!"

8:26   And He said to them, "Why are you timid, you men of little faith?" Then He arose, and rebuked the winds and the sea; and it became perfectly calm.

After Jesus and His disciples had boarded the boat, Jesus fell asleep. A powerful storm soon hit with savage force; the boat was being tossed around by the wind and the waves. The disciples awoke Him to inform Him of their state of affairs. They believed they were in a very bad situation; they believed they were about ready to sink and head for Davy Jones' locker.

Any normal person might have replied, "Wow! Am I glad you awakened me! I had no idea there was such a storm raging! I suggest you put your life jackets on and prepare for the worst. This craft can't stand much more of this storm! Prepare to meet thy God!"

However, that is not what Jesus said. Instead He *rebuked* them. Why? Look at these verses again. In verse 18 He had told them to depart to the other side. He had indicated, "Guys, we are here, but we are going over there. That is where we will be shortly."

After saying this, there were some interruptions with seemingly unrelated discussions. Then Jesus and his disciples got into the boat and headed for the other side of the lake. As their journey progressed, a great storm hit with full force. This was not your average afternoon squall. This must have been a horrendous storm to cause such fear in these disciples, who were fishermen. Fishermen operate from boats all the time. They know about storms and how to deal with them. This storm, however, had them scared. They thought they were about to perish. Even with all the knowledge and experience they had, they did not feel capable of dealing with the situation at hand.

Have you ever been in a situation—a great storm of circumstances— and felt like you were not going to survive? Then you said, "God, I'm not going to make it! I am going to sink and drown!" You may even have accused Him of not caring. Faced with such frightening circumstances, we usually begin to muster all the resources at our disposal; anything and everything we can find. With every ounce of strength we have emotionally, physically, and financially, we religiously try to overcome the storm we are facing. But isn't God good! He makes sure the storm is more than we can handle on our own!

While we are in the midst of a great storm and begin thinking that God doesn't care about what is going on in our life, the Lord will rebuke us just as He did His disciples.

Jesus had already told His disciples that they were going to the other side. He had also directed the focus upon Himself as leader to those who had interrupted their journey across the lake. To the one who promised to follow Him anywhere, He reminded how filled with difficulty the way would be. To the other—who was more concerned with getting every responsibility of life settled before following—He focused the first priority upon following Him without reservation.

Once the disciples found themselves in the storm, they lost sight of what Jesus had instructed previously. It was as though He had never said anything about their going to the other side, about the difficulties that would be encountered while following Him, or about focusing their priority on following Him.

When we find ourselves in the middle of a great storm, God permits Satan and his kingdom to sift us like wheat. Satan will do whatever he can to cause us to doubt God's care, to abandon ship, or to turn back. He wants us to do anything—except keep going forward, trusting God no matter what the situation may seem to be.

When God gives us a word and tells us the way He wants us to go, it is our responsibility to obey. Satan knows that if we continue doing things God's way, we will wind up where He directs us with an even stronger faith. Once we do, Satan's kingdom will suffer a defeat. Satan will try to discourage us, sifting us like wheat. Satan and his kingdom do not want us to grow through experiences, but to lose heart and turn back. But God means the journey and the sifting for our good.

So we must learn to stand on the promises that God gives us. Before we make any major decisions, we need to know exactly what God wants us to do. Then, when He shows us our direction, we need to begin the journey He has for us. If we believe God and persevere, we will find ourselves right where He sent us, stronger in the Lord.

Review: Essentials of Warfare
The Firm Stand

In this chapter we have looked at . . .

1.   The result of standing firm on our own.

2.   Standing firm on God's promises.

3.   A principle for standing firm.

> It does not do much good to grow strong or to put on the full armor of God if we are unwilling to stand firm in obedience to God.

Part 3: Putting on God's Armor

An Important Sequence

Ephesians 6 gives instruction on preparing for battle and the equipment that will be needed in the war.

6:10 Finally, be strong in the Lord, and in the strength of His might.

6:11 Put on the full armor of God, that you may be able to stand firm against the schemes of the devil.

Notice the sequence that has been given here: Verse 10 says, "Be strong in the Lord." We have seen that as Joshua led the children of Israel and they obeyed God, they were strong.

Verse 11 says, "Put on the full armor." There is the sequence. First, be strong; second, put on the armor. We do not put on the armor in order to be strong. The sequence is to first be strong, and then put on the armor.

Why Put on the Full Armor?

If we are strong, why should we have to put on the full armor? Look at verses 12 and 13,

6:12 For our struggle is not against flesh and blood, but against the rulers, against the powers, against the world forces of this darkness, against the spiritual forces of wickedness in the heavenly places.

6:13 Therefore, take up the full armor of God, that you may be able to resist in the evil day, and having done everything, to stand firm.

We need to wear the full armor of God in order to oppose and be immovable against the onslaught of the enemy. We need to put on the full armor because we are vulnerable.

An Armored Tank

Let's say that you decide to go into the business of building armored tanks. You decide you want to build a very strong tank—one that will stand up to and surpass anything the enemy might have in the field. You mobilize it with caterpillar tread that enables your tank to operate effectively on ice, marshy ground, mud, rocks, sand, and uneven ground. Your tank is given a powerful engine. You weave the latest technological advances into your mechanics. Then you take the same gauge sheet metal that is on your new car and rivet it to your tank. You look at your powerful tank in pride and decide to market it to the armed forces. You display it to all the important brass. They are impressed with all but two aspects: your tank has no protection and no weaponry. The sheet metal will protect neither the tank nor those inside. Therefore, your tank is of no military value. A tank requires heavy armor plating to withstand the rigors of war. It also must have a powerful system of defense.

Armed with your new information, you equip your tank with heavy armor and implement the most powerful weaponry available through modern technology; you also mount several of the largest caliber machine guns in the industry on it. Now your tank is ready to meet the enemy head-on.

Without the full armor of God, our natural defenses won't protect us from our enemies.

We have a real enemy; we are not merely playing war games. First Peter 5 tells us about one of the enemy's tactics and how to recognize it.

5:8   Be of sober spirit, be on the alert. Your adversary, the devil, prowls around like a roaring lion, seeking someone to devour.

Since the enemy is seeking someone to devour, we should be sensible and on the alert in the same way we safely drive a car. There are two types of drivers. The first—who could be compared to a believer with no armor—has the attitude of one oblivious to everyone and everything around as though they are the only one on the road. They see in short distances only. You've probably seen them; their nose seldom points away from the hood ornament on their car. You wonder how they get from home to their destination without killing themselves or someone else.

The second type of driver is the defensive driver—who could be compared to an armor-wearing believer. A defensive driver doesn't watch just the car ahead of him, but he is continually aware of the traffic flow. If he sees illuminated brake lights on the cars ahead of him, he begins to back off. If he decides to pass someone, he makes certain it is safe to do so before proceeding.

Why is he carefully watching the other drivers? By being on the alert, he can more accurately determine beforehand any potential danger that might come his way. He is prepared to take defensive action at all times in order to maintain safety for himself and his passengers.

Demonic forces are continually looking for ways to cause trouble. We as believers need to be on the alert, just like a defensive driver, to prevent any unnecessary trouble before it starts. If we are wearing the full armor of God, when the smoke of battle clears we will not be a battle casualty. Instead, we will still be standing firm.

Belt of Truth

Paul continues his exhortation in Ephesians.

6:14   Stand firm therefore, having girded your loins with truth, and having put on the breastplate of righteousness,

6:15   and having shod your feet with the preparation of the gospel of peace;

The Scripture tells us to stand firm, encompassed in truth. Ephesians 6:14 says, "Stand firm therefore, having girded your loins with truth . . ."

First Peter 1:13 speaks of girding up the loins of the mind for action. The word *gird* means "to surround or hem in." So the believer is to surround or hem in his mind with something. That something is God's truth, which He has given us in His Word. Bear in mind it is not God's job to gird the believer's mind with truth. That is the job of each individual. When Peter talked about girding up the loins of the mind, the sentence structure is in the imperative; *we* are to do the girding.

Adam and Eve gave the first Scriptural example of how *not* to stand firm in truth. In Genesis 2 and 3 we find:

2:16   And the LORD God commanded the man, saying, "From any tree of the garden you may eat freely;

2:17   but from the tree of the knowledge of good and evil you shall not eat, for in the day that you eat from it you shall surely die."

3:4   And the serpent said to the woman, "You surely shall not die!"

The truth is given in Genesis 2:17: "For in the day you eat from it you shall surely die." The lie is given in Genesis 3:4: "You surely shall not die!" Because our first ancestors did not stand firm, we were born incapable of standing firm. But we have been born-again, and our Father has set us apart as holy. He wants us standing firm in the truth He has given us. The prerequisites for standing in that truth are given in 2 Corinthians 10.

10:3   For though we walk in the flesh, we do not war according to the flesh,

10:4   for the weapons of our warfare are not of the flesh, but divinely powerful for the destruction of fortresses.

10:5   We are destroying speculations and every lofty thing raised up against the knowledge of God, and we are taking every thought captive to the obedience of Christ.

Neither Adam nor Eve did what these verses tell us to do. They did not take their every thought captive. God gave them the truth. The serpent gave them a lie. They rejected the truth and embraced the lie. Satan and his demonic forces are using the same strategy today. They have used this strategy unchanged for so long because it is incredibly effective. If we are going to be effectual against the attacks of the enemy, we must first listen to and believe the truth. Only then can we recognize and reject any lies.

Not only do we have the Scriptures to provide the truth, we have the living Truth as our very life. He is in us, and we are in Him. As we study the truth about the weapons God has provided, we will begin to recognize the armament we wear is the Lord Jesus Christ. No wonder Paul told us to "put on the Lord Jesus Christ, and to make no provision for the flesh in regard to its lust" (Romans 13:14). We must stand in Him for victory.

Put on the Breastplate of Righteousness

A breastplate is essential to our armament, for it covers all the vital organs we depend upon to survive in life. A blow to any of these essential organs can spell defeat, so we must learn to wear righteousness at all times with full understanding.

Two Kinds of Righteousness

The last phrase of Ephesians 6:14 says, ". . . and having put on the breastplate of righteousness." There are two kinds of righteousness. The word *righteousness* means "the character or quality of being right or just." [36]

Self-Righteousness

The first kind of righteousness is self-righteousness. The first part of verse 9 in Philippians Chapter 3 tells us about it.

3:9   and may be found in Him, not having a righteousness of my own derived from the Law . . .

Any righteousness we establish on our own, according to Isaiah 64:6, is "as filthy rags" (KJV). This refers to dirty menstrual cloths—evidence that no life has been produced in this cycle of living. By saying our righteousness is as filthy rags, the prophet is showing how our own self-righteousness cannot produce life, just a smelly mess. A person can try to live a better life, turn over a new leaf, determine to do what is right, read the Bible more, pray more, and do lots of good things for the Lord, but he cannot make himself righteous. He cannot give himself the character or quality of being right or just before God. If he depends upon his own actions, they must all be absolutely perfect; to fail in only one is equivalent to total failure.

The Righteousness of God

Since the fall of man, the only right standing any person could obtain came by receiving it as a gift of God's grace through faith. The first specific reference in Scripture that explains God's method of imputing righteousness to man's account is found in Genesis Chapter 15 in regard to Abram.

15:6   Then he believed in the Lord; and He reckoned it to him as righteousness.

Abram was not the first to be reckoned as righteous, however, for the Faith Hall of Fame framed in Chapter 11 of Hebrews begins with Abel.

11:4   By faith Abel offered to God a better sacrifice than Cain, through which he obtained the testimony that he was righteous, God testifying about his gifts, and through faith, though he is dead, he still speaks.

Regardless of the law that came later, no man established his own righteousness, but received it by faith, then lived it out by faith in God's promises. Throughout the Old Testament this was true, though they never fully realized all the promises they received.

We, however, have been provided something better. We have received the revelation of Christ and His Spirit. Through the Lord Jesus Christ we become the righteousness of God, according to 2 Corinthians Chapter 5.

5:17   Therefore if any man is in Christ, he is a new creature; the old things passed away; behold, new things have come.

5:18   Now all these things are from God, who reconciled us to Himself through Christ, and gave us the ministry of reconciliation.

5:21   He made Him who knew no sin to be sin on our behalf, that we might become the righteousness of God in Him.

This is all the work of God; He placed in us a new spirit, the Spirit of Christ, who has become our life and our righteousness. It has been accomplished by grace through God's gift of faith; sealed by the Holy Spirit. There is nothing about which we may boast. Colossians 2, however, reveals that receiving is not enough.

2:6   As you therefore have received Christ Jesus the Lord, so walk in Him.

As children of God, we can now illustrate His righteousness, fulfilling His purpose for us to the praise of the glory of His grace. Look at the following verses in Ephesians Chapter 2:

2:8   For by grace you have been saved through faith; and that not of yourselves, it is the gift of God;

2:9   not as a result of works, that no one should boast.

2:10   For we are His workmanship, created in Christ Jesus for good works, which God prepared beforehand, that we should walk in them.

We see our need to practice righteousness in 1 John Chapter 2 and 3.

2:29   If you know that He is righteous, you know that everyone also who practices righteousness is born of Him.

3:7   Little children, let no one deceive you; the one who practices righteousness is righteous, just as He is righteous.

The importance of confessing our sin is evident from 1 John Chapter 1.

1:6   If we say that we have fellowship with Him and yet walk in the darkness, we lie and do not practice the truth;

1:7   but if we walk in the light as He Himself is in the light, we have fellowship with one another, and the blood of Jesus His Son cleanses us from all sin.

1:8   If we say that we have no sin, we are deceiving ourselves, and the truth is not in us.

1:9   If we confess our sins, He is faithful and righteous to forgive us our sins and to cleanse us from all unrighteousness.

These verses make it plain that we, as believers, are to walk in righteousness; that is, as God's children we are to practice righteousness. When we fail and confess our sin, God cleanses us from the unrighteous programming of our flesh. If a person has demons oppressing him and there is some unconfessed sin in his life, that person could not force a demon to leave him alone. Because of the unconfessed sin, the demon is not required to leave; he retains his legal right to afflict.

We are to gird our minds with truth. Jesus prayed for us, saying, "Sanctify them in the truth; Thy word is truth" (John 17:17).

Sanctification

The word *sanctification* means "to separate from evil things and ways."[37] Sanctification means "to separate from the world and to consecrate to God. To sanctify anything is to declare that it belongs to God. . . . In an ethical sense sanctification means the progressive conforming of the believer into the image of Christ, or the process by which the life is made morally holy."[38]

According to 2 Thessalonians Chapter 2, sanctification is God's purpose for believers.

2:13   But we should always give thanks to God for you, brethren beloved by the Lord, because God has chosen you from the beginning for salvation through sanctification by the Spirit and faith in the truth.

Do you want to know God's will? Sanctification is part of it. God disciples His people and expects them to be obedient. He wants them to choose to live their life in a manner consistent with His holiness. To willfully go against what we know Scripture says is to rebel against God our Father!

Sanctification is not something that comes automatically to our soul.[39] It must be learned and perfected by obedience to God's Word. No one can accomplish it for us. Each of us must go through the experiences God allows in order to mature us. The righteousness of our new spirit is worked into our soul, becoming the basis of our actions.

We received righteousness from God. When we practice that righteousness, it becomes a part of our mind, our emotions, and the exercising of our will. In the course of our life, we receive training in how to live life in a righteous manner. In 2 Timothy Chapter 3 we find that . . .

3:16   All Scripture is inspired by God and profitable for teaching, for reproof, for correction, for training in righteousness.

How to Put on the Breastplate of Righteousness

When Ephesians 6:14 talks about our putting on the breastplate of righteousness, what does that mean? First, we must believe we are in right standing with God on the basis of what the Lord Jesus Christ has done for us on the cross. God placed Jesus' Spirit into each believer. It is a gift. It cannot be earned.

Secondly, Christians must practice righteousness based on the belief that we are now God's righteousness. Righteousness becomes a part of our mind, emotions, and will; that is, it becomes an essential element of our personality. In turn, our righteous thoughts, emotions, and decisions of the will are expressed by our physical actions.

As a person begins to practice the righteousness of his spirit, he will not think like he did before being born-again. Instead, he will begin making more Christ-like choices, and his soul will be conformed more and more into the image of Christ. His actions will demonstrate the character of God. That occurs because righteousness is becoming a part of his personality. Righteousness becomes a lifestyle. It supernaturally becomes a natural part of the believer through practice.

Shod Your Feet

Ephesians 6:15 says, "And having shod your feet with the preparation of the gospel of peace." Having our feet shod with the gospel is like having new tires on our car. New tires will provide confidence as we drive on muddy or snowy roads. New tires are dependable; they decrease or eliminate our worrying about flats or blowouts. A brand new set of tires provides maximum traction and increased mobility in any circumstance. The same is true in regard to having new shoes for our feet. If we put carefully constructed shoes on our feet, we are prepared to walk anywhere required. What is necessary in preparing the proper spiritual shoes?

The word *preparation* means "the state of being prepared or ready." First Peter 3:15 instructs us to always be ready to present our reasons for the hope we hold in life so we can reply to anyone who asks. We must each study to learn the truth of God's promises to us, to put in our own words why we look forward with confidence—for Jesus Christ in us is our hope and peace. Without Him there is no true peace with God, with ourselves, or with any other person. There is no possibility for us to walk in peace or to share that peace with others.

Romans 5 says,

5:1   Therefore having been justified by faith, we have peace with God through our Lord Jesus Christ.

When we become Christians, there is no longer any warfare with God. We are at peace with Him, because we are now accepted in His Son and we are a part of His family. With this assurance, Philippians 4 continues the good news with instruction and promise for every circumstance.

4:6   Be anxious for nothing, but in everything by prayer and supplication with thanksgiving let your requests be made known to God.

4:7   And the peace of God, which surpasses all comprehension, shall guard your hearts and your minds in Christ Jesus.

We have *peace with God* at salvation. We also need to have the *peace of God*, especially during a storm. We need it when the waves come in over us and we don't understand all that is crashing around us. It is in those times we don't know how to escape or survive on our own. Although that may be going on in our life, if we have our armor on, we can experience the peace of God because of the faithfulness of the Lord Jesus Christ. Those situations that would normally devastate us have little or no effect; the peace of God guards our heart and our mind.

However, we must learn to walk in God's peace at all times. If we are walking after the flesh, we cannot enjoy the peace of God because Romans 8:6 says, "The mind set on the flesh is death, but the mind set on the Spirit is life and peace." A part of our spiritual fruit is peace. It is only by walking in the Spirit that we can obey the commands of Colossians 3:15, which tells us to let the peace of Christ rule in our hearts—and Hebrews 12:14, which instructs us to pursue peace with all men.

The Shield of Faith

Ephesians 6 continues,

6:16   In addition to all, taking up the shield of faith with which you will be able to extinguish all the flaming missiles of the evil one.

We are to pick up, hold, and be ready to use the shield of faith in order to put out the fiery arrows that the enemy shoots at us. Satan and his demons are completely familiar with all our points of vulnerability. They know exactly what ammunition will bore a hole right through us to provoke hurt, anger, and every sinful response. But God has provided a shield the size of a door—that's the root word for *shield*—to protect us completely! That door is Christ, our truth, our righteousness, our hope, and our peace; He provides the basis for our faith.

Word: Logos or Rhema

The word for *word* can be translated two ways in the Greek. *Logos* refers to "the content of communication." *Rhema* refers to the "communication of that content." The Spirit of Christ communicates the content of God's truth to us as the way of life. When God's Spirit reveals something to us, He makes it living truth. Luke 2 gives us an example:

2:25   And behold, there was a man in Jerusalem whose name was Simeon; and this man was righteous and devout, looking for the consolation of Israel; and the Holy Spirit was upon him.

2:26   And it had been revealed to him by the Holy Spirit that he would not see death before he had seen the Lord's Christ.

2:27   And he came in the Spirit into the temple; and when the parents brought in the child Jesus, to carry out for Him the custom of the Law,

2:28   then he took Him into his arms, and blessed God, and said,

2:29   "Now Lord, Thou dost let Thy bond-servant depart in peace, according to Thy word;

2:30   for my eyes have seen Thy salvation."

The Greek word in verse 29 translated "word" is not logos; it is *rhema*. We could read it, " . . . let Thy bond-servant depart in peace according to Thy *rhema*"—according to that which has been communicated to me. Verse 26 says it had been revealed or communicated to him by the Holy Spirit.

Romans 10:17 uses the same term: "So faith comes from hearing, and hearing by the word (*rhema*) of Christ." Faith comes from what we hear by the word of Christ. In John 10 the Lord gave these promises to us:

10:27   "My sheep hear My voice, and I know them, and they follow Me;

10:28   and I give eternal life to them, and they shall never perish; and no one shall snatch them out of My hand.

10:29　"My Father, who has given them to Me, is greater than all; and no one is able to snatch them out of the Father's hand.

10:30　"I and the Father are one."

What greater shield of protection could we ask for than to be safely in the hand of God?

Faith Defined

The word *faith* means "trust, reliance." The background of the word comes from the idea of rolling one's complete weight over upon something as trustworthy. Faith is active when we trust the faithfulness of the Lord Jesus Christ, the truth of His teaching, and the redemptive work He accomplished at Calvary. As a result, we totally submit to Him and His message, which are accepted as God's truth. Vine defines *faith* as a "firm persuasion or conviction based on hearing."[40] As an example, when the Scripture says that God created the earth, most believers have no problem trusting that God created the earth. It is easier to believe what God says about creation than to believe man's speculations about it! But faith includes more than one element.

Elements of Faith

First, faith requires a basis of truth. Second, faith requires a knowledge, or awareness of that truth. We have been given the mind of Christ, which activates that truth in our soul. When God reveals something to us, He uses that part of man's spirit that some theologians call the intuition.[41] We know that we know it is true, although we may not know how we know, nor do we know how to explain it.

The third element of faith is our assent with truth. We choose to be in agreement with what God has shown us intuitively. The fourth element of faith is our committal to that truth. We act according to what we believe. The emotions may or may not play a part in all this. We may experience an emotion when we decide to obey God, but it doesn't necessarily have to be there. The emotions should never control the decisions we make.

The Use of the Shield of Faith

We are told to take up the shield of faith. How does the shield of faith work? What do we do with it? Verse 16 says, "In addition to all, taking up the shield of faith with which you will be able to extinguish all the flaming missiles of the evil one." Faith is used to extinguish or quench the ammunition that the enemy fires at us. Remember, these missiles are not something we can see physically coming toward us. These missiles are the contaminated thoughts or imaginations that come our way. They are the accusations and doubts that Satan throws at us; even his distorting of God's Word, which is intended to sidetrack our faith.

What, then, does it mean to take up the shield of faith? It means we respond to Satan's attacks with an unyielding resolve to implement the truth as the Holy Spirit has revealed it. Then we must stand firm in faith despite what our thoughts may be telling us or how our feelings may be trying to manipulate us. We must choose to act upon what God has revealed to us. Jesus responded to Satan's fiery tests with, "It is written . . ." and submitted to God.

That is very easy to say, yet it is very difficult to do. When we are honest, we will acknowledge that the hardest thing we ever do in our life is to learn unconditional trust in God. Yet, if we talk to people and ask them if they trust God, they would probably feel insulted because they had been asked. We say we trust God, but if the truth were really known, it is often only lip service. When we are in our great storm, the easiest thing to do is to base our thinking upon the information we receive from the world, focusing on circumstances we can physically see. It is easier to respond according to the natural than to respond to what we Scripturally know to be true in our heart. However, it's not nearly as rewarding, nor does it reflect the wisdom of God.

We have talked about the "great storms" of life. There is another storm we face that may not be as easily recognized. Some of our worst times of trusting God come when we are experiencing the easy times of life. During these times, reliance upon habit patterns that have worked in the past are resorted to because we don't "need" God and His ways when our situation is comfortable. During a great storm, we often are able to understand our own inadequacy to provide solutions to our problems and turn to God, who uses spiritually turbulent weather to bring us to greater dependence on Him rather than the world system.

If we are going to take up the shield of faith as we go through one of these storms, we must listen to the truth God recalls to our memory. We must choose to agree with the truth we have received. Then we must choose to act on that truth instead of reacting according to what our circumstances are telling us is true.

The truth is undeniable: God has begun a good work in the life of every believer. He will not be sidetracked; He will complete what he has begun. Each Christian has to practice standing firm in faith throughout every part of life, not just when the enemy says, "Ha! Where is your God now? Where is He in this situation?" The enemy may test us through thoughts put directly into our mind, or he may use a friend or a neighbor to shoot his fiery missiles.

When we go through a great storm, if we have previously accepted God's truth, His Spirit will recall to our remembrance the *rhema* that He has given us. Then we can stand on His word and say, "God, the storm is great. It's more than I can bear alone; I feel like I'm going under. I feel like no one cares. I feel deserted and rejected. I feel like I am on a one-man trail that leads nowhere, and I feel useless and hopeless. I know my thoughts and feelings do not line up with your Word. Therefore, I am making the choice to keep believing and trusting that Your Word is true and You are in control of my life. You began a good work in me, and I know that You won't quit until that work is complete. I want You to do whatever You need to do in my life to get me to Your goal."

At the point of our need when we have no reserve strength or resources of our own, God will give us what we need to continue even though the circumstances may get worse. His power is perfectly displayed through our weaknesses, which He will use to shame the world's strengths (1 Corinthians 10:13; 2 Corinthians 12:9).

The enemy wants us to feel useless and hopeless. He wants to sift us like wheat and reveal us as being weaklings and failures. If we don't stand on the *rhema* that God has given, the enemy will divert us from God's direction. Should that happen, Satan and his kingdom may be the winners of a battle, but God will still win the war. He must then get us back on track to complete His work in us. In the meantime, He must find someone else to do what He wanted us to do, and we will lose a reward.

The Helmet of Salvation

Ephesians 6 goes on to say,

6:17   And take the helmet of salvation . . ."

This helmet of salvation does not refer to being born-again. Paul is not saying, "Oh, by the way, now you need to be saved!"

What does a helmet cover? It covers the head. What is in our head? Our brain. Thayer's Lexicon defines *salvation* as the "deliverance from the molestation of enemies."[42] Paul is telling us to take hold of the saving work of Christ, allowing it to deliver and preserve our mind from the world, the flesh, and the devil. By instructing us to take up the full armor of God, Paul wants us to be delivered from the molestation of enemies.

Not only are we to take up the helmet of salvation, but we are also to take up the sword of the Spirit.

The Sword of the Spirit

Paul continues his discourse in Ephesians:

6:17   . . . and the sword of the Spirit, which is the word of God.

A sword is a weapon of war. It is used to defend ourselves, others, or possessions. It is also used to cut down the enemy. What is the Christian's sword? It is the Word of God. In this verse, the Greek word used is not logos; it is *rhema*.

To be engaged in spiritual warfare, we cannot simply take any Scripture (*logos*) we have read. The written word is not the sword of the Spirit. To take up the sword of the Spirit, we need to listen for *rhema*. We must take that which the Holy Spirit reveals to us through our spirit and use that specific truth in our battle against the enemy—it will always agree with the *logos*. That is the way the Lord Jesus Christ exercised His authority. When Satan came against Him, Jesus said, "It is written. . . ." If we are using God's *rhema*, we are speaking what the Holy Spirit has revealed. We are not simply quoting a verse off the top of our head. We are using God's specific truth for each unique battle.

Getting the Order Right

Look at the following elements of these verses again.

6:14   having girded your loins with truth
        having put on the breastplate of righteousness

6:15   *having shod* your feet

6:16   *taking up* the shield of faith

6:17   *take* the helmet of salvation
        take the sword of the Spirit

Verse 14 tells us first to gird our loins with truth. If we are listening to the lies of the enemy, we are not wrapped about with truth. We cannot pay attention to the enemies' distortions and the truth of God simultaneously. They are like oil and water; they don't mix.

Verse 14 continues by telling us to put on the breastplate of righteousness. If we don't know that we have been made righteous in our spirit and that we are in the process of learning to act righteously in our soul and body, we are missing a vital piece of armor.

Verse 15 instructs us to shod our feet with the preparation of the gospel of peace. If a believer does not understand his full acceptance in Christ and the fullness of Christ's payment for the sins of the whole world, he can neither walk in the peace of God as he interacts with abrasive others, nor can he effectively share the Good News with them because his feet are not shod with the gospel of peace. That piece of armor is not in place.

Verses 16 and 17 tell us to take up the shield of faith, the helmet of salvation, and the sword of the Spirit. The believer must first gird, put on, and shod. It is only after this initial action that he can proceed to take up the shield of faith, the helmet of salvation, and the sword of the Spirit.

We cannot take up the shield of faith or take negative thoughts captive if we don't know the truth. If we have not girded, put on, and shod, neither can we wield the sword of the Spirit because we will not be dressed in the armor of God.

Without this full armor of God in place, we will not be able to recognize and defeat the maneuvers of our enemy. Nor will we be able to pray continually in the Spirit or intercede for the body of Christ.

Perseverance in Prayer

The Apostle Paul makes another important point in the sixth chapter of Ephesians:

6:18   With all prayer and petition pray at all times in the Spirit, and with this in view, be on the alert with all perseverance and petition for all the saints.

How little or how much importance we give to prayer will determine the effectiveness of our warfare.

In this study of the full armor of God, we have considered the battle weaponry that has been given to us through the Lord Jesus Christ. But unless we stand in His truth, living our lives in proof that He is our way, our truth, and our life, we will never experience His victory.

Pray in the Spirit

We have been encouraged to walk in the Spirit in order to manifest the righteousness of God. The basic essential of that walk is prayer; James 5:16 tells us that the prayers of the righteous are greatly effective. Since this is God's evaluation, we must set our hearts to pray—to pray at all times from our righteous spirit. When we do not know how we should pray, God has already provided His Holy Spirit in answer to our need. Consider Romans 8:

8:26   And in the same way the Spirit also helps our weakness; for we do not know how to pray as we should, but the Spirit Himself intercedes for us with groanings too deep for words;

8:27   and He who searches the hearts knows what the mind of the Spirit is, because He intercedes for the saints according to the will of God.

From this second verse we see that our resurrected High Priest is also active on our behalf. Along with the prayers of the Holy Spirit, He is interceding for us (Hebrews 7:25).

Kinds of Prayers

When we read our instructions to pray with prayers and petitions, we may think the statement is repetitive. We are not, however, as knowledgeable as we ought to be on this subject. Though a later chapter is devoted to a more complete study of warfare praying, we will deal here with the subject in the context of Ephesians Chapter 6.

The Greek word translated *prayer* is a general term denoting "communication with God, offering devotion, speaking intimately in worshipful conversation." It is the regular giving and receiving of meaningful communication with our heavenly Father. This intimate association day by day strengthens our faith and our fellowship with Him. Those with whom we never converse, we never truly get to know.

Jesus spent much time in prayer regardless of the pressures in His daily life on this earth. Though the crowds and their demands pressed heavily upon Him, it was through prayer He discerned His direction for the day. We get a glimpse of this in Luke 4:42–44. Jesus had spent the previous day speaking in the synagogue and delivering a man there of an unclean demon. He had then healed Peter's mother-in-law before sitting down to rest. But the crowds poured in and He spent the remainder of the day and into the night laying hands on every one of them, delivering them from demons and healing their diseases. Did He "sleep in" the next day for a well-deserved rest? Look at the beginning of verse 42.

4:42   And when the day came, He departed and went to a lonely place
        . . .

His habit was to spend time alone, drawing apart to be with His Father. Time after time we read of His need for this fellowship. It is what kept Him on track with His Father's direction, as we see in the remainder of these verses in Luke 4.

4:42   . . . and the multitudes were searching for Him, and came to Him, and tried to keep Him from going away from them.

4:43   But He said to them, "I must preach the kingdom of God to the other cities also, for I was sent for this purpose."

4:44   And He kept on preaching in the synagogues of Judea.

Exciting victories over the enemy's destructive work upon man must never dictate our response to any situation. Only prayer at all times can keep us in the work God has designed for us.

Petitions

The Greek word translated *petition* denotes "the expression of personal needs, asking God and seeking after His provision for them." He is our supply and He has revealed to us the means to receive them, respectively, in 1 John 5:15 and Philippians 4.

5:15   And if we know that he hears us, whatsoever we ask, we know that we have the petitions that we desired of him (KJV).

4:19   But my God shall supply all your need according to his riches in glory by Christ Jesus (KJV).

Our needs have been fulfilled in Christ and we receive that provision by request. We must not forget that we are each a part of the whole body of Christ and that our own prosperity of spirit, soul, and body is dependent on the well-being of all the saints. We do not fight our battles alone; we are a part of the army of God. United in our stand together, we will experience greater victory. Look at how God is glorified through our interdependence in Chapter 1 of 2 Corinthians. It was God . . .

1:10   who delivered us from so great a peril of death, and will deliver us, He on whom we have set our hope. And He will yet deliver us,

1:11   you also joining in helping us through your prayers, that thanks may be given by many persons on our behalf for the favor bestowed upon us through the prayers of many.

It will do no good to put on the whole armor of God's provision in Christ if we do not keep alert with our prayers and intercessions.

Review: Essentials of Warfare
Putting on God's Armor

To put on the full armor of God, we need to . . .

1.　put on the belt of truth (6:14).

2.　put on the breastplate of righteousness (6:14).

3.　shod our feet (6:15).

4.　take up the shield of faith (6:16).

5.　take the helmet of salvation (6:17).

6.　take the sword of the Spirit (6:17).

7.　persevere in prayer (6:18).

8.　pray in the Spirit (6:18).

> Christians must put on the full armor of God; our natural defenses will not protect us from spiritual enemies.

Chapter 8

Names of God

Part 1: Meaning Behind the Names

To help equip us to better deal with demonic oppression, we need to ponder the names of God and learn about the character of the Lord Jesus Christ. As we study His names, if you do not know God as described, note the name so you can refer to it later. Even better, ask God to make that name real in your experience. We have been given eternal life that we may know our God.

Adonai

Adonai, a plural Hebrew word usually written as "Lord" in most translations, means "Master or Lord"; it denotes ownership. Adonai is the one who must be obeyed. The Septuagint, a Greek Old Testament used during the days that the Lord Jesus Christ walked the earth, used the word *kurios* for it's translation of Adonai—the same word the New Testament uses in reference to the Lord Jesus Christ; it denotes not only the possessor and owner of all things, but the absolute ruler over every other rank and relationship. The name implies that all those who submit to Him can enter Christ's perfect rest, expecting to receive God's direction, supervision, and provision.

David was a man after God's own heart. Though his life was not always above reproach, his heart was always tender before God and easily broken over his sin. His trust was firm and unshakable in his Lord. He respected the authorities the Lord established and though they threatened his life, his faith remained firm in his Lord as avenger. In adversity and in triumph, in pain and in pleasure, in understanding and in perplexity, in flight and in pursuit, in positions of submission and authority David's praise pours forth in the Psalms to Adonai, his Lord.

- His hope was placed in Adonai as he waited for Him (Psalm 39:7).

- He saw Adonai as the sustainer of his soul—as the One to whom he looked to keep his soul from giving way when under trial or affliction (Psalm 54:4).

- He saw Adonai as the source of his hope and confidence (Psalm 71:5).

- He saw Adonai as his refuge; a place of shelter, protection, or safety (Psalm 73:28).

- He trusted Adonai to make his soul glad (Psalm 86:4).

- He saw Adonai as good and ready to forgive. He saw Him as abundant in lovingkindness (Psalm 86:5).

- He chose to glorify Adonai forever (Psalm 86:12).

- He saw Adonai as merciful, gracious, slow to anger, yet abundant in lovingkindness and truth (Psalm 86:15).

- He saw his Adonai as the strength of his salvation (Psalm 140:7).

Isaiah saw Adonai sitting on a throne, lofty and exalted (Isaiah 6:1). The prophet heard Adonai asking for volunteers to speak to His people and answered the call (Isaiah 6:8).

Ezekiel informs us of Israel's permissive attitude in defiance of Adonai when they said, "The way of the Lord is not right" (Ezekiel 18:25).

How many in the church today live as though the information in Ezekiel's statement about Israel were true, and look at the values of our society for verification? The numbers might reveal part of the reason the church is lacking in spiritual power. Listen to Adonai's response in the same verse to the people's statement.

18:25 ". . . Hear now, O house of Israel! Is My way not right? Is it not your ways that are not right?

The Lord Jesus Christ in striking similarity asked this question in Luke Chapter 6.

6:46 "And why do you call Me, 'Lord, Lord,' and do not do what I say?"

It is essential that we recognize Adonai as absolute ruler over every authority in rank and relationship. It is He who is master over all. It is He who has established "right." In a society filled with demands about individual rights, we can become deceived into thinking that those perceived rights overrule His ways that are right. Should we fall into that trap, we would be as wrong as were the people of Ezekiel's day.

Elohim

Elohim is a plural Hebrew word usually written as *God* in most translations. It means "the strong, faithful One—the only true God."

In the beginning, Elohim created the heavens and the earth. Whatever Elohim spoke came to pass. Everything He created and brought into being He pronounced as "good." He created man in His own image and enjoyed fellowship with him in the garden. He observed as Adam named all the creatures that He had made. Elohim saw that it was not good for Adam to be alone; He took a rib from Adam's side and formed it into a suitable mate to help him.

After Adam and Eve were driven from the garden, the earth's population began to grow. All the earth became corrupt in the sight of Elohim the Creator; therefore, He determined to destroy it.

However, one man had found favor with Elohim. That man was Noah. Elohim told Noah to build an ark, and to fill it with two of every kind of animal. Elohim then destroyed His corrupted creation with the flood. After the flood waters had covered the entire earth, Elohim remembered Noah and the animals in the ark. It was Elohim who caused the wind to pass over the earth and to dry the waters. It was Elohim who told Noah and his family when to leave the ark and release the animals. It was Elohim who blessed Noah and his sons, and told them to be fruitful, multiply, and fill the earth. It was Elohim who accomplished all things by His Word.

Abram fell on his face before Elohim, who promised to be his God and to establish an everlasting covenant with him and his descendants. It was Elohim who remembered Abraham and sent Lot from the midst of Sodom and Gomorrah before He destroyed them. It was Elohim who tested Abraham's faith in the proposed sacrifice of his only son and provided a substitute sacrifice at just the right moment.

Elohim gave Jacob a new name and formed a nation through him, a people called by His name. He purposed through Joseph to lead them into Egypt. There He made them strong through adversity, then delivered them into the wilderness. He kept them, fed them, and clothed them in their wilderness journey until they learned His character and ways. It was then that Elohim brought them into the land of promise—the land filled with milk and honey.

Elohim did not forsake His people, though they did not remain faithful to Him. Over and over He disciplined them until, after many years in captivity, they learned to have no other gods before Him.

Elohim, who sent Moses to deliver His people, promised that He would raise up a prophet from Israel. This One would be their savior and establish an eternal kingdom for God's people. This One came as promised and was crucified. But He was also raised from the dead and seated at the right hand of God where He ever lives as our God and Savior, the Lord Jesus Christ.

It is the Lord Jesus Christ who is our Elohim, our strong, faithful one—the true God who delivers us from all our enemies and failures. He faithfully accomplished the work His father sent Him to do, and His faithfulness continues even now as He intercedes for us.

El Elyon

El is the singular form of Elohim. *Elyon* means "the Supreme Highest, all others are below Him." El Elyon is usually translated "the Most High." He is sovereign over all. Andrew Jukes makes this comment:

El, like in El Shaddai, means might or power. "Thus the word "Elyon" or "Most High" here applied to God, reveals, that, though He is the "Highest" there are others below Him, endowed by Him with like natures, and therefore in some way related to Him; but that, because He is the "Highest" He has the power to rule and turn them as He will should they be disobedient or seek to exalt themselves against Him."[43]

An example of this comes from the archives of heaven itself. Recorded in Isaiah 14 we find:

14:12 "How have you fallen from heaven, O star of the morning, son of the dawn! You have been cut down to the earth, you who have weakened the nations!

14:13 "But you said in your heart, 'I will ascend to heaven; I will raise my throne above the stars of God, and I will sit on the mount of the assembly in the recesses of the north.

14:14 'I will ascend above the heights of the clouds; I will make myself like the Most High (El Elyon).'

14:15 "Nevertheless you will be thrust down to Sheol, to the recesses of the pit."

These verses are spoken to the King of Babylon, but they also refer to Satan.[44] Satan was created Lucifer, the shining one, the bright star of the heavens. The seal of perfection—both in wisdom and beauty—was upon him. God placed him on the holy mountain of God, blameless from the day he was created. Then, with only six words, Scripture tells us how Lucifer fell from his high position of anointed cherub. The last phrase in Ezekiel 28 gives us the sad commentary:

28:15 "You were blameless in your ways from the day you were created, until unrighteousness was found in you."

Unrighteousness was found in Lucifer. What was this unrighteousness? Charles Ryrie gives some insight on Isaiah 14:13, 14, which is believed to describe Satan's fall.

Five phrases beginning with *I will* describe Satan's sin. He wished to occupy heaven, the abode of God Himself. To exalt his throne above the stars of God may refer to his desire to rule all the angelic creatures, or it may simply be another way to indicate his self-exaltation. North, in heathen literature, indicated the abode of the gods; thus, Satan was ambitious to govern the universe as the council (assembly) of Babylonian gods supposedly did. He wanted the glory that belonged to God alone and his entire goal was to be like the Most High (Heb., Elyon).[45]

Satan became unrighteous, was cast from the mountain of God (Ezekiel 28:16), and was thrown down to the earth with his followers (Revelation 12:7–9). El Elyon will have no other gods before Him; this is His first commandment.

Daniel was told that the saints of the Highest One would receive the kingdom and possess it forever (Daniel 7:27). Jesus, the son of the Most High, provided entrance to the kingdom of heaven and believers are referred to as sons of the kingdom. We receive all that pertains to the kingdom of God by faith walked out in obedience to Him.

The Lord Jesus Christ has given us an example of faithfulness and humility to the Most High God by His submissive obedience. As a result, He is set over every name named. Our victory in warfare can only be accomplished with the same submissiveness, tearing down every thought within our mind which lifts itself in opposition to the Truth, the Most High God.

El Olam

Olam means "eternal, perpetual, from before time began to beyond the end of future time." El Olam is the Everlasting God, the God of Ages, the God of Eternity.

Because He is the God of eternity, what He does transcends what we call "time." His actions rise above and go beyond the limits of time. Webster defines *eternity* as "infinite time; endless. It is duration without beginning or end." Look at some of what God does with His eye beholding eternity.

- He establishes everlasting covenants (Genesis 9:16).

- What He gives to His people, He gives as an everlasting possession (Genesis 17:8).

- His anointing qualified priests to minister through a perpetual (eternal) priesthood (Exodus 40:15).

- He is our eternal, safe refuge (Deuteronomy 33:27).

- He established the righteous with an everlasting foundation in the passing storm (Proverbs 10:25).

- He provides Israel with everlasting salvation (Isaiah 45:17).

- He shames and brings everlasting disgrace to our persecutors (Jeremiah 20:11).

- He loves us with an everlasting love (Jeremiah 31:3).

- His kingdom and dominion is everlasting (Daniel 4:3).

- His ways are everlasting (Habakkuk 3:6).

- He gives all men the opportunity to inherit eternal life because of His great love (John 3:16).

- He deals out retribution to those who don't know God. Their penalty will be eternal destruction away from the presence, glory, and power of the Lord (2 Thessalonians 1:8, 9).

- He provides believers with eternal comfort and hope by His grace (2 Thessalonians 2:16).

- He provides eternal salvation through the Lord Jesus Christ (Hebrews 5:9).

His reproach is everlasting as well. He has kept rebellious angels in eternal chains under darkness for His judgment (Jude 6). His enemies can look forward only to everlasting fire, punishment, and destruction. El Olam is truly the Eternal God.

El Roi

Roi comes from the Hebrew root meaning "to see, to perceive, understand, and know." El Roi is the God who sees.

A Christian working in real estate told of a man he'd met from a different denomination who had been visiting one of the houses of prostitution in Nevada. The Christian asked if he was not concerned that God would see what he was doing.

The man replied, "Oh, no. . . . God is in His temple, and I'm in Nevada. There is no way He's going to see me."

Do we think that God does not see us and know what we are doing on a moment-to-moment basis? Do we think He does not care what we are doing? As we come to better understand each of God's names, we more clearly comprehend His character. This named attribute describes His ability to not only see, but to understand everything. We can see this attribute even in creation. God saw each thing He created and saw that it was good. As the years passed, however, God saw that man's thoughts and actions were evil. Not only did He see the physical man, he also saw the inward man. David, in Psalm 139, describes this attribute of God.

139:1   O LORD, Thou hast searched me and known me.

139:2   Thou dost know when I sit down and when I rise up; Thou dost understand my thought from afar.

139:7   Where can I go from Thy Spirit? Or where can I flee from Thy presence?

David went on to say that it didn't matter if he were in heaven, Sheol, or the remotest part of the sea; God would be there to lead him. Scripture continually reveals God as seeing and knowing all.

We have already seen how God saw the oppression of His people in Egypt and raised up Moses to deliver them from their suffering. Man, however, is often deceived. Pharaoh, just like the real estate man's acquaintance, thought God was not around. Man's complacent attitude is exposed in Psalm 10.

10:11   He says to himself, "God has forgotten; He has hidden His face; He will never see it."

Not only does El Roi see, but He endows His children with the ability to see from His perspective. Jesus gave sight to blind physical eyes; but He also told Nicodemus that a man must be born-again before he is able to see the kingdom of God. The Lord Jesus Christ validates the importance of seeing things from God's perspective in John Chapter 5:

5:19 "Truly, truly, I say to you, the Son can do nothing of Himself, unless it is something He sees the Father doing; for whatever the Father does, these things the Son also does in like manner."

This is the law of the Spirit of life in Christ Jesus that sets us free from the law of sin and death—doing only what the Father shows us to do. Consider the work the Lord Jesus Christ was sent to earth to do: that He might destroy the works of the devil. In the same way the Father sent Him, He sends us with this promise in the gospel of John.

14:12 "Truly, truly, I say to you, he who believes in Me, the works that I do shall he do also; and greater works than these shall he do; because I go to the Father."

We can only do the works that our Father prepared for us by exercising spiritual eyes given by El Roi—by seeing circumstances from His perspective. This is seeing things hoped for, giving substance to things unseen; this is the life of faith walked out in obedience.

El Shaddai

The Hebrew word *Shaddai* means "most powerful in strength, omnipotent." El Shaddai is translated either "God Almighty" or "Almighty God."

Early in Genesis, the LORD told Abram to leave his country and his family and go to a place He would show him. Before Abram and Sarai ever had children, the LORD promised to make Abram a great nation with so many descendants they could not be counted. Later the LORD came to Abram in a vision and told him he would have a son. Abram believed, thus He considered Abram as righteous due to his faith. The LORD made a covenant with Abram; He would give the land of Canaan to his descendants.

Something happened in Abram's life that we sometimes find happening in our own lives as we stand on the promises of God: time passed! A great deal of time passed! To Abram and Sarai it no doubt seemed like the LORD had forgotten His promise to give them a child of their own. With the intention of helping out, Sarai gave her Egyptian maid, Hagar, to Abram as his wife. Joy of all joys, when Abram was 86 years of age, Hagar conceived. She bore a son and Abram was content, but this was not the son that had been promised. Ishmael was the product of the will of man and the will of the flesh; it was the result of Abram and Sarai trying to assist the LORD.

Thirteen more years passed after Ishmael was born without seeing the promise of God. Then, when Abram was ninety-nine, El Shaddai spoke these words in Genesis 17.

17:1   "I am God Almighty (El Shaddai); walk before Me, and be blameless.

17:2   "And I will establish My covenant between Me and you, and I will multiply you exceedingly."

The LORD, as El Shaddai, told Abram that He would establish His covenant with Abram. To *establish* means "to make, to build or to bring into being." The LORD made the covenant, but it was God as El Shaddai that would make it happen. To emphasize what He was doing, He changed Abram's name, meaning "exalted father" to Abraham, meaning "father of a great number." Again He told Abraham that his wife Sarah would conceive his child. How did Abraham respond to the news? He laughed at the prospect that he, at one hundred years of age, and Sarah, at age of 90, would have a child; it was humanly impossible. The covenant that the LORD made was established and brought into being by El Shaddai. The fulfillment of this promise is recorded in the book of Genesis Chapter 21.

21:1   Then the LORD took note of Sarah as He had said, and the LORD did for Sarah as He had promised.

21:2   So Sarah conceived and bore a son to Abraham in his old age, at the appointed time of which God had spoken to him.

Abraham and Sarah could not produce the promise by the works of the flesh. The bodies of both had to come to the point they could no longer produce naturally to make them realize it was all of God.

Nathan Stone, the author of *Names of God*, provides a noteworthy statement.

> Abraham and Sarah had to learn that what God promises, only God can give . . . Thus this name also taught Abraham his own insufficiency, the futility of relying upon his own efforts and the folly of impatiently running ahead of God.[46]

In God's first revelation of Himself as El Shaddai, we see that He is almighty, all powerful, and able to accomplish what is impossible in the physical realm. That is the meaning of the first part of the name, El.

The word *Shaddai* is translated "Almighty." This word, according to Nathan Stone, "is used in connection with judging, chastening and purging."[47] This is shown to be true in the book of Job, where the name El Shaddai is used 31 of its 48 occurrences; the book of Job is the story of a man learning to know El Shaddai.

Because of the circumstances in Job's life, he argued with El Shaddai while others smeared Him with lies (Job 13:3, 4). Rather than taking responsibility for his own hostile attitude to what was happening in his life, Job accused the Almighty of embittering his soul (Job 27:2). Job acknowledged El Shaddai should do these things to the unjust who perform iniquity, but proceeded to proclaim his own innocence, inferring God was indeed guilty of injustice (31:2–40). Finally, Job went so far as to label El Shaddai his adversary, calling Him to answer for the indictment which had been written against him (31:35).

The Lord's response to Job is given in Chapter 40:

40:2   "Will the faultfinder contend with the Almighty? Let him who reproves God answer it."

When Job heard God ask that question, he wisely concluded that he should say no more. Ryrie makes this comment about God's response:

> When Job criticized God's ways, he was in effect trying to usurp God's position as governor of the world. In this paragraph full of irony, God asks if Job can really perform those things which only God can do.[48]

After the LORD finished His verbal reprimand, Job repented. Ryrie's comment is significant:

> Job repents of his pride and rebellion and finds contentment in the knowledge that he has God's fellowship. This is the great lesson of the book: If we know God, we do not need to know why He allows us to experience what we do. He is not only in control of the universe and all its facets but also of our lives; and He loves us. Though His ways are sometimes beyond our comprehension, we should not criticize Him for His dealings with us or with others. God is always in control of all things, even when He appears not to be.[49]

The ways of El Shaddai as listed below give us a clear picture of a God who is faithful to keep His covenants with His people.

- When El Shaddai concludes a work in our life, we will delight in Him (Job 22:25), and we will have understanding (Job 32:8).

- El Shaddai gives life. John 10:10 tells us that the Lord Jesus Christ came that we might have an abundant life. Job had life, but El Shaddai wanted him to experience life abundantly. After taking Job through his ordeal, Job's fellowship was restored, along with his fortunes; all he had increased twofold (Job 42:10). The life Job lived after El Shaddai had taken him through his tribulation was more abundant. A person can experience life even while imprisoned by an enemy. Once that person escapes or is released from his prison and experiences freedom, he'll live life more abundantly. El Shaddai wants us out of our bondage from the world, the flesh, and the devil.

- El Shaddai does not treat us wrongly (Job 34:10).

- El Shaddai will not pervert justice (Job 34:12).

- El Shaddai will not heed nor give regard to an empty cry (Job 35:13). He is not moved by pity parties.

- El Shaddai finds us, we don't find Him. He is exalted in power. He will not do violence to justice or abundant righteousness. The worldly wisdom of men does not impress Him (Job 37:23, 24).

- El Shaddai brings destruction (Isaiah 13:6). Since He does not treat us wrongly nor pervert justice, El Shaddai brings destruction to our fleshly, worldly, demonic ways.

Immanuel

The Hebrew word *Immanuel*, meaning "God with us" is used specifically only twice in the Old Testament, and transliterated into Greek only once in the New Testament.

In our study of the names of God we have already seen how God created the heavens and the earth; whatever He spoke came into being. He even created man in His own image. It was not long, however, until mankind became corrupt in the eyes of God. Because of His love for His creation, God raised up prophets who were to warn the people and were to give His instruction.

The Apostle Paul, in Galatians 4, tells us . . .

4:4   But when the fulness of the time came, God sent forth His Son, born of a woman, born under the Law,

4:5   in order that He might redeem those who were under the Law, that we might receive the adoption as sons.

It was God's Son, Immanuel, of which it is spoken in Matthew's first chapter:

1:23   "Behold, the virgin shall be with child, and shall bear a Son, and they shall call His name Immanuel," which translated means, "God with us."

This verse is, of course, referring to the Lord Jesus Christ. The author of the letter to the Hebrews, speaking of the Lord Jesus Christ, tells us He is God (Hebrews 1:8). He was born of a virgin as prophesied by Isaiah. Speaking about this same Jesus, John's gospel tells us that. . . .

1:3   All things came into being by Him; and apart from Him nothing came into being that has come into being.

1:12   But as many as received Him, to them He gave the right to become children of God, even to those who believe in His name.

1:14   And the Word became flesh, and dwelt among us, and we beheld His glory, glory as of the only begotten from the Father, full of grace and truth.

Jesus Christ spent three years on earth teaching and discipling. He healed the sick, raised the dead, cleansed lepers, and cast out demons. He was tempted by Satan—tempted in all things as we are—yet was without sin (Hebrews 4:15). When Immanuel came to this earth, He didn't come for a visit to see how things were going. He came with a mission: He knew the blood of goats and bulls would not take away sins (Hebrews 10:14), therefore, He became a sacrifice for us, taking all our sins upon Himself. Peter, in his first epistle, explains:

2:24   and He Himself bore our sins in His body on the cross, that we might die to sin and live to righteousness; for by His wounds you were healed.

Although He knew the shame and suffering to come, Immanuel was willing to submit to His Father's will. Men despised and rejected Him, yet He willingly gave His own life by dying on the cross to enable mankind to inherit eternal life.

Death, however, knew victory for only three days; then God raised His Son from the dead (Acts 2:24). Since our Immanuel is the source of eternal life, death could hold Him no longer. By His resurrection, Jesus Christ rendered the devil, who had the power of death, powerless.

His resurrection provides indisputable evidence of our justification. The book of Romans gives the facts.

4:25   He who was delivered up because of our transgressions, and was raised because of our justification.

Merrill C. Tenney defines *Justification* as . . .

> That judicial act of God, by which, on the basis of the meritorious work of Christ, imputed to the sinner and received by him through faith, He declares the sinner absolved from his sin, released from its penalty, and restored as righteous.[50]

In other words, because of Christ's death on the cross, God considers those who in faith receive His Son as being free from the consequences or penalties of sin. That person is then considered righteous. The reason? The Lord Jesus Christ paid the full price for the sin of the world.

Jesus' resurrection was "proof of God's acceptance of His Son's sacrifice."[51] The reason Christ—our Immanuel—went to the cross to die was because of our transgressions. His death served a purpose; He secured our right to become children of God. His resurrection came about because of our justification (Romans 4:25). Jesus' mission fully accomplished, the Father raised His Son from the dead. Ephesians 1:6 tells us that He also raised us with Christ, seating us in heavenly places in Christ Jesus.

In John Chapter 14, Jesus spoke of the Holy Spirit.

14:16   "And I will ask the Father, and He will give you another Helper, that He may be with you forever;

14:17   that is the Spirit of truth, whom the world cannot receive, because it does not behold Him or know Him, but you know Him because He abides with you, and will be in you."

14:18   "I will not leave you as orphans; I will come to you."

Jesus Christ came to this earth, lived, and worked among us. He came to purchase our redemption and enable us to become the children of God. He told His disciples it would be better for them if He left—only then would the Holy Spirit come. Jesus had one body and was limited to being in one place at one time. The Holy Spirit, on the other hand, has no such limitations. He would live in each believer. Truly the Lord Jesus Christ is Immanuel—God with us.

Jehovah

Yahweh is a Hebrew verb form meaning "I Am." Yahweh is the active, self-existent One.[52] Jehovah—the English rendering of the Hebrew tetragram[53]—is written "LORD" in most translations. Sometimes it is written as "GOD." Yahweh, or Jehovah, means much more than self-existence. It is like an unfinished statement to which we may provide the ending with our need of Him. He Himself has told us many times who He is for His people. You might not have ever thought of Jehovah in this way as you have studied the Bible, but from now on you may want to keep your eyes open for His revelation of Himself as His provision for your every need.

In Genesis 1, Scripture tells us that Elohim created everything, including man, and that He loved His creation. In the next chapter we are introduced to Jehovah. The first words that Jehovah spoke to man are recorded in Genesis Chapter 2.

2:16   And the LORD God commanded the man, saying, "From any tree of the garden you may eat freely;

2:17   but from the tree of the knowledge of good and evil you shall not eat, for in the day that you eat from it you shall surely die."

Jehovah gave Adam specific instructions concerning his provisions, telling him what would happen if he disobeyed. Then, when the serpent arrived on the scene with Adam and Eve, it was their responsibility to make a choice to either believe Jehovah or to believe the serpent. Unfortunately, they chose to go along with the serpent's program. Nathan Stone tells of the attributes of Jehovah:

> It is as Jehovah that God places man under moral obligations with a warning of punishment for disobedience. . . . God is revealed as righteousness and true holiness in Ephesians 4:24 . . . Jehovah . . . is righteous in all His works (Daniel 9:14). . . . His first requirement of those who should be His witnesses is 'Ye shall be holy: for I Jehovah your Elohim, am holy' (Leviticus 19:2). . . . And a righteous Jehovah whose holiness is thus violated and outraged must condemn unrighteousness and punish it. So it is Jehovah who pronounces judgment and metes out punishment."[54]

That is exactly what Jehovah did with Adam and Eve. He listened to their excuses and then pronounced judgment first on the serpent, then on Eve, and lastly on Adam. Jehovah then clothed them and sent them out of the garden.

It was Jehovah that had seen the oppression of His people and commissioned Moses and Aaron to take the sons of Israel out of Egypt. How were His people to know who had commissioned Moses? God answered Moses' inquiry in Exodus Chapter 3.

3:14   And God said to Moses, "I AM WHO I AM"; and He said, "Thus you shall say to the sons of Israel, 'I AM has sent me to you.'"

3:15   And God, furthermore, said to Moses, "Thus you shall say to the sons of Israel, 'The LORD, the God of your fathers, the God of Abraham, the God of Isaac, and the God of Jacob, has sent me to you.' This is My name forever, and this is My memorial-name to all generations."

His name is the same forever because He is the same forever. James 1:17 informs us that He is the giver of everything good; there is no variation in Him. The prophet Malachi tells us that the Lord does not change (Malachi 3:6). His consistency is our security. The same thing was said of His Son in Hebrews 13:

13:8   Jesus Christ is the same yesterday and today, yes and forever.

Jesus Christ's *I AM* Statements:

Jehovah revealed Himself to His people; looking briefly at the gospel of John, we find it to be filled with Jesus' Jehovah-statements of Himself:

* I AM He—the Messiah (John 4:25, 26).

* I AM the bread of life (John 6:35).

* I AM the light of the world (John 8:12).

* I AM the Son of Man (John 8:28).

* I AM before Abraham was born (John 8:58).

* I AM the door—of salvation (John 10:9).

* I AM the good shepherd (John 10:11).

* I AM the Son of God (John 10:36).

* I AM the resurrection and the life (John 11:25).

* I AM teacher and Lord (John 13:13).

* I AM the way, and the truth, and the life (John 14:6).

* I AM the true vine (John 15:1).

The "Jehovah" names that follow are not all-inclusive, but will give you a start for your own personal study. Listen closely for His word spoken to you (rhema) as we continue our study of the names of God.

Jehovah-jireh

"The name Jehovah-jireh is one of many names compounded with Jehovah. Most of these compound names of God arise out of some historic incident, and portray Jehovah in some aspect of His character as meeting human need."[55]

The Hebrew root of the word *jireh* means "to have regard for the one seen, to see to their every need with provision and care." Jehovah-jireh is the LORD who Provides.

The name Jehovah-jireh was first used by Abraham in memorial to his mountain top experience of testing. After Abraham and Sarah had received their promised son, Isaac, God sent Abraham to the land of Moriah to offer the lad as a burnt offering. Abraham obeyed without question, believing the promise of God that this very son would still become a great nation in spite of His request. Once Isaac and his father arrived at the altar site, Abraham built an altar. Prior to their arrival, Isaac had seen the wood and fire, and inquired about the missing lamb needed for the offering. His father gave this answer: "God will provide for Himself the lamb for the burnt offering, my son" (Genesis 22:8). He then arranged the wood, bound his son, and placed him on top of the wood.

As he picked up the knife to slay Isaac, the angel of the LORD interceded, telling Abraham not to harm the boy. Looking up, Abraham saw a ram caught in a thicket by his horns. God had provided! Abraham gladly made the substitution and sacrificed the ram instead of his son. That day father and son both saw the provision of God. In the KJV and the NASB, respectively, Genesis 22 says,

22:14   and Abraham called the name of that place Jehovah-jireh: as it is said to this day, In the mount of the LORD it shall be seen. (KJV)

And Abraham called the name of that place The LORD Will Provide, as it is said to this day, "In the mount of the LORD it will be provided." (NASB)

The account given in Genesis Chapter 22 is amplified in Hebrews Chapter 11:

11:17   By faith Abraham, when he was tested, offered up Isaac; and he who had received the promises was offering up his only begotten son;

11:18   it was he to whom it was said, "In Isaac your descendants shall be called."

11:19   He considered that God is able to raise men even from the dead; from which he also received him back as a type.

Jehovah-m'kaddesh

The Hebrew word *m'kaddesh* means "to purify, cleanse, set apart as sacred; to declare holy and consecrated to God." Jehovah-m'kaddesh is the LORD who makes us holy.

Repeatedly in Scripture we are reminded of the awesomeness of our holy God. Moses was instructed to remove his shoes in the presence of a holy God. Only the high priest could enter into God's holy presence once a year, and then was required to be covered with a blood sacrifice for his sin. David's Psalm declares the holiness of his God.

103:1   Bless the LORD, O my soul; and all that is within me, bless His holy name.

David's son, Solomon, asserted in Proverbs that . . .

9:10   The fear of the LORD is the beginning of wisdom, and the knowledge of the Holy One is understanding.

One of the first things we need to understand about God is that He is holy and He desires holy behavior of us. Scripture explains the concept well in 1 Peter Chapter 1.

1:15   But like the Holy One who called you, be holy yourselves also in all your behavior;

1:16   because it is written, "You shall be holy, for I am holy."

Merrill C. Tenney says this about holiness:

> Holiness is first applied to God, and is early associated with ideas of purity and righteousness . . . *Holiness* means the pure, loving nature of God, separate from evil.[56]

The Apostle Paul, in Romans Chapter 12, makes this bold declaration:

12:1   I beseech you therefore, brethren, by the mercies of God, that ye present your bodies a living sacrifice, holy, acceptable unto God, which is your reasonable service (KJV).

In the Old Testament, people were instructed to offer some *thing* to God. In the New Testament, *we* are to be that living, holy, and acceptable sacrifice offered to God. Paul concluded that such action on the part of a believer was reasonable.

In Christ we were not only accepted, but made acceptable. We were made the very righteousness of God in Him, born-again as a new species with the character and nature of God's holiness. We are now to work out what is true within.

Jehovah-nissi

The Hebrew word *nissi* comes from a root meaning "something lifted up, a token to be seen far off; in particular it is a banner set up on a high place in case of invasion, showing the people where to assemble." Jehovah-nissi is the LORD My Banner.

After the children of Israel had been released from Egyptian captivity, a new situation emerged. Pharaoh and his army had come to take them back into custody; the LORD, however, delivered them without their having to fight. They simply passed through the Red Sea to freedom; God fought their enemies as the people remained silent. There was nothing for them to do except cross over into the wilderness. The symbolism is of a slave crossing the line of demarcation from a state of being in bondage to the state of being free. There is no work involved—we are saved by grace, not by works (Ephesians 2:8, 9). Our part is to simply believe and receive the truth of the gospel.

When a person passes from death into life, he is delivered from the domain of darkness and is transferred into the kingdom of the Lord Jesus Christ (Colossians 1:13), but he, too, enters the wilderness spiritually. While there, he may find himself in situations where he is forced to learn to trust God to supply his physical needs and may choose to grumble and complain against God, as did the children of Israel.

In the wilderness, a new crisis arose: Israel found themselves under attack by Amalek. This time there was not a hint of Moses telling the people to stand by and watch the salvation of the LORD; He would not fight for them as He did at the Red Sea. Instead, Moses instructed Joshua to pick some able-bodied men to defend them physically from Amalek.

As Joshua fought against Amalek, Moses held up the staff of God in his hand. As he did, Israel prevailed in the battle. When Moses became tired and lowered the staff, Amalek prevailed. Victory was theirs only when the staff was raised; and the staff remained raised only when Aaron and Hur rallied round to support Moses as he held the staff.

After Amalek's defeat, the LORD told Moses His plans: He would blot out the memory of Amalek from under heaven. How did Moses respond to the victory that had just been won? Exodus 17 tells us.

17:15   And Moses built an altar, and called the name of it Jehovah-nissi:

17:16   For he said, Because the LORD hath sworn that the LORD will have war with Amalek from generation to generation (KJV).

The NASB tells us that Moses built an altar and called it "The LORD is My Banner."

We are told in 1 Corinthians 10:1–11 that the things which took place with the children of Israel happened as examples for our instruction. What significance does this hold for us?

When Moses lifted high the staff of God, Israel prevailed because God was at work in the place where they had assembled. Today that is representative of us as we engage in our battles against the world, the flesh, and the devil. As long as we remain under the upheld banner of God, we will prevail—as did Moses and the children of Israel. Being born-again, however, does not automatically keep us under His banner. To remain under God's banner, we must be practicing obedience. Disobedience destroys our fellowship with God, which forces us to operate from our own resources. When we do, our rebellion allows the enemy to prevail. This is clearly shown in Numbers Chapters 13 and 14. Moses had sent 12 spies to investigate the Promised Land. Although they were highly impressed with the land itself, only two of them—Caleb and Joshua—were willing to take possession of the land. The others gave such a negative report that the whole congregation was ready to stone any would-be conquerors, including Moses and Aaron.

The LORD told Moses that everyone from age 20 and older who grumbled against God would die in the wilderness because of their unbelief. The next morning, however, Moses' listeners acknowledged they had sinned but were now ready to forcefully conquer the land. Moses assured them the LORD would not go with them; they would be going up against the enemy under their own banner and in their own resources. Instead of listening to their leader, they went into battle and were defeated.

As Moses reviewed all that had happened in the lives of the children of Israel since Kadesh-barnea, he found their attitudes had turned to one of bereavement.

There is a lesson in this for us. If we want to be victorious over the world, the flesh and the devil, we must enter the battle under God's direction and banner. It is there we will experience supernatural power to accomplish His desires.

Jehovah-rapha

The LORD had delivered the children of Israel from the hand of Pharaoh, had parted the Red Sea, and had confounded the pursuing Egyptians in its midst. Moses stretched his hand over the sea, which resumed its natural course, and destroyed Pharaoh's army. After leaving the Red Sea, Moses took his group for a 3-day's journey into the wilderness of Shur. There they found water, but since it was not fit for human consumption, they complained to Moses. It was there, in the dry wilderness of Shur, that the Lord tested the children of Israel. Then in Exodus 15 God spoke.

15:26   And He said, "If you will give earnest heed to the voice of the LORD your God, and do what is right in His sight, and give ear to His commandments, and keep all His statutes, I will put none of the diseases on you which I have put on the Egyptians; for I, the LORD, am your healer."

The words LORD and *healer* made into a compound word is "*Jehovah-rapha.*"

Prior to the time that the children of Israel spied out the land of Canaan, Aaron and Miriam had murmured against Moses for marrying a Cushite woman. Because of their murmuring, the LORD had come down in a pillar of cloud and severely reprimanded them for their actions. Once the cloud had withdrawn, Miriam was leprous. In desperation, Moses called to the LORD and said, "O, God, heal her, I pray!" When Moses used the word *heal,* he was using the word "rapha." He no doubt remembered when the children of Israel were complaining about having no water to drink that the LORD had spoken to him and said, "I, the LORD, am your healer." Miriam required healing, but was required to remain outside the camp for seven days; only then was she received back into camp free of her leprosy.

In the book of 2 Kings, we find Hezekiah, the king of Judah, had become mortally ill. The LORD spoke to Isaiah the prophet and told him to tell the king to set his house in order because he was about to die. After the prophet delivered the message, Hezekiah prayed. That prayer is recorded in 2 Kings Chapter 20:

20:3 "Remember now, O LORD, I beseech You, how I have walked before You in truth and with a whole heart and have done what is good in Your sight."

Afterward, Hezekiah wept bitterly. The LORD heard his prayer and had Isaiah return to King Hezekiah with this message:

20:5 . . . 'Thus says the LORD, the God of your father David, "I have heard your prayer, I have seen your tears; behold, I will heal you. On the third day you shall go up to the house of the LORD.

20:6 "And I will add fifteen years to your life . . . "

In the Psalms David petitions the LORD to be his healer.

6:2 Be gracious to me, O LORD, for I am pining away; Heal me, O LORD, for my bones are dismayed.

103:2 Bless the LORD, O my soul, And forget none of His benefits;

103:3 Who pardons all your iniquities, Who heals all your diseases.

The Lord Jesus Christ performed the works of Jehovah-rapha in the flesh. During his public ministry, Jesus healed those suffering with various diseases and pains: demoniacs, epileptics, paralytics, the blind, the deaf, lepers, the lame, the crippled, the mute, even the feverish found healing. The Scripture abounds with irrefutable evidence of Christ operating as Jehovah-rapha.

Jehovah-rohi

The Hebrew word *rohi* is from the root meaning "to tend as one cares for sheep." Inclusive in this definition is feeding, governing, guarding, nurturing, healing, and delighting in all that is in one's care; this is Jehovah-rohi—the LORD, our Shepherd.

Isaiah foresaw the time when the LORD God Himself would come like a mighty shepherd to tend His flock; He would gather His lambs into His arms, nurture, and carry them close to Himself (40:10, 11). The gospel of John records the words of the Lord Jesus Christ who said . . .

10:11   "I am the good shepherd; the good shepherd lays down His life for the sheep."

Jesus called Himself the good shepherd who guards the sheep with His life; He does not flee in the face of the enemy. He knows each of His sheep intimately, caring for their well-being, speaking to them until they are familiar with His voice and will safely follow His direction. If one in His flock strays, He does not abandon it to its own wanderings but searches it out, cleansing, and restoring it.

The twenty-third Psalm is a beautiful word picture, drawn to help us understand the character of our Shepherd.

23:4   Even though I walk through the valley of the shadow of death, I fear no evil; for Thou art with me; Thy rod and Thy staff, they comfort me.

God Glorified

As our Shepherd, the Lord Jesus Christ wants the best for us. It is His desire, therefore, that we die to our own way of doing things. When we choose to honor Jesus Christ as Lord, we will follow Him wherever He leads. When we choose to honor Him as Jehovah-rohi, we are acknowledging Him as our shepherd. As Shepherd, He leads us by the way of death to the flesh; only then is His life expressed from our spirit to our soul, and then exhibited through our body. When that happens, God receives glory.

Kingdom of Darkness Steals Glory

We know that Satan purposefully comes as an angel of light in order to deceive us. He also wants to steal glory that belongs to God. That is accomplished as he controls our lives in any way. Demonic forces want to prevent us from practicing Godly principles; that honors their efforts. As we act upon what they interject into our minds and emotions, demonic spirits can exhibit their lives through us. If they can achieve that, they are glorified by the believer.

The Shepherd's Leadership

It is one thing to choose to receive the Lord Jesus Christ as Savior. That step transfers us into eternal life. Once we have the life of the Lord Jesus Christ in us, He desires that we make Him Lord by choosing to obey Him in everything. We learn to be obedient, as we come unquestionably under His leadership as Shepherd. A shepherd will lead his sheep into areas of pasture that are best for them; our Shepherd does the same, knowing our every need. In our journey He will lead us in ways that will bring death to our own fleshly desires and ambitions so that He can be the controlling factor in our lives. He wants to exchange His life for ours, thereby living His life through us. Our enemy wants us to think that is a horrible, frightful way to go.

Commercial Airline

The truth of the matter is we frequently allow other people to be the controlling factor in our lives. An example might be when we fly with a commercial airline. We board an aircraft and allow the pilot and crew, whom we have probably never personally met, to take control of our destiny for several hours. It may be foggy, cloudy, or snowy, yet we will literally trust them with our lives, and expect them to deliver us safely to our destination.

Satan and demons do not care if we trust the aircraft's pilot to deliver us to our destination. However, they become highly irate anytime we decide to trust Christ as the Pilot of our life and let Him lead us as Shepherd.

We must learn to keep our eyes upon Him and listen for His voice. He is our Jehovah-rohi who has our welfare at heart. He is our supply of every need. He feeds us with rich, life-sustaining truth in the quietness of His peace. He restores us by guiding us into all righteousness for His glory. He, who is our eternal life, removes all fear of death with His comforting presence. In the face of our enemies we may feast on every spiritual blessing in security, anointed, and overflowing. His goodness and lovingkindness continually surround us, for our life is hidden with Him in God.

Jehovah-sabaoth

The Hebrew word *sabaoth* is defined as "an army, soldiers; warriors who stand and fight against an enemy." Jehovah-sabaoth is the LORD of hosts; He is the captain of our salvation.

Jehovah-sabaoth has been actively delivering His people from their enemies since the time He first called Abram to become the father of a people unto Himself. But it was not until they were ready to enter the Promised Land as a nation that He was called by this name. He appeared to Joshua standing before the city of Jericho, identifying Himself as the captain of the host of the LORD. Joshua bowed his face to the earth in submission, removing his sandals in the presence of holiness.

Hannah prayed in great sorrow and distress to Jehovah-sabaoth to deliver her from the great affliction she suffered from childlessness. Listen to her prayer in 1 Samuel Chapter 1.

1:11   And she made a vow and said, "O LORD of hosts, if Thou wilt indeed look on the affliction of Thy maid-servant and remember me, and not forget Thy maidservant, but wilt give Thy maidservant a son, then I will give him to the LORD all the days of his life, and a razor shall never come on his head."

The LORD remembered Hannah's request and the vow she had made and gave her a son. She named him Samuel; he later became a judge over Israel. There is no situation too insignificant—or any opposing force too great—for our LORD of hosts to become involved.

We must, however, be ever watchful, lest we presume upon the Lord's promises as Saul did. We must never believe the ways that seem right to us are better than obedience to the LORD of hosts. The enemy may fill our minds with fear as we stand in overwhelming situations, but we must look to Him who is greater than any circumstance we could see in this world. Elisha prayed that the Lord would open his servant's eyes to see the spiritual battle then in progress. If we desire to see the reality of that battle, we must also keep in mind the source of our victory. The book of Zechariah said it well:

4:6 " . . . This is the word of the LORD to Zerubbabel saying, 'Not by might nor by power, but by My Spirit,' says the LORD of hosts."

As we learned in the previous chapter, our warfare is in the spiritual realm. We must not allow the enemy to focus our warfare on people or circumstances; these are merely used as opportunities for the enemy to distract us from the true battle. The real war is fought in our spirit as we are led by the Spirit of God to stand strong in the Lord Jesus Christ, His ways, His truth, and His life. In Him we have authority over every name named. In Him we are not simply survivors, we are more than conquerors. We are the children of God, joint-heirs with the Lord Jesus Christ who is Head of the church and the mighty hosts of heaven.

As we walk obediently in the law of the Spirit of life in Christ Jesus, we are set free from destructive deceptions planted deep and built strong within our flesh. In that freedom we have the potential of becoming part of the mighty army led by Jehovah-sabaoth, destroying the works of the enemy in our own lives and in the lives of those around us.

Jehovah-shalom

The specific name *Jehovah-shalom* is used only once in Scripture. The NASB translates the name as, "The LORD is Peace."

Gideon experienced the peace of God when his circumstances told him there was no peace available. The sons of Israel had not obeyed God and as a result, He allowed Midian to oppress them for seven years. During this time, the Midianites fought against Israel, destroying their crops and their animals. The Midianites brought their own livestock with them, allowing them to over-graze the land to help devastate it. The Midianite oppression was so severe that the sons of Israel had to live in dens and caves in the surrounding mountains.

This fierce oppression caused the sons of Israel to cry out to the LORD. He heard their cry and sent them a prophet to remind them that it was He who had brought them out of bondage from Egypt, and that they were not to fear their oppressors.

One day Gideon was working to save a portion of the wheat crop from the marauding Midianites. Little did he realize that not far away was an angel of the LORD, observing. The angel spoke to Gideon, assuring him the LORD was with him; then he called Gideon a valiant warrior. Gideon's response was classic. He asked a question that we may have asked when things are not going as we would like. His words are recorded in Judges 6:

6:13 "Oh my lord, if the LORD is with us, why then has all this happened to us? And where are all His miracles which our fathers told us about, saying, 'Did not the LORD bring us up from Egypt?' But now the LORD has abandoned us and given us into the hand of Midian."

The angel did not answer Gideon's question. God's prophet had already delivered the answer: they had not obeyed the LORD their God. Then the angel told Gideon he would be the one who would deliver Israel from the Midianites.

Gideon was concerned about the insignificance of his ancestry and that he was the youngest in the family. This did not seem to concern his heavenly visitor. He would accompany the valiant warrior who would defeat Midian. Gideon was not as confident as was his caller, and asked for a sign and prepared an offering. Once prepared, Gideon presented it to the angel of God, who had him lay the meat and the bread on a rock and pour out the broth. The angel touched it with his staff, and fire sprang up from the rock, consuming the sacrifice. The angel then silently vanished from Gideon's sight.

By this time, Gideon—convinced he had been speaking to the angel of the LORD—became very fearful that he would die. The LORD must have known what he was thinking because He said, "Peace to you, do not fear; you shall not die" (verse 23).

That was good enough for Gideon. He proceeded to build an altar to the LORD and named it "The LORD is Peace." The King James Bible tells us that Gideon called the altar "Jehovah-shalom" (Judges 6:24).

That night the LORD told Gideon to tear down the altar of Baal and to cut down the Asherah; the wood was to be used to offer a burnt offering. Because of his great fear, Gideon took ten of his servants with him to do what the LORD had instructed.

The men of the city were furious when they discovered what had happened and tried to get his father, Joash, to release Gideon to them. His father wisely responded, "If Baal is a god, let him contend for himself."

Meanwhile, the Midianites and the Amalekites were preparing to return to the land to remove everything of value and destroy the rest. Before that could occur, however, the Spirit of the LORD came upon Gideon and he rallied the people. Gideon must have been unsure of himself; he twice asked for a sign in order to ascertain that he was doing the right thing. The LORD, however, honored his requests.

As Gideon and his followers gathered, the LORD told him he had too many men; they could have boasted in their own ability and strength. Therefore, the Lord cut his army from 32,000 down to a mere 300! At that point, their newly appointed leader probably felt he had a legitimate reason to be afraid! That night God gave him even further confirmation that he was doing the right thing.

Therefore, Gideon took his small army to confront the enemy. Gideon's army was not as heavily armed as an army normally would be. Instead, they were equipped with the armament of God: trumpets, and pitchers containing flaming torches inside! At Gideon's signal, they blew the trumpets, broke their pitchers, and said, "For the LORD and for Gideon." Now don't you just know that would bring tremendous fear to the enemy! Can you imagine the Midianites and the Amalekites being overly alarmed by hearing the sound of trumpets, breaking pitchers, and the sight of 300 torches burning in the night? Normally, that would not send any great enemy reeling. This time was different, however. As Gideon and his men were obedient to God, "the LORD set the sword of one against another even throughout the whole army; and the army fled" (Judges 7:22).

Remember the situation. In his own eyes, Gideon was nobody. God had heard the sons of Israel crying out because of their oppressors. He approached Gideon and told him to go fight an innumerable enemy. Once Gideon received his commission to confront the enemy, he built an altar to the LORD and called it *Jehovah-shalom*, meaning, "The LORD is Peace." The angel of the LORD had not come to Gideon during a long reign of peace; he came during a time of national crisis. This angel had required something of Gideon that no military leader in his right mind would ever consider as a plan of military action. Gideon used the unlikely tools that God had given him—trumpets, pitchers, and torches—yet he won the war. The heavenly messenger had helped Gideon work through his doubts and fears, using him in a way that Gideon had never thought possible.

Jehovah-shalom: the LORD my peace. Philippians 4 says,

4:5   . . . The Lord is near.

4:6   Be anxious for nothing, but in everything by prayer and supplication with thanksgiving let your requests be made known to God.

4:7   And the peace of God, which surpasses all comprehension, shall guard your hearts and your minds in Christ Jesus.

Jehovah-shammah

The Hebrew word *shammah* is defined as "there, in that place, therein." Jehovah-shammah means "The LORD is there." This was the name given in description of the New Jerusalem envisioned by Ezekiel (Ezekiel 48:35). This city was measured and built meticulously, being apportioned and assigned for the people of God.

In Chapter 14 of John's gospel, Jesus culminated His talk with His disciples during His final Passover feast with them. He had told them of His upcoming betrayal, the necessity of His leaving them, and their need to love one another as He had loved them. To encourage their troubled hearts and give them an eternal view toward which to hope, He left them with this promise:

14:2   "In My Father's house are many dwelling places; if it were not so, I would have told you; for I go to prepare a place for you.

14:3   "And if I go and prepare a place for you, I will come again, and receive you to Myself; that where I am, there you may be also."

When Jesus left His disciples, He told them He was going to prepare a place for them in order that they may, at a later time, join Him. During the interim, all of us as His disciples must be prepared through the work of the Holy Spirit. First Corinthians Chapter 6 sheds this light . . .

6:17   But the one who joins himself to the Lord is one spirit with Him.

As believers, we have been born-again with a new spirit, birthed by His spirit, sinless and unable to sin. Now He is in the process of saving our souls—teaching us to renew our mind, working in us to will and to do His good pleasure. He is educating us on how to correctly use our emotions, just as we might learn to read the gauges and lights on our car to alert us to any problems in the making. He will make evident what He has accomplished in our inner man by saving our body, eventually transforming it into a flawless, spiritual dwelling place.

This salvation process is not just individual; it is collective. We are not independent of one another. We are parts of a whole, essential to each other; our own well-being depends upon the health of every other member in the body of Christ, the church. Because He is holy, his bride must also be holy. He gave Himself for His bride to save her, sanctifying and cleansing her with His word, so He might receive her unto Himself without spot or wrinkle. At the marriage supper of the Lamb, His bride, the church, will be clothed in fine linen, which is the righteous acts of the saints.

Jehovah-shammah is the God who is there; He delights to be where His people are. When the marriage feast is over and the millennial honeymoon is complete; when the enemy, his armies and followers have been judged and sentenced, God will make a new heaven and a new earth. This is the consummation of God's timeless plan for us. Revelation 21 gives us God's viewpoint.

21:2   And I saw the holy city, new Jerusalem, coming down out of heaven from God, made ready as a bride adorned for her husband.

21:3   And I heard a loud voice from the throne, saying, "Behold, the tabernacle of God is among men, and He shall dwell among them, and they shall be His people, and God Himself shall be among them."

Once God reveals this vision, we can only respond, "Yes, come quickly, Lord Jesus!" We who have this hope are purifying ourselves, just as He is pure (1 John 3:3).

Jehovah-tsidkenu

The Hebrew word *tsidkenu* means "righteousness, or rightness." *Jehovah-tsidkenu* is the LORD our righteousness.

The name Jehovah-tsidkenu is given in Jeremiah 23.

23:5   "Behold, the days are coming," declares the LORD, "When I shall raise up for David a righteous Branch; and He will reign as king and act wisely and do justice and righteousness in the land.

23:6   "In His days Judah will be saved, and Israel will dwell securely; and this is His name by which He will be called, 'The LORD our righteousness.'"

Throughout the Bible we see the provision of a just God for the sins of mankind. God did not save Noah because he was sinless. Noah and his family were delivered because he refused to walk in the wickedness of the world; instead he walked with God. Can two walk together except they be agreed?

There is no particular goodness noted in Abram when the LORD called him from his country and relatives to a new land to make him a great nation, to bless him, or to become his God. It was not until he was promised an offspring of his own and believed God that the LORD accounted his faith as righteousness. This has been the way of the LORD down through the ages—without faith it is impossible to please God (Hebrews 11:6); whatever is not of faith is sin (Romans 14:23).

Our righteous God who establishes truth has proclaimed that the Lord Jesus Christ is our righteousness; apart from Him we can do nothing. The New Testament shows us that eternal life is the free gift of God given through the Lord Jesus Christ (Romans 6:23). The only response He asks is our exercise of faith to what we have heard from the word of Christ, lived out in obedience.

Jehovah-tsidkenu is the LORD our righteousness. God expects us to live out the righteousness we have been given at salvation; it must take root in our souls and bodies. Paul sums it up nicely in Romans Chapter 6.

6:11   Even so consider yourselves to be dead to sin, but alive to God in Christ Jesus.

6:12   Therefore do not let sin reign in your mortal body that you should obey its lusts,

6:13   and do not go on presenting the members of your body to sin as instruments of unrighteousness; but present yourselves to God as those alive from the dead, and your members as instruments of righteousness to God.

Review: Names of God
Meaning Behind the Names

1. Adonai	Master or Lord. Usually written as "Lord."
2. Elohim	The strong, faithful One. The true God. Usually written as *"God."*
3. El Elyon	The Most High.
4. El Olam	The Everlasting God, the God of Ages, the God of Eternity.
5. El Roi	The God who sees.
6. El Shaddai	God Almighty, or Almighty God.
7. Immanuel	God with us.
8. Jehovah	(Heb. Yahweh) LORD; I AM WHO I AM.
9. Jehovah-jireh	The LORD who Provides.
10. Jehovah-m'kaddesh	The LORD who makes us holy.
11. Jehovah-nissi	The LORD is My banner.
12. Jehovah-rapha	The LORD, your healer.
13. Jehovah-rohi	The LORD, our Shepherd.
14. Jehovah-sabaoth	The LORD of hosts.
15. Jehovah-shalom	The LORD is Peace.
16. Jehovah-shammah	The LORD is there.
17. Jehovah-tsidkenu	The LORD our righteousness.

This is not an exhaustive list, but enough to introduce you to the inexhaustible Person upon whom our salvation rests. As we grow in our knowledge of who He is, we rejoice in the fact that by His victory we can continue to grow in that knowledge eternally.

Part 2: The Life of Total Commitment

In our study thus far, we have seen the importance of obeying God. Total commitment, therefore, is imperative to the Lord Jesus Christ. There are three basic statements a believer needs to consider in completely yielding to the authority of Christ.

Three Statements Of Total Commitment:
I Yield My Will

The first statement of total commitment makes this declaration: "I choose to yield my will to You and to commit to Your will as You reveal it to me."

Buying a Used Car

We can compare this first statement of total commitment to the process of buying a used car. In your search for a used vehicle, you find exactly the kind of car you want to buy. The salesman is waiting for you to close the transaction, but because of an upcoming appointment, you need to leave. You know the salesman you are dealing with has a shady reputation, but he also has the kind of car you are looking for.

Before leaving the dealership, the salesman makes an offer by saying, "Let's do something to tie up this car so no one else can buy it while you are gone. I know you want this car, and the price is reasonable. Would you be willing to leave five thousand dollars as a cash deposit and sign my blank contract? If so, I will put the car on hold for you. You can then leave; I'll fill in all the blanks on your contract—the make and model, the equipment on the car, the condition of the tires, engine, and paint. I will take care of all that information; you won't have to worry about a thing. Then, on my way to the airport, I'll bring the car described on the signed contract to where you have your appointment. I'll leave the keys under the seat and we will have a completed car sale!"

Would you be willing to accept the salesman's offer? He could fill in the blanks, describing a car you would never consider. He could even deliver a different vehicle. If you signed the contract and paid in advance, you could be in for a very bad shopping experience. No, you would not sign the sales contract.

Total Commitment is more than Words

The Lord Jesus Christ, in Luke 6, warns us that commitment is not simply a matter of words.

6:46   "And why do you call Me, 'Lord, Lord,' and do not do what I say?

6:47   "Everyone who comes to Me, and hears My words, and acts upon them, I will show you whom he is like."

Jesus then continues to relate the parable of the man who built a house upon the rock and another who built a house upon the ground without any foundation.

Although it may not be wise to trust a shady used car salesman, we can always build upon a solid foundation by trusting God. We can take a blank sheet of paper and sign our name at the bottom of the page, saying, "God, You fill in the blanks on this contract. I don't fear what You will write in the blanks. I am choosing now to submit unconditionally to Your will, whatever it may be."

I Yield My Rights

The second statement of total commitment says, "I choose to yield all my rights to You."

To what kind of rights do we refer? We are surrendering our right to be defensive when wronged; our right to dictate what is right when we disagree; our right to hide when we are vulnerable; our right to quit when we become tired; our right to feel good when we begin to suffer.

We are yielding our right to trust ourselves more than we trust God. We are yielding our right to believe anything about ourselves in any way that contradicts what Scripture says about us: feelings of inferiority, insecurity, or inadequacy might be examples. A child of the God of the universe has no reason for low self-esteem. We must surrender all our rights to be or act in any way that is contrary to God's will for us.

We live in a world obsessed with rights; getting all that we presume is ours by right. Christians may unintentionally embrace this deception and be swept along into something even worse—false doctrine. We perceive God as combination errand boy and body guard. We expect Him to prevent all harm and keep us happy with our every desire. We tend to think such an arrangement would prove God's love for us.

Have we forgotten who God is? Have we assumed our way is His way because we think what we believe is right? When confronted with the truth of His Word, we squirm and search for some loophole and call it grace without realizing the grace of God equips us for obedience. Until we humble ourselves, yielding our rights to Him, we will experience neither victory nor maturity. The fear of God is the beginning of wisdom.

Humble obedience to Christ must become our lifestyle according to Philippians Chapter 2.

2:5   Have this attitude in yourselves which was also in Christ Jesus,

2:6   who, although He existed in the form of God, did not regard equality with God a thing to be grasped,

2:7   but emptied Himself, taking the form of a bondservant, and being made in the likeness of men.

2:8   And being found in appearance as a man, He humbled Himself by becoming obedient to the point of death, even death on a cross.

2:12   So then, my beloved, just as you have always obeyed, not as in my presence only, but now much more in my absence, work out your salvation with fear and trembling;

2:13   for it is God who is at work in you, both to will and to work for His good pleasure.

I Surrender My Life

The third statement of total commitment makes this announcement: "I choose to unconditionally yield every part of my life—spirit, soul, and body—to anything You choose to do with it."

Although we consider Jesus Christ to be our Lord, we often withhold areas which are special to us. For one reason or another we retain authority over them, proving the incompleteness of our faith.

Paul confronts us with a reminder of God's awesome sovereignty and our proper response of worship in Romans 11:33–12:2.

11:33   Oh, the depth of the riches both of the wisdom and knowledge of God! How unsearchable are His judgments and unfathomable His ways!

11:34   For who has known the mind of the LORD, or who became His counselor?

11:35   Or who has first given to Him that it might be paid back to Him again?

11:36   For from Him and through Him and to Him are all things. To Him be the glory forever. Amen.

12:1   I urge you therefore, brethren, by the mercies of God, to present your bodies a living and holy sacrifice, acceptable to God, which is your spiritual service of worship.

12:2   And do not be conformed to this world, but be transformed by the renewing of your mind, that you may prove what the will of God is, that which is good and acceptable and perfect.

We must yield the consent of our will, surrender our rights, and every integral part of our being to God. We owe our very existence to an awesome God; our total commitment to Him would be a reasonable response. It would be almost humorous to refuse if it were not so tragic.

Let's return to the illustration of buying a used car. On your way to your appointment, you drive past another dealership that hires top quality salesmen; they have the same make vehicle you want to buy. After your appointment, you return and find the vehicle in question to be in remarkable condition. You work out all the details of the car sale satisfactorily and are ready to buy. The dealership is reputable; it will stand behind what it sells. At this point it would be reasonable to sign the contract. Consider how ridiculous non-compliance looks as we continue our illustration.

You have completed negotiations; the contract is ready. It is time to commit. Instead of signing, however, you hesitate. You think of all that could go wrong with a used car and recall horror stories of others who have purchased used vehicles. Your fears win out as you walk out of the dealership.

The Danger of Compromise

The above story may sound ludicrous, but we find believers doing that very thing with God! We say, "God, I want to be totally committed. I want to be all You want me to be." But when God desires our commitment, we say, "Forget it! I don't need to go that far; just make my life run smoothly." In God's economy, we must submit to God's way, or continue on the painful road of self-destruction.

A Misconception

Believers often embrace a misconception concerning total commitment; they assume they can take it back. When we totally commit our life to God, the Creator considers us committed. We have made a vow, saying, "God, I choose to yield my will to You and to commit to Your will as You reveal it to me; I am choosing to yield all my rights to You; I choose to unconditionally surrender every part of my life—spirit, soul, and body—to anything You choose to do with it." We have asked Him to put us through whatever circumstance we need to cleanse our heart. We desire to be conformed to Christ's image. Once that step takes place, God accepts our commitment and holds us to it. Deuteronomy 23 says,

23:21 When you make a vow to the Lord your God, you shall not delay to pay it, for it would be sin in you, and the Lord your God will surely require it of you.

Once we totally commit our lives to God, He will, without exception, require it of us. Do you know God as His names have revealed Him? Have you surrendered to Him as Lord? From your perspective, is the Lord Jesus Christ the One you *must* obey? If you have not made a total commitment to Him, you need to consider carefully all you have read in this chapter. The following prayer of total commitment is included for your prayerful consideration.

A Prayer of Total Commitment

Heavenly Father, I choose to totally commit my life to You. I choose to yield my will to You and to commit to Your will as You reveal it to me. I choose to yield all my rights to You. I choose to unconditionally surrender every part of my life—spirit, soul, and body—to anything You choose to do with it.

I recognize that my total commitment cannot be taken back. Thank You for being committed to my commitment.

All this I pray in the name, the power, and the authority of the Lord Jesus Christ.

Review: Names of God
The Life of Total Commitment

In this chapter, we have examined:

1.   Three statements of total commitment:

   •   I choose to yield my will to You and to commit to Your will as You reveal it to me.

   •   I choose to yield all my rights to You.

   •   I choose to unconditionally surrender every part of my life—spirit, soul, and body—to anything You choose to do with it.

2.   The danger of compromise.

3.   A prayer of total commitment.

I beseech you therefore, brethren, by the mercies of God, that ye present your bodies a living sacrifice, holy, acceptable unto God, which is your reasonable service.

And be not conformed to this world: but be ye transformed by the renewing of your mind, that ye may prove what is that good, and acceptable, and perfect, will of God.

Romans 12:1, 2 (KJV)

Part 3: A Proper Perspective

If we don't have a proper perspective of who God is, the enemy can more easily lie to us. He will attempt to convince us that his version of life is true. Without a proper perspective, we have no sharp two-edged sword—no *rhema*—for our defense.

Psalm 9 tells us,

9:9   The LORD also will be a stronghold for the oppressed, a stronghold in times of trouble,

9:10   And those who know Thy name will put their trust in Thee; for Thou, O LORD, hast not forsaken those who seek Thee.

Knowing the names of God needs to be more than just an intellectual knowing. To know His names requires a revelation—something that God speaks to us personally in our spirit. Verse 10 declares that it is those who know His Name who will put their trust in Him. This word *know* carries within its definition "an understanding gained through experience."

Job said, "I have heard of Thee by the hearing of the ear; but now my eye sees Thee" (Job 42:5). Job had first known God because of what others had told him. After Job had been through forty-two chapters of God's discipline, training, and revelation, his eyes had been opened to see God as He really is. As a result, Job saw himself from God's perspective. Because of that, Job says in verse 6, "Therefore I retract, and I repent in dust and ashes." His experiential knowledge of God had turned his life around.

We need to remember that when God takes us through a great storm, He is doing so with a purpose. As He reveals who He is, we—like Job—will see ourselves as we are apart from Him. Then we, too, will say, "Therefore I retract, and I repent in dust and ashes." His plan is to mature us and conform us more closely to the image of the Lord Jesus Christ.

The more we understand about God, the fewer lies the forces of darkness will be able to propagate in our mind. If we have an opinion about God that is contrary to what His name reveals, then our concept of God is faulty. That flawed concept is the basis for the enemy to build a fortress or stronghold from which to work. God sets us free from that bondage with truth concerning Himself.

We are not in a Fleshly War

2 Corinthians 10 says,

10:3   For though we walk in the flesh, we do not war according to the flesh,

10:4   for the weapons of our warfare are not of the flesh, but divinely powerful for the destruction of fortresses.

10:5   We are destroying speculations and every lofty thing raised up against the knowledge of God, and we are taking every thought captive to the obedience of Christ.

10:6   and we are ready to punish all disobedience, whenever your obedience is complete.

We do not war according to the flesh because John 6:63 tells us that the flesh profits nothing. When we are oppressed, it is our job to make war against the enemy. It is not God's job. God has already provided our means of victory against the enemy. Satan's power has been broken because the Lord Jesus Christ defeated him at the cross. Now it is our job to stand in His victory against the enemy.

When we are demonically oppressed, we must focus our warfare against the oppressor. We may ask how we can accomplish such a frightening task. The way is given in Scripture. In Luke 9:1 Jesus gave His disciples power and authority over all the demons. In James 4:7 we are told to submit ourselves to God and to resist the devil. However, we cannot focus the war against the oppressor by fighting according to the flesh; not if we desire to be effective in spiritual warfare.

2 Corinthians 10:4 says, "For the weapons of our warfare are not of the flesh, but divinely powerful for the destruction of fortresses." This tells us the weapons we use are powerful because of God. Being divinely powerful weapons, they will destroy fortresses, or strongholds. A stronghold is a place built for security; it is well-fortified. When a demon finds ground to afflict us, he plants thoughts into our mind or feelings into our emotions. When accepted, those thoughts and feelings become our own. Then the demon can begin to contribute more of the same, thus building a pattern or stronghold—a place of security, a place where he can hide and control safely. Every time a demon lies to us and we believe the lie, that demon is fortifying his stronghold. The demon may do this by giving us thoughts declaring we are no good, or that God doesn't care about us or our situation. He may tell us we are about to go under. He puts these thoughts into our mind and manipulates our feelings, which seem to verify the thoughts. If we do not take those thoughts captive, the enemy continues to build his stronghold. Before long, the demon is well-fortified with a whole system of lies, and it will take a great deal of truth and persistence to tear down his stronghold. It won't happen instantly!

Speculations

2 Corinthians 10:5 says, "We are destroying speculations and every lofty thing raised up against the knowledge of God, and we are taking every thought captive to the obedience of Christ." A *speculation* is a "conjectured thought, which is the formation or expression of an opinion without sufficient evidence or proof." In Acts 5:4 Ananias and Sapphira speculated in their heart that they could lie to the Holy Spirit, win the praise of man, and live happily ever after. In reality, this speculation turned out to cost them their lives.

Another example of speculation might be seen in the lives of the children of Israel. They had been led out of Egypt; Pharaoh had been in hot pursuit. The Red Sea had been divided and the children of Israel, under Moses' leadership, had crossed over safely and had witnessed the destruction of Pharaoh's army. Shortly afterward, they came to water that was unfit to drink and witnessed God make it useable. With all that in mind, this is the complaint that the children of Israel later voiced against Moses and Aaron in Exodus Chapter 16:

16:2 And the whole congregation of the sons of Israel grumbled against Moses and Aaron in the wilderness.

16:3 And the sons of Israel said to them, "Would that we had died by the LORD's hand in the land of Egypt, when we sat by the pots of meat, when we ate bread to the full; for you have brought us out into this wilderness to kill this whole assembly with hunger."

What a speculation! This was the opinion they formed without any evidence for a conviction. In reality, previous evidence should have overwhelmingly convinced them that God was on their side, providing for all their needs.

Have we ever had an experience of God's miracle in our life, and then a short time later grumbled because we didn't think God was doing anything? Is God pleased with this kind of response? Do we accept negative experiences as evidence of God's negligence? Are we accepting what we see or feel as true, or do we believe what God says is true? Have we been caught in the enemy's snare, making faulty speculations?

Here is a good way my wife and I have found to destroy speculations. When God blesses us, my wife writes down the date, noting what had happened. Then she makes a list of what we have seen God do. When we later find ourselves in another great storm, we review that list to help us remember what God has done. You will be amazed at how this can give you a lift spiritually. This was the reason for the Sabbaths, the feasts, and holy days in the Old Testament: to recall the great things that God had done for His people.

A Barrier Wall

2 Corinthians 10:5 goes on to say, "We are destroying speculations and every lofty thing raised up against the knowledge of God." These lofty things are high or elevated places; anything that is lifted up as a barrier. They are like walls built around a fortress as part of a defense system. We believe the barriers we erect protect us, but instead they prevent us from really knowing God.

A barrier is anything that restrains or obstructs progress or access. Police officers will set up a barrier at the scene of a crime to prevent unauthorized access. They want to obstruct passage to the crime scene so evidence is not destroyed. A barrier is meant to keep people out. That is what demons try to do. They raise these barriers in an attempt to prevent us from getting close to God. First John 1:7 tells us that as we walk in the light, in fellowship with one another, the blood of Jesus, the Son of God, cleanses us from all sin. From this we see the importance of remaining open and vulnerable to God and to the people around us, not hiding behind a system of defense barriers. Our job is to destroy every high place or barrier we have allowed the enemy—or ourselves—to build between us and the experiential knowledge of God.

The Knowledge of God

2 Corinthians 10:5 continues, "We are destroying speculations and every lofty thing raised up against the knowledge of God." These speculations and lofty things really have been raised against the knowledge of God. What is meant by the knowledge of God? This is not referring to God's knowledge or wisdom. Rather, it is our experiential knowledge of Him. If a demon tells us that God is not going to supply our needs and we believe him, we will not experience God as Jehovah-jireh. If we witness God blessing a neighbor, we may view Him as Jehovah-jireh to our neighbor; however, we may not perceive Him as Jehovah-jireh to us. Therefore, we don't know Him as the LORD Who Provides. We must destroy these speculations that are raised up against knowing who God really is in our lives. Demons do not want us to know experientially the love and grace of God.

We probably know about and recognize the President of the United States. But how many of us can make a casual phone call to the White House and speak to the President as a friend? For most of us, that simply is not the case. Intellectually, we may know the President. In our experience, however, he may not be a close friend. How similar is our relationship with God!

How can we make that relationship intimate in our experience? We read what the Scripture reveals about Him, we study His names that tell us about His character and who He is. But it is only by staying vulnerable to His truth and open to the Spirit's *rhema* that the facts about Him will be transformed into a personal experience with Him.

The book of 2 Corinthians, Chapter 10, verse 6 provides us with a goal: to be made obedient, both individually and collectively. When we discipline ourselves to walk in fellowship with one another, even when it is painful, our ungodly systems of defense will rise to the surface, needing to be confessed and replaced with God's love and acceptance. God often brings people into our lives for this purpose.

Like mirrors held before us, they practice sins that are offensive in our eyes, yet allowed in our own lives. We become angry at God's patience with them, not realizing it is to bring us to repentance. When we understand His reproof and bring our own life into obedience, it will be more meaningful to watch God do a work in their life.

The Making of an Overcomer

Revelation 12 says,

12:11 "And they overcame him because of the blood of the Lamb and because of the word of their testimony, and they did not love their life even to death."

They overcame him; they whom the accuser of the brethren had indicted. These believers overcame Satan. These whom Satan had daily accused before God were overcomers because of three things: because of the blood of the Lamb, because of the word of their testimony, and because they did not love their life even when faced with imminent death.

Because of the Blood

The first basis upon which believers overcome Satan is the blood of the Lamb. The Lord Jesus Christ shed His blood for the remission, or forgiveness, of sins. By releasing us from our bondage to sin, we are set apart from the ways of sin so that all believers can be released from a life of continual sinning. This speaks of the salvation of our soul—not of spirit, not of entering the kingdom, but learning to live apart from sinful ways in the kingdom. Without the shed blood of the Lord Jesus Christ, no one would ever experience this freedom from sin.

It is the blood of the Lord Jesus Christ that gives Christians the Scriptural right to be overcomers. So let's consider the shed blood of the Lamb and see what Scripture tells us about what it does in the life of a believer.

The Blood of the Lord Jesus Christ ...

- was shed in covenant on behalf of many. The benefits are available to everyone who enters that covenant through belief in Jesus Christ (Mark 14:24).

- justifies us. It releases us from the penalty of our sins, paying all debts for sin in full (Romans 5:9).

- brings us close to God. Because His blood was shed, the sin which separated us has been removed (Ephesians 2:13).

- makes peace with God, reconciling us to Himself (Colossians 1:20).

- cleanses our conscience from dead, religious works to serve God (Hebrews 9:14).

- initiates a covenant of salvation between ourselves and God (Hebrews 9:18).

- provides forgiveness. Without His shed blood there is no forgiveness for sin (Hebrews 9:22).

- makes believers clean with the right to enter the holy presence of God (Hebrews 10:19).

- sanctifies His people, setting them apart as God's possession, cleansed, and fit for Him (Hebrews 13:12).

- is used by the Spirit in sanctifying believers, sprinkling them with His blood in the personal application of the sacrifice of Christ (1 Peter 1:2).

- redeems us, purchasing our freedom from slavery to sin (1 Peter 1:18, 19).

- cleanses us from all sin as we walk in the light. We must walk in openness, submissive to the Holy Spirit's work in us (1 John 1:7).

- released us from our sins, setting us free to live in His righteousness (Revelation 1:5).

- purchased us from slavery to the ruler of this world. We are to be His priests and rulers on earth (Revelation 5:9, 10).

- empowers believers to overcome Satan. We overcome Satan *because* of the blood, not *with* the blood (Revelation 12:11).

- represents His life in payment for our sin. Placing the blood of the Lord Jesus Christ between us and a demon reminds the demon that the Lord Jesus Christ is between us and him (Leviticus 17:11, 14).

- is the acceptable substitution for my life in payment for my sin, for the wages of sin is death but the gift of God is life by the blood of the Lord Jesus Christ (Leviticus 1:2–5).

We may ask, "What is accomplished when I put the blood of the Lord Jesus Christ between myself and a demon?"

1. I notify the demon that I believe Christ's blood was shed for my sins, and that I have accepted His substitutionary death.

2. I notify the demon that I have been purchased by the Lord Jesus Christ.

3. I notify the demon that my sins can no longer be held against me. Therefore, he has no ground; nothing to lay claim to.

As we act in belief upon what the blood of the Lord Jesus Christ does, we are qualified to walk in freedom from oppression. Demons know what the blood of Christ accomplished. If we are going to be effective in spiritual warfare, we need to know what it has done, too.

The Word of Their Testimony

Something else was basic to believers overcoming Satan and his demons. Not only did they overcome him because of the blood of the Lamb, but because of their word of testimony.

A *testimony* is "an open declaration or evidence given in support of a fact or statement." They spoke their testimony and what they said lined up with the Scriptures. Proverbs 18 tells us that . . .

18:21 Death and life are in the power of the tongue, and those who love it will eat its fruit.

We have the power of death and life in our tongue. The power of the tongue is loosed by the words we speak. We will eat the fruit produced by the tongue: either death or life. That is a different way of saying we who love to talk are going to have to eat our words! The words we eat might be sweet or bitter, depending upon what we choose to say.

Philemon 6 says, "And I pray that the fellowship of your faith may become effective through the knowledge of every good thing which is in you for Christ's sake." The word the NASB translates *fellowship*, the KJV renders *communication*—the literal meaning being "the sharing of what is jointly held in common." The circumstances we face are used by God in order that we might be conformed to the image of the Lord Jesus Christ. They help teach us the truth about the good things we have received in our lives. As we communicate our expanding faith with others, our words become an effective tool of warfare, exposing and dissipating the lies perpetrated by the kingdom of darkness. As we share our knowledge with others, we grow stronger in spirit, able to stand in righteousness, more easily resisting the enemy's lies, thus enjoying the fruit of Jesus' ministry on earth.

But if we choose to doubt God's truth and accept and spread the enemy's lies, our words will negate the victory of Christ in our life, and our faith needed for victory will be ineffective.

They Did Not Love Their Life

The third reason believers overcame Satan was because they did not hold their life dear even when threatened with death. When we really want to be all that the Lord Jesus Christ wants us to be, the Lord will take us through a death process that destroys our own fleshly identity. We learn to reckon ourselves dead to sin as a new creature alive to God. We must come to the place in our walk with God where we want our flesh-life dead and buried so that the life of the Lord Jesus Christ can be lived out through us. When we get to that place, demons find it difficult to influence us.

Though very few of us have had to face the threat of physical death that early Christians faced, we need to grow strong enough in our own faith to be able to face any end-time test we may encounter.

Examples of Faith
Positive Faith

In Mark 11 we are told about true faith in action.

11:22 And Jesus answered saying to them, "Have faith in God.

11:23 "Truly I say to you, whoever says to this mountain, 'Be taken up and cast into the sea,' and does not doubt in his heart, but believes that what he says is going to happen, it shall be granted him.

11:24 "Therefore I say to you, all things for which you pray and ask, believe that you have received them, and they shall be granted you."

Jesus was speaking in these verses to His disciples about their faith in God. We know that true, positive faith comes from hearing the word of Christ (Romans 10:17). Remember that there are four elements required for faith. First, faith requires a basis of truth. Second is the person's knowledge or awareness of the truth. Third is his agreement or assent with the truth. Fourth is his committal to that truth. When we hear Christ's word spoken and believe it is true, we respond differently to the situations of life because we are in agreement with truth. By our actions, a non-functional faith declares that we live contrary to any truth we have received.

Negative Faith

Just as there is positive faith, so is there also negative faith. Once a demon plants a lie in our mind and we agree with it, we begin to act on that lie. The thought may be, "I am worthless."[57] If we agree, the demon may stir up our emotions so that we feel worthless. Once we begin thinking and feeling something is true, it's relatively easy to become convinced that our thoughts and feelings are accurate. Sadly, that is as true with children as it is with adults.

Portraits from Faith's Hall of Fame

The following verses from Chapter 11 of Hebrews give some of God's phenomenal portraits from Faith's Hall of Fame:

11:6   And without faith it is impossible to please Him, for he who comes to God must believe that He is, and that He is a rewarder of those who seek Him.

11:7   By faith Noah, being warned by God about things not yet seen, in reverence prepared an ark for the salvation of his household, by which he condemned the world, and became an heir of the righteousness which is according to faith.

11:8   By faith Abraham, when he was called, obeyed by going out to a place which he was to receive for an inheritance; and he went out, not knowing where he was going.

11:17   By faith Abraham, when he was tested, offered up Isaac; and he who had received the promises was offering up his only begotten son;

11:29   By faith they passed through the Red Sea as though they were passing through dry land; and the Egyptians, when they attempted it, were drowned.

11:30   By faith the walls of Jericho fell down, after they had been encircled for seven days.

If we will review these stories in the Bible, we will notice an important fact: none of these people acted until they had received a revelation from God. Often we act according to our emotional ups and downs, or upon our circumstances, rather than submitting all things to God's will. Sometimes we may receive *rhema* through other people, but must always discern that we are responding only to what He has revealed. The soldiers of faith in Hebrews 11 acted on what they knew to be true based on what God had already revealed to them.

Faith versus Presumption

There is a major difference between faith and presumption. Bob George makes an excellent distinction between the two in his book *Classic Christianity*:

> In true faith, God is always the initiator, and man is always the responder. In presumption the order is reversed: Man assumes the role of initiator and tries to use "faith" as a power to force God to be the responder![58]

The Making of a Stronghold

We must pay attention to what we ponder! Do any of our patterns fall into these ways of thinking?

- I will obey God if His will doesn't conflict with my lifestyle, or if it is convenient.

- I am afraid to obey God in this particular situation.

- I don't need God's direction or supervision. All I want from God is His provision and blessing.

- I don't want God's chastening in order to be fruitful. I don't want to suffer.

- God does not supply my needs very well. I see Him as "Jehovah-cheapo" instead of as Jehovah-jireh; otherwise I would be rich and could have everything I want.

- God could never use me. I'm no good. Everything I do turns sour.

- He is my fair-weather Captain. As long as things go smoothly, He is my friend. Where is He when the going gets tough?

- Why doesn't God give me peace? My life is a wreck and my insides are tied in knots. I know I'm going to end up with ulcers.

- The situation I am going through is never going to improve. My marriage, my family situation, my job, my finances, etc. will never recover. God doesn't care, so I would be better off dead.

If we are thinking these kinds of thoughts, we have a stronghold. We have an area where the enemy has successfully gained a foothold. We have given him a right to work in our lives. It is important to begin our warfare by tearing down these lies, replacing them with God's truth. We must seek out what He says and then believe and act on the truth, renewing our minds with Christ-like obedience. Only when we become strong in faithful submission to the will of God can we stand fast in effective warfare for ourselves or others, helping them to understand the important role of obedience to God for their own victory.

Review: Names of God
A Proper Perspective

In this chapter we have investigated several areas:

1.   We are not in a fleshly war.
     • Speculations
     • A barrier wall

2.   The knowledge of God.

3.   The making of an overcomer.
     • Because of the blood
     • The blood of the Lord Jesus Christ

4.   The word of their testimony.
     • They did not love their life

5.   Examples of faith.
     • Positive faith
     • Negative faith
     • Portraits from Faith's Hall of Fame
     • Faith versus presumption

6.   The making of a stronghold.

> The name of the LORD is a strong tower;
> the righteous runs into it and is safe.
>
> Proverbs 18:10

Chapter 9

Prayers for Warfare

Kinds of Prayers

Many things are meant by the word "prayer." There are a number of words in Biblical Hebrew and Greek languages that are translated "prayer," with each sharing something in common, yet denoting something different.

Prayer can refer to our personal times with God in worshipful conversation. How intimate it becomes depends upon how well we have come to know God and trust Him. It can be the most fulfilling communication of our lives, sharing with full vulnerability and receiving in return His unconditional love and encouragement.

Prayer can refer to our expression of worship in adoration of the awesome greatness and goodness of God. As we speak out our commendation, He draws even nearer, for He inhabits the praise of His people. "My mouth will speak the praise of the Lord; and all flesh will bless His holy name forever and ever" (Psalm 145:21). Should this not be the Scriptural cry of our hearts?

Prayer can refer to our thanksgiving for the blessings He heaps upon us. As we recall His specific faithfulness to us, we grow in our realization of how great His lovingkindness has been toward us, even before our earthly life began. Our thanksgiving and praise minister to the heart of God and fulfill our very purpose.

Prayer can refer to our confession of sins—speaking out in agreement with God as to what is right. It is through this act of repentance that we align ourselves to walk in open fellowship with Him. His promise is that He hears our confession, and then He forgives and cleanses us from all the unrighteousness of the sin.

Prayer can refer to our requests regarding our personal needs. It is an acknowledgment that He is our resource and that we are totally dependent upon Him in every part of our lives. It is also our confirmation of His promise: ask and it shall be given to you.

Prayer can refer to our intercession for the needs of others. In prayer we can stand in the gap, seeing what may not be seen by others and loosing the powers of heaven into any situation. It is not only the work of the Lord Jesus Christ today on our behalf; it is also our work on behalf of each other.

Prayer can refer to an act of submission as we abandon our will and align ourselves with God's will. It is not humiliation to humble one's self before God; being in awe of God is the beginning of wisdom and knowledge. When we humble ourselves before Him, He will, in due time, lift us up. He has, in fact, already seated us in heavenly places with Him in Christ Jesus.

Warfare Praying

Prayer can also refer to something quite different from the above. Prayer, in the context of warfare, refers to our open verbal stand in the spirit realm. It often expresses our submission to God in humility and confession of any sin which has yielded ground to the enemy. However, it also includes our resistance toward the devil and his work, taking back authority which has been yielded to him and the powers of darkness. Three such prayers are included in this study.[59]

> With all prayer and petition pray at all times in the Spirit, and with this in view, be on the alert with all perseverance and petition for all the saints.
>
> Ephesians 6:18

Part 1: Knitting-of-Souls' Prayer

Father, if my soul has been knit to the soul of any of the following people in any manner that would not bring glory and honor to the Lord Jesus Christ, I choose to loose my soul from the soul of each of the following: (Name them).

As best I know, I have chosen, or do now choose, to forgive them for any way they may have sinned against me. I bless them, and I ask You to bless them. If, according to Your wisdom and knowledge, I have not genuinely forgiven any of them, I'm asking You to reveal that to me and to prepare me and enable me to truly forgive each one of them. I choose to allow You to produce in me the attitude toward them that the Lord Jesus Christ wants me to have.

If I have listened to any lies that Satan or any demonic forces have given me concerning any of these people, I confess that as sin, and I ask You to forgive me. I put the blood of the Lord Jesus Christ between me and each person I have named and any demons that may be in or around them.

All this I pray in the name, the power, and the authority of the Lord Jesus Christ.

Understanding the Scriptures

We will look first at the Scriptural foundation for the Knitting-of-Souls' Prayer.

1 Samuel:

18:1 Now it came about when he (David) had finished speaking to Saul, that the soul of Jonathan was knit to the soul of David, and Jonathan loved him as himself.

Jeremiah:

11:9 Then the LORD said to me, "A conspiracy has been found among the men of Judah and among the inhabitants of Jerusalem."

Ezekiel:

22:25 "There is a conspiracy of her prophets in her midst, like a roaring lion tearing the prey. They have devoured lives; they have taken treasure and precious things; they have made many widows in the midst of her."

Hebrew Definitions

Soul (nephesh) is defined as the "inner being of man; seat of emotions, mental acts, and acts of the will."[60]

Knit (qashar) means "to bind, join, knot; to be in league together, confederate, conspire; to be knitted together, bound fast."[61]

Our soul is the function of our mind, emotions, and will; it is the expression of our personality. David's soul and Jonathan's soul were knit together in a good bond; there was nothing wrong with that bond. However, since a good bond is possible between two people, an evil bond is possible as well, especially if demons are afflicting either or both of them. We know Satan is a counterfeiter and that he will do anything he can to deceive people in any way possible. An evil bond between two people would give him the opening, or ground, to oppress.

In the references cited above we read of the *conspiracy* that God found in the hearts of His people. All Israel was bound together in their pursuit of false gods, while their prophets were also in league, growing fat through their plundering of the people and the temple wealth. This kind of conspiracy, or knitting together, was not limited to Bible times. We need only to read the headlines of our newspapers to realize that not only are fame and fortune pursued as idols by our society, but by many within the church as well. The lure of compromise and deception incapacitates the church, limiting its power because we have united our mind, will, and emotions with those who have succumbed to demonic, fleshly, or worldly allure. We are each answerable for our own personal part in this. Individual repentance is necessary for the church as a whole to be cleansed. This is the root of revival, restoring us to our "first love."

Colossians 2 says:

2:2   that their hearts may be encouraged, having been knit together in love . . .

2:19   and not holding fast to the head, from whom the entire body, being supplied and held together . . .

In verse 2 Paul was concerned that those who had not experienced the benefit of his personal teaching should be knit together with those who had. This bonding was to be accomplished with love, reinforced by the exchange of true experiential knowledge of Christ. In this way their hearts would be encouraged with understanding and resulting confidence.

In verse 19 Paul was also concerned that no one disqualify them from receiving their prize by delighting in self-abasement, the worship of angels, or taking their stand on visions; all of which are products of an inflated mind. This could happen if they were not bound fast to the head, knit together with the body, and growing by God's grace.

These Scriptures reveal the importance of our relationships; the people who become a part of our thoughts, emotions, and decisions are powerful influences. These Scriptures also reveal how essential it is for us to continually review our affiliations so we not become entangled with deceptions, which give demonic forces the legal ground to work in our lives.

Preventive action is always best in maintaining spiritual health. But God, through the Lord Jesus Christ, has provided for healing in each damaged area. Therefore, we need not fear or deny wrong entanglements; we need instead to deal with them in prayer.

Analyzing the Prayer

Father, if my soul has been knit to the soul of any of the following people in any manner that would not bring glory and honor to the Lord Jesus Christ, I choose to loose my soul from the soul of each of the following: (Name them).

When working with people, I have them name any person they can recall who may have hurt them, wronged them, rejected them, hated them, or cursed them in any way during their lifetime.

To start, I normally have a person name their father and mother, even if they don't think their parents have hurt them in any way. Demons afflicting a person could very well have gained access through ancestral bloodlines. Therefore, the oppression could come from the father's or mother's family—or there could be something coming from both. I have them give their father's name and include his family, friends and ancestors. For example: "I choose to loose my soul from the soul of my natural father, Jeremiah Ebenezer Smorkendorf, his family, his friends, and his ancestors."

If there are any specific people within that group who need particular attention, I ask the person to add those names: "I choose to loose my soul from the soul of my father's father, Jeremiah Clarence Smorkendorf— who was an adulterer—and from his family, friends, and ancestors. I also choose to loose my soul from my father's friend, Josh Elias, who tried to molest me as a child, and his family, friends, and ancestors." I have them name the person, using the full name when possible.

When they loose their soul from the soul of their mother, I have them use her maiden name and married name(s) always including, as above, their family, friends, and ancestors.

Then I go through a list with them to help them think of anyone that may have hurt, wronged, rejected, abused, hated, or spoken negatively toward them in any way during their lifetime.

A List of Those Who May Have Rejected You

Father:

Mother:

Step-father(s):

Step-mother(s):

Anyone: who may have incested or raped you.

Anyone at church: Pastor, elders, deacons, Sunday School teacher, etc.

Anyone at work: Boss, co-worker, supervisor, etc.

Ex-spouse: Name each of them, even if married only a short time.

Spouse: Whether living or deceased.

Children: from a spouse's previous marriage or your own.

Anyone: you have been involved with in sex, drugs, or alcohol. If you cannot think of specific names say, "I choose to loose my soul from the soul of anyone I've joined with in sex, drugs, or alcohol and their families, friends, and any of their sexual partners."

Anyone: who continually wants to put you down, lord it over you, or that is domineering, or manipulative.

This is not an all-inclusive list, but it gives you an idea of whom you might want to include while reading the Knitting-of-Souls' Prayer for yourself.

Include people who have wronged you, even if they have died. If the deceased had demons afflicting them, the demons do not die; they are free to afflict someone else. If you didn't get along with that person while they were living, it is highly recommended you break any evil soul-tie you might have developed with them.

As best I know, I have chosen, or do now choose, to forgive them for any way they may have sinned against me. I bless them, and I ask You to bless them.

When we are choosing to forgive someone for something, we cannot depend upon our feelings; we are making a choice. When Christ died on the cross, it is seriously doubtful that He emotionally felt like forgiving anyone. People were spitting at Him and ridiculing Him. They shoved a crown of thorns on His head after nearly beating Him to death. His tormentors kneeled and bowed before Him to mock Him. They crucified Him between two robbers. They challenged His deity: "He saved others; let Him save Himself if this is the Christ of God, His Chosen One. Let this Christ, the King of Israel, now come down from the cross, so that we may see and believe! Hail, King of the Jews."

Do you think His emotions were saying, "Wow! Look at all this attention I'm getting. People have flocked to see this event that will mark world history. I am so excited to be here with you today. All these words you have spoken and all your gestures make me feel like someone very special!"

No! During the time of His darkest hour He felt like bailing out, but He remained true to the wishes of His Father (Luke 22:41–44). His body had been beaten. He was in physical pain. He was in emotional pain. He was in spiritual pain—He felt abandoned. Just before His death He cried out, "My God, My God, why hast Thou forsaken Me?" Psalm 22 gives a descriptive account of the great agony He suffered. The people witnessing the events of that day rejected Him and the cause for which He came to this earth.

Jesus did what He did because He had chosen to be obedient to His Father. He did not go to the cross thinking it was a wonderful place to spend the weekend! He made the choice to forgive those who were rejecting Him, knowing it was the right thing to do. He had received *rhema* from His Father. Jesus Christ did not make His choice because He was on an emotional high or was having a good day.

There is no implication in this that Jesus was emotionally depressed or feeling sorry for Himself. He was without sin. He knew He had come for this purpose. The point is, He did not make His decision based upon what

He emotionally felt. He made the decision to die on the cross long before He took the trip to Golgotha. He said in Mark 14:36, "Abba! Father! All things are possible for Thee; remove this cup from Me; yet not what I will, but what Thou wilt." Even as Jesus was on the cross being crucified He said, "Father, forgive them; for they do not know what they are doing . . ." (Luke 23:34). We also need to forgive those who have wronged us because it is God's resolve, not because we may be able to muster up a few good feelings about the situation. The Lord Jesus Christ has paid the price for their sin. As the righteousness of God in Christ Jesus, we must also be willing to forgive those who have wronged us.

I was once working with a man experiencing demonic oppression, walking him through this prayer. As I read the part concerning forgiveness, he had the thought that he did not have the ability or the desire to forgive his mother. A demon, however, cannot prevent a person from forgiving an offender if they choose to forgive. A willing believer has the ability to forgive. If we can say, "I am making the choice to forgive," then we are able to forgive. A demon may still venture near and put thoughts into our mind, stir up our emotions, and try to convince us we cannot forgive. That is a lie. If we were not able to forgive, God would not have instructed us to forgive others; He would be asking us to do the impossible. God will not do that.

This was not the man's own thinking; a demon was oppressing him, presenting his mind with thoughts contrary to the wishes of his spirit. The oppressive spirit did not wish to lose his ground; unforgiveness provided the legal right for its continued affliction. Earlier, during counseling, the man had disclosed his desire to forgive his mother; he knew that God had spoken and revealed his need to forgive. Due to his feelings, he wasn't sure he could forgive some terrible things she had done to him. Because the man had not made the choice to forgive, the demon had been able to exercise power over him, thus building an unsuspected stronghold. Forgiveness was the pivotal point. Once he realized how the evil spirit had been influencing his mind and emotions, he exercised his will and forgave. He confessed his sin of unforgiveness, and resisted the demon. The result? The demon, devoid of rights and armor, immediately fled from him.

If, according to Your wisdom and knowledge, I have not genuinely forgiven any of them, I'm asking You to reveal that to me and to prepare me and enable me to truly forgive each one of them. I choose to allow You to produce in me the attitude toward them that the Lord Jesus Christ wants me to have.

By praying in this manner, we are giving God the opportunity to reveal whether or not we have truly forgiven someone. We are asking God to prepare us and then enable us to deal with any unforgiveness.

If I have listened to any lies that Satan or any demonic forces have given me concerning any of these people, I confess that as sin, and I ask You to forgive me.

It is a sin to listen to the lies of a demon! Should a demon come alongside us in order to manipulate our thoughts or emotions, our response reveals our true faith. If we accept the demon's thoughts and feelings as though they were our own and act upon what we have received, then we are in rebellion against God. That is sin. We must confess our sin of listening to, believing, and acting upon information given to us by demonic forces.

I put the blood of the Lord Jesus Christ between me and each person I have named and any demons that may be in or around them.

We need to remember what it means to put the blood of the Lord Jesus Christ between ourselves and a demon. It lets the demon know we know the blood was shed for our sins and that we have accepted Christ's substitutionary death. It notifies the oppressing demon that we have been purchased by the blood of the Lord Jesus Christ, and that we are not our own. In addition, it lets a demon know our sins are forgiven, therefore, the demon has no ground to claim; our sins are confessed.

All this I pray in the name, the power, and the authority of the Lord Jesus Christ.

We are standing against the enemy, resisting not in our own strength, but in the almighty power of the Lord Jesus Christ, who has been given all authority over every name named. In Him we exercise that authority, learning to rule with Him over His creation.

Review: Prayers for Warfare
Knitting-of-Souls' Prayer

We have looked at:

1. The Knitting-of-Soul's Prayer.

2. Understanding the Scriptures.

3. Hebrew definitions.

4. Analyzing the prayer.

5. A list of those who may have rejected you.

Lord, teach us to pray.

Part 2: Iniquities-of-the-Fathers' Prayer

Heavenly Father, because of what I have learned from Scripture, I humble myself before You in prayer, and I confess that my father, his family and his ancestors; my mother, her family and her ancestors and I have sinned against You by not following after You fully. We have not kept Your commandments, nor have we walked fully in Your teaching. We have committed iniquity, acted wickedly, and rebelled against You and, as a result, we stand shamed before You. Because we have transgressed Your law and have not obeyed Your Word, and because You are righteous and keep the covenant You made with Abraham and his descendants, You have poured out the curse and brought great calamity upon us instead of Your blessing; thus You have confirmed Your words that You spoke against those that disobey You. You have kept this calamity in store for us and brought it upon us because You are righteous and we are disobedient. We have sinned. We have been wicked. (Be more specific here.)

Father, in accordance with Your righteous acts, I humbly request that You turn Your anger and wrath away from me that has come upon me because of the iniquities of my father, mother, and our ancestors to the third and fourth generations and beyond. I'm asking You to hear my prayer, and I request that You review my situation, not because of any merit of my own, but because of Your great compassion, and I ask You to forgive and to take action on my behalf that I may be spared. All this I pray in the name, the power, and the authority of the Lord Jesus Christ.

2 Chronicles:

7:12   Then the LORD appeared to Solomon at night and said to him, "I have heard your prayer, and have chosen this place for Myself as a house of sacrifice.

7:13   "If I shut up the heavens so that there is no rain, or if I command the locust to devour the land, or if I send pestilence among My people,

7:14   "and My people who are called by My name humble themselves and pray, and seek My face and turn from their wicked ways, then I will hear from heaven, will forgive their sin, and will heal their land."

The Lord appeared to Solomon after He had completed the temple of the Lord, proclaiming it to be His chosen house of sacrifice. In advance, He provided a way for the people to receive forgiveness and healing for the devastation that would come as a result of the sins they would commit.

Whenever unconfessed sin is found in the lives of God's people, they must turn from their wicked ways. His people need to humble themselves, pray, and seek His face. This verse speaks to believers. As children of God, we all need to humble ourselves. Humility is not insignificance; it is having the proper perspective of one's importance, neither higher nor lower than it really is. When we humble ourselves, we are no greater in our own eyes than in God's sight. We see ourselves as subservient to God. It is His opinion that counts. When we humble ourselves, we are not strutting up to God giving our opinion, advice, or our instruction. We are coming to Him, listening for and seeking His advice and instruction.

We must make the choice to repent—to stop going in our direction and head in His direction. We must choose to turn from our wicked ways. Obviously that means overt sin such as stealing, lying, murder, sexual sin, etc. It must also include covert sins that are not quite as obvious: hate, anger, unforgiveness, bitterness, fear, unbelief, insistence upon our own way instead of God's way, etc. These are all equally evil in God's sight. We need to be open to God's showing us any evil in our own lives and to His completely removing it from us.

Only after we humble ourselves, pray, seek God, and turn from our wicked ways does He hear us. He will forgive our sin and cleanse us from its unrighteousness. Then He will even heal our land.

The Fathers' Iniquities

Exodus 20:

20:5   " . . . I, the LORD your God, am a jealous God, visiting the iniquity of the fathers on the children, on the third and the fourth generations of those who hate Me,

20:6   but showing lovingkindness to thousands, to those who love Me and keep My commandments."

A Hebrew Definition

Visit: (paqad) means "to pay attention to, observe; to visit in order to inspect, to investigate, to discover, to find; to review in order to appoint reward or assignment."[62]

When God heard the outcry of Sodom and Gomorrah's great sin, He went down to investigate all He had heard before establishing His judgment (Genesis 18:20, 21). God is not mocked; what is sown will be reaped. But neither is He unjust, for He will not punish children for their father's sins. Each person is dealt with according to his own heart (Ezekiel 18:18–20). The Lord's ways do not change; His patience and kindness leads to repentance. Those who hate Him and His ways suffer.

The flesh of man does not change either. Just as it has been since man first fell into sin, we are each born without the capacity to receive the things of God. We learn to survive and live in this world by watching the values and methods of our parents. We hear what they say, see how they respond to circumstances, and we store this away until we later need it. These ways can become strongholds for the enemy and even though we become born-again, these fortresses remain intact until we tear them down by repentance and obedience, renewing our minds with the ways of God.

God heard the outcry of His people in Egypt and provided them with a great deliverer. He has sent a Savior for us as well. We need to turn from any unrighteous ways of our natural fathers and look to His way of deliverance.

You might not like the idea of the above Scriptures being used as a basis for this prayer, thinking the Old Testament is not for today or that it does not apply now. However, the New Testament has no misgiving about it.

1 Corinthians 10 says . . .

10:1   For I do not want you to be unaware, brethren, that our fathers were all under the cloud, and all passed through the sea;

10:2   and all were baptized into Moses in the cloud and in the sea;

10:3   and all ate the same spiritual food;

10:4   and all drank the same spiritual drink, for they were drinking from a spiritual rock which followed them; and the rock was Christ.

10:5   Nevertheless, with most of them God was not well-pleased; for they were laid low in the wilderness.

10:6   Now these things happened as examples for us, that we should not crave evil things, as they also craved.

10:7   And do not be idolaters, as some of them were; as it is written, "The people sat down to eat and drink, and stood up to play."

10:8   Nor let us act immorally, as some of them did, and twenty-three thousand fell in one day.

10:9   Nor let us try the Lord, as some of them did, and were destroyed by the serpents,

10:10 Nor grumble, as some of them did, and were destroyed by the destroyer.

10:11 Now these things happened to them as an example, and they were written for our instruction, upon whom the ends of the ages has come.

The things which occurred in the Old Testament were written as examples from which we may learn. As parents, we would be delighted if our children would learn from our mistakes. We can tell them to watch for certain pitfalls, but they are the ones who ultimately must decide what to learn and use from our experiences. Spiritually, we have the same choice. We can learn from the mistakes of those who lived during Old Testament days, or we can ignore what they experienced and make the same mistakes ourselves. God's ways have not changed. The choice is ours to make from the moment we are born-again with freedom to choose.

Personalizing the Prayer

This Iniquities-of-the-Fathers' Prayer was adapted from Daniel 9:1–22. Instead of naming the whole nation, however, it names our parents and their ancestors. They are the individuals through whom sin is passed to us as individuals. The wording has been changed somewhat to make it more contemporary, but the meaning is still true to the Word of God and has been applied to us personally; we alone are responsible for our relationship and fellowship before God.

Directions for Using the Prayer

The ending of the prayer's first paragraph refers to "being more specific." We must confess the sins of our father and those of his bloodline.[63] When we do that, we are simply acknowledging to God that this is a list of sins you know your father and/or his family have committed. Confessing their sins will not help them in any way. We are simply naming the sins of which we are aware, telling God that we want nothing to do with those sins. To enjoy God's forgiveness and freedom from those sins, our family would need to confess their own sins. In essence, we are saying, "Father, I recognize the sins that my father and his ancestry have committed and view them from your perspective; I want nothing to do with their sin. I want to be pure before You."

When we have confessed every sin we can remember that our father's bloodline has committed, we must do the same thing concerning our mother's bloodline. Then continue reading the prayer as written.

If demons have gained access to oppress us through our bloodline, this prayer will take the ground back that our ancestors have given the enemy through their sins. After that has been completed, we must keep the slate clean for our own life and our family's sake.

Life Is Like a Computer

An illustration might be helpful to show the necessity to pray this kind of prayer. You just inherited your family's personal computer, but you only know enough to turn it on. Nevertheless, you begin to type a story. Since you are not familiar with the computer, at times you may randomly use keys which tell the computer to do something more than you desire. You finally finish writing your story, but when you print your first draft, it does not look the way it should. You made inappropriate commands without canceling them, and the computer seems to have a mind of its own. Although the computer followed your commands, the finished product is unsatisfactory. There are spaces and gaps where they don't belong. You accidentally set the first page in bold; the right margin was not justified; there were redundant words you didn't catch; there were misspelled words; there were all kinds of typing imperfections in your document.

Our life is similar to typing on a computer. Our ancestors also made some inappropriate commands in the computer and didn't correct them. We are now using the computer that we inherited from our ancestors and all their inappropriate commands are still in the computer. We sometimes make improper commands of our own, not knowing how to correct them. Our program is not printing out like we think it should. Our life is permeated with areas we can't seem to do anything about. No matter how hard we try to change the outcome, we can't.

The solution for a personal computer is to learn how to go through the text with an understanding of all the "codes" that have been fed into it. These codes are like commandments. As our text is read and the codes deciphered, we can see what "inappropriate commands" were given. When these are deleted and replaced by proper commands, our text will print out as it was meant to be.

Inappropriate codes or commands were given in our ancestry. If these are still in force because they have never been deleted—cancelled with confession and repentance—those codes allow demonic forces to work in our life because they are still in our computer's memory. This Iniquities-of-the-Fathers' prayer is designed to delete improper codes from our past.

Review: Prayers for Warfare
Iniquities-of-the-Fathers' Prayer

We have looked at:

1.   The Iniquities-of-the-Fathers' Prayer.

2.   Understanding the Scriptures.

3.   The Fathers' Iniquities.

4.   A Hebrew definition.

5.   Personalizing the prayer.

6.   Directions for using the prayer.

7.   An illustration: Life is Like a Computer.

Humility is not insignificance; it is having the proper perspective of one's importance, neither higher nor lower than it really is.

272   From Darkness to Light

Part 3: Warfare Prayer

Father, in the name of the Lord Jesus Christ, I take authority over and bind this demon that is afflicting me, along with those under his authority. You evil, afflicting spirit, I bring the blood of the Lord Jesus Christ between you and me. Any negative words, thoughts, or feelings you have given or put upon me, I bind in the name of the Lord Jesus Christ. Any negative words, thoughts, or feelings you give _____ that are against me, I bind those words, thoughts, and feelings and put them back on you. I break any curse you've put upon me or that you are trying to carry out in my life, and I break any evil soul-tie between me and _____. I take back all the ground I have given you, and I confess my sins if I have listened to your lies, thoughts, or feelings. Now, you evil spirit from _____, I command you to go to the place the Lord Jesus Christ wants you to go. Be gone in the name of the Lord Jesus Christ.

Analyzing the Prayer

Father, in the name of the Lord Jesus Christ . . .

Anytime we purpose to resist demons, we should never come against them in the name of "Jesus" by itself. This is based on the fact that demons themselves sometimes take that name. It was a shock to my theological system the first time I encountered a demon taking the name "Jesus." Since then, I have seen quite a few people who have had demons using that name. These demons masquerading as "Jesus" very commonly will give the person false information, hoping they will accept it and act upon it. Should this occur, the demon would gain more strength and more ground in the person's life.

It is recommended that authority over demons always be taken in the full name of the Lord Jesus Christ. I never use the name Jesus by itself when I'm dealing with demonic forces. Demons need to know that we are aware of the difference. Demons will talk about "Jesus" far more readily than they will talk about the Lord Jesus Christ.

I take authority over . . .

If a demon is afflicting you, you can ask God, you can beg God to get rid of it, but He will not do it. Luke 9 tells us Jesus gave His disciples power and authority over all demons.

God will not force a demon to leave you because it would be incorrect and inconsistent for Him to do so. Had it been the right thing to do, He would have done it back in the Garden of Eden before Eve had been deceived by the serpent and Adam chose to join her in sin. However, He did not intervene. He had given man authority over the serpent; we have the same authority over Satan and his demons today. God promises us that when we submit to Him and we resist the devil, the oppressor will flee from us (James 4:7). If a demon is oppressing us, we are the ones who need to take authority over it.

and bind this demon that is afflicting me along with those under his authority.

The Bible never recommends nor suggests you ask God to bind any demon that may be oppressing you. Read the literal translation of what the Lord Jesus Christ spoke in Matthew 18:18, "Truly I say to you, whatever you bind on the earth shall occur, being bound in heaven; and whatever you loose on the earth shall occur, being loosed in heaven."[64] When we bind on earth, we are putting into effect on earth Christ's work which has already been accomplished in the heavenly realm. In Matthew 12:29 Jesus says, "Or how can anyone enter the strong man's house and carry off his property, unless he first binds the strong man? And then he will plunder his house." Those verses instruct us in our authority and tell us how and why we are to use it.

You evil spirit, I bring the blood of the Lord Jesus Christ between you and me.

When we say this, we are reminding the demon that the blood of the Lord Jesus Christ was shed for our redemption. It informs the demon we are bringing the life of the Lord Jesus Christ between him and us as a legal "off limit" sign. As believers, our sins have been paid for and can no longer be held against us. Demons do not like to be reminded of the blood of Christ.

Demons Hate the Blood of the Lord Jesus Christ

I witnessed an example of their dislike for His blood one evening when a woman's husband and friend brought her to investigate the possibility of any demonic oppression in her life. We were approaching the stairs that led to my office. As I began walking down the stairs ahead of them, I heard this woman say, "I am not going down those stairs into his office."

Her husband and friend assured her that everything would be all right. With a determined conviction in her voice she reiterated, "I am *not* going down into his office!"

The woman's friend had briefed me earlier on the situation. She had told me the woman really did want help, but that at times she appeared to be controlled by demonic forces. Remembering this, I turned on the stairs and looked at the woman. I quietly spoke to a demon, informing it that the Lord Jesus Christ with His shed blood was behind him, coming his way. If he didn't come into my office, that blood would remind him of Satan's defeat at the cross of Calvary.

As soon as this was spoken, the lady responded by saying, "Why are we just standing here? I thought we were going to go into his office." She then proceeded down the stairs and entered the office with no further hesitation.

Any negative words, thoughts, or feelings you have given or put upon me, I bind in the name of the Lord Jesus Christ. Any negative words, thoughts, or feelings you give _____ ...

The blank represents the name of a person you suspect has a demon afflicting them that may be plaguing you. For example: you are around someone by the name of "Jochebed." After you and Jochebed have parted, you begin feeling depressed, thinking life is terrible because God is not doing much for you. But when you stop to think about it, you remember you were not feeling this way until after you had talked with Jochebed. You wonder if you might be oppressed by some demon that may be afflicting him. If this kind of situation is true of your case, you would put *Jochebed's* name in the blank.

Any negative words, thoughts, or feelings you give <u>Jochebed</u> that are against me, I bind those words, thoughts, and feelings and put them back on you (the demon). I break any curse you've put upon me or that you are trying to carry out in my life, and I break any evil soul-tie between me and <u>Jochebed</u>. I take back all the ground I've given you, and I confess my sins if I've listened to your lies, thoughts, or feelings.

We rarely realize how important it is to confess our sin of listening to the lies, thoughts, and feelings of demons. If we don't do this, the warfare prayer will not be effective because this prayer is based on James 4:7: "Submit therefore to God. Resist the devil and he will flee from you." We must first submit to God. If we do not confess as sin our believing whatever the demon has persuaded us to believe, he will continue using the same lies and maintain his oppressive work. He will not leave because he is not required to leave. If he does leave, he will return in short order to intensify what he was doing earlier. Our sin of listening to the demon must first be confessed.

Now, you evil spirit from <u>Jochebed</u>, I command you to go to the place the Lord Jesus Christ wants you to go. Be gone in the name of the Lord Jesus Christ!

If we have covered all the ground and cancelled the legal right demons have to oppress us, when we tell them to go, they will leave without any fanfare. They will just leave. After the demons leave, whatever demonic symptoms they caused will have gone with them.

A Pretty Vase

Most of us either have children, know people who have children, or have baby-sat children. Think about this example: You take a three year old with you to a friend's house to visit. You walk into your friend's house and see an expensive vase placed on the coffee table. What might you say to the three year old? You might say, "I do not want you to touch that vase!" You would also probably give one of your "looks" to make sure the child understood exactly what you meant. You would warn the child because you know toddlers are curious and like pretty things; they like to touch them and carry them around. In the enthusiasm of the moment, you know that the child could knock the vase over or drop it. Then you would be the proud owner of a newly broken, expensive vase, or have a very upset friend, or both.

Here's an alternate of this example. When you walk in your friend's house you see a very expensive vase on an exceptionally sturdy shelf which is out of reach. Would you say anything to the child? Probably not, unless you just wanted the child to see the vase. Why wouldn't you say anything? You are not concerned about the safety of the vase. It is out of the child's reach.

Fellowship with Demons

When Paul says, "I do not want you to," it must imply there is a possibility that a believer is able to do whatever Paul does not want that person to do! Paul says this in 1 Corinthians 10.

10:20 . . . I do not want you to become sharers in demons (NASB).

The KJV says it like this: . . . and I would not that ye should have fellowship with devils.

The word *sharers* (or *fellowship*) in the Greek is defined as "a partaker, a partner, an associate, or a companion; one who shares life in common or in agreement with." Paul instructs Christians, "I do not want you to become a partaker, a partner, an associate, or a companion with a demon. I do not want you to share your life being in agreement with a demon." Are you wondering how it would be possible to do that? All a demon has to do is come alongside us, put his thoughts into our mind, or stir up our emotions. If we accept these as our own thoughts or feelings, we have become a partaker, a partner, an associate, or a companion with a demon.

Beelzebub, Lord of Flies

Look at another example. You are home alone. Your wife has gone out of town for a wedding, and you must fend for yourself. You decide to fix eggs for breakfast and accidentally drop some egg yolk on the table. Since you are rushed for time, you decide to clean up the mess later, and go to work. You return home for lunch and heat up some spaghetti. One of those slippery strands of spaghetti slips off your fork and falls to the table top. You're running late again, so you decide to clean up the spaghetti later, when you clean up the egg yolk from breakfast.

After work, you return home. As you walk into the kitchen you see flies on the table, dining on egg yolk and spaghetti. Because of your dislike for flies, you shoo them away as you head to the kitchen for a drink of water. While you are drinking your water, what are the flies going to do? They are going to return to the egg yolk and spaghetti. You could shoo those flies off all evening until you and the flies are so exhausted that you and the flies go to bed.

If you wanted to keep those flies off your table, what must you do? You need to get some warm, soapy water and a dish rag, go over to your messy table, and clean up the mess. The flies may still be buzzing around, but they are no longer interested in your table because there is nothing there to attract them.

Demons act in a similar manner—maybe this is why another name for Satan is *Beelzebub, lord of flies*.[65] Demonic forces are buzzing around us, so to speak. If there is any unconfessed sin in our life, it's like we have egg on our face. In that condition, demonic forces are attracted to us, and they will come like flies to honey. That is why it is so essential to confess our sins with repentance.

Why would a demon want to have fellowship with a believer? The next verse in 1 Corinthians Chapter 10 gives us the answer.

10:21   You cannot drink the cup of the Lord and the cup of demons; you cannot partake of the table of the Lord and the table of demons.

Cup in Scripture signifies "fellowship." Therefore, Paul is saying that you cannot have fellowship with God and have fellowship with a demon simultaneously. You cannot partake of the table of the Lord and the table of demons at the same time. Bear in mind, Paul is leaving no room for the possibility of drinking the cup of the Lord along with the cup of demons. The Apostle was specific: "You *cannot* drink the cup of the Lord *and* the cup of demons."

Look at what God says about eating at His table. "You cannot partake of the table of the Lord and the table of demons." From His table God offers salvation, love, joy, peace, patience, kindness, goodness, gentleness, etc. His table is loaded with spiritual food. But this verse says, "You cannot." We *cannot* partake of the table of the Lord *and* the table of demons simultaneously. It is one or the other. If we are listening to and accepting the lies of demons, in any area, we are feasting at their table—not the table of the Lord.

Spiritual Rebellion

Why would demons want us to partake of their table? What happens when a believer has fellowship with a demon? Look at Deuteronomy Chapter 9.

9:23 "And when the LORD sent you from Kadesh-barnea, saying, 'Go up and possess the land which I have given you,' then you rebelled against the command of the LORD Your God; you neither believed Him nor listened to His voice."

This verse provides us with God's definition of rebellion: " . . . you neither believed Him nor listened to His voice." Demons are trying to prevent us from listening to or believing what God says. That is why they put distracting thoughts into our minds and stir our emotions. If we accept the demon's thoughts, do we believe what God has said? No. If we act on what the demon tells us, are we obeying God? No. If we don't listen to God or believe Him, we are in a state of rebellion against God! Isaiah 63 tells us the result of rebelling against God.

63:10 But they rebelled and grieved His Holy Spirit; therefore, He turned Himself to become their enemy, He fought against them.

There is no reference in the New Testament of God's people being His enemies nor His being their enemy. Once we are in a state of rebellion, however, God will not go along with our thinking and ways. He will do the same kind of thing with us as He did with Job, who accused

God of being his adversary and of treating him unjustly. Of course, none of that was true. Although Job perceived it to be true, God did not put up with Job's pity party. In reference to Job's sin, God was his adversary and fought against him in the area of his sin. His whole purpose was to bring Job back into fellowship with Him.

Rebellion is a serious thing. When we are in rebellion, we grieve the Holy Spirit—displeasing and hurting Him, causing Him sorrow and pain. We are commanded not to grieve the Holy Spirit (Ephesians 4:30) for very good reason: When we grieve the Spirit of God, He cannot have the kind of ministry *through* us that He desires because His ministry, at that time, must be *to* us. Believers are already in relationship with God. Once we grieve the Holy Spirit, God needs to return us to fellowship with Him before He can use us as He desires. As long as we are entertaining the lies of demons in any given area, we *cannot partake* of the table of the Lord in that particular area. This is why we must submit to God and resist the devil. Only then will he flee from us.

Review: Prayers for Warfare
Warfare Prayer

We have looked at the following:

1. A Warfare Prayer.

2. Analyzing the prayer.

3. How Demons Hate the Blood of the Lord Jesus Christ.

4. An illustration: A Pretty Vase.

5. The possibility of having fellowship with demons.

6. Beelzebub, Lord of Flies.

7. Spiritual Rebellion.

> ...I do not want you to become sharers in demons.
>
> 1 Corinthians 10:20

Chapter 10

Questions and Answers

Here are a few questions that people have asked in reference to the subject of demonic oppression.

1.   Is there any authenticity to the book entitled *This Present Darkness?*

I have read *This Present Darkness* by Frank Peretti and it makes for very interesting reading. Once I began reading, I didn't want to put it down. There is more truth in Peretti's book than the kingdom of darkness would like believers to know. *This Present Darkness* vividly portrays that there really are demons in our world, scheming and plotting against us. It also shows their purpose: not only to steal, kill, and destroy, but to manipulate humans and get them to carry out demonic schemes. I would recommend this book to anyone interested in obtaining a better understanding of how demons work in our world today.

2.   If it is true that demons cannot take away a believer's salvation, why do they bother to oppress believers at all?

If someone could hurt you only by indirect means, a good way would be to somehow hurt your children. How often, when we see our children suffer, would we gladly change places with them? We desire to prevent them from going through unnecessary pain and suffering.

I think Satan and his demons—apart from the fact that it is their nature to destroy—want to hurt God in some way. They obviously cannot hurt God directly, so they try to do so indirectly. Demons will come to afflict and oppress us, God's children, trying to get us to turn against Him in some way. If we do, don't you think that must grieve the heart of God? We are His children and He loves us very much. He loves us enough that He sent His only Son to suffer and die for us. When we fall into the same trap as Adam and Eve, you know that must cause God pain. Adam and Eve's sin was believing Satan's lie instead of God's truth. Eve sought to be like God—the very purpose for which she had been fashioned. The serpent had told her if she ate the fruit she would be like God, knowing good and evil. She chose to fulfill that goal by a means forbidden by God and was deceived into believing the means were justified because the goal was right.

God is watching us. When we choose to believe a demon's lie, He knows the suffering we will endure. As He sees us making a bad choice, I'm sure He also suffers.

3. Can you give an example to show how a demon might put its thoughts into our mind or its feelings into our emotions?

A young married couple is in church listening to a guest missionary. During the meeting, God impresses upon them to give to the missionary's support. They intuitively know what God wants; however, they do not know the amount they are to give. Let's look at their situation from two perspectives.

Perspective #1

The next day at the breakfast table John and Marcia discuss the idea of giving to the missionary's support. They are not aware there is a demon in the room listening intently to their conversation.

"John, have you given any thought to how much we should give to the missionary holding special services at our church?" Marcia asked.

John responded, "Not much. Have you?"

Marcia replied, "Well, I was thinking maybe we could give him one hundred dollars. I know that sounds like a lot of money, but I'm convinced God would honor our giving."

At this point, the demon gets involved and begins putting thoughts into John's mind and stirs up feelings of depression in John's emotions. He reminds John how he has had a hard time providing food for the table. The demon suggests to John that though they tithe, they are still poor. Therefore, God has not kept His promise or honored their giving. Without realizing what is really happening, John has listened to the thoughts the demon had given him and fallen prey to the feelings the demon had manipulated.

With a hint of frustration in his voice, John begins to react to Marcia using the very thoughts the demon had given. "You say, 'God will honor our giving?' We pay our tithe faithfully every payday, yet we barely have enough money to keep food on the table! We need to fix the washing machine and you think we should give that much money? I think we should buy a few groceries and call a repairman. Then if God gives us extra, we can send it to the missionary at a later date."

The matter is settled; John and Marcia go with this decision. They are being double-minded. In double-mindedness we receive information from two sources: one holy and one unholy. God had given them information by way of their spirits; John and Marcia both sensed God leading them to give to the missionary.

The demon had given John thoughts in reference to a real life situation—the washing machine had broken down and they did not have the money needed to have it repaired. Some thoughts the demon had given to John were accurate and some were not. Then the demon manipulated John's emotions causing him to experience feelings of anxiety and doubt patterned after his flesh. John felt depressed and his feelings seemed to be justified; they *had* tithed, yet they were still tight financially.

It was easy for the demon to interject a plausible question in conjunction with the feelings he had already induced in John—"Why hasn't God given us more money anyway? Doesn't He care about us?"

Upon which source of information did John choose to act? He chose not to give to the missionary at this time; he would keep back what God had prompted him to give, using it to buy extra food and to have the washing machine repaired. This decision was actually in rebellion against God and grieved the Spirit of God. The demon had won a victory.

Perspective #2

In the first perspective, John and Marcia had just finished their conversation at the breakfast table. Now let's look at their situation from a different perspective.

John is feeling depressed and thinks it best not to talk about this anymore right now. It is time to go to work anyway, so he leaves the table, says good-bye to Marcia, and suggests they talk about it later. Off he goes to work. The demon working on John's thoughts and feelings stays close to John, hoping to get another opportunity to influence him in some way.

In his spirit, John knows that Marcia is right in what she said, but he does not *feel* like doing what he knows he should do. On his way to work, John starts praying aloud. "Father, I know Your word is true. I just don't understand why we are having such a hard time financially. If You are trying to teach me something, I'm willing for You to do whatever is necessary in my life to get me where You want me to be. I know this depression is not from You and I certainly don't enjoy being depressed. Lord, Your word says that You will meet all my needs, but I don't see the evidence of that in the area of our finances. However, I am making the choice to believe You no matter what the circumstances may be telling me. I know You want us to give to the missionary, but I don't know how much to give. If You'll let us know exactly how much You want us to give, we'll give it."

When John started praying, the demon listened in disgust and anger. He was more determined than ever to see this poor, miserable wretch suffer.

John is feeling about the same, but he's glad he has decided to give to the missionary. Then John recalls having heard someone teach how a demon can interfere in a Christian's life and saying that we need to take authority over it. John doesn't know if there is a demon bothering him, but he decides to act on what he has heard to see if it makes any difference.

John cautiously begins, "If there is a demon around me influencing me in any way, I command you to listen to what I have to say."

As John says this, the demon can not believe what he is hearing. However, he *has* to listen to John. "That is not the way it is supposed to be," thinks the demon. "He is supposed to be listening to me! Who says I have to listen to him!"

John, completely unaware that the demon is actually there listening, carefully continues. "I take authority over you and command you to listen to me in the name of the Lord Jesus Christ."

"*Oh, no*, don't use *that* Name! That is not fair!" fumes the demon. "I do not want to listen to you!"

But the demon knows he must listen, even though that is not his desire.

John continues, "Any demon afflicting me in any way, or causing me to think negatively or to feel depressed, I command you to stop doing that in the name of the Lord Jesus Christ."

Keeping his thoughts to himself, the demon thinks, "Ha! I don't have to stop. I can give you any thought I want to give you, and I am not going to stop. I am going to torment you until you lose whatever 'faith' you have in your God. I have a legal right to oppress you because you have listened to me and believed what I have told you!"

Then the Holy Spirit, living in John's spirit, speaks quietly reminding him of the teaching he had heard: "If you have a demon oppressing you, that demon will put thoughts into your mind and manipulate your emotions. If you choose to act upon those thoughts and feelings, you will become a partner with that demon. That sin will grieve the Holy Spirit."

Tears come to John's eyes as he thinks about that. He *really* feels terrible now. John's new feeling is not a feeling of depression. He is under conviction because he knows he has grieved the Holy Spirit; he has not wanted to do that. Still driving, with tears in his eyes, John confesses, "Father, I am guilty. I have grieved Your Spirit by listening to a demon! I have believed what that demon has told me. He has even provoked me to be angry toward You, blaming You for my financial problems! I had no awareness of there being a demon anywhere around me! Even so, I was wrong. I confess my sin of unbelief—of believing this demon instead of believing You. I ask You to forgive me."

The demon knows his operation is in trouble. The seething creature cannot believe what has happened. He knows if John maintains his position he will no longer be able to manipulate John's thoughts or emotions.

John wipes away the tears and continues with a new spark of determination, "Demon, I bind you in the name of the Lord Jesus Christ. It is written, 'Whatsoever things I bind on earth shall be bound in heaven; and whatsoever things I loose on earth shall be loosed in heaven.' I loose my spirit from your hold. I loose my mind, my emotions, and my will. I loose my body. Now, you evil spirit, I command you to go to wherever the Lord Jesus Christ wants you to go! Be gone in the name of the Lord Jesus Christ!"

One of God's holy angels immediately escorted the frustrated, angry demon away from John's presence.

John has no proof there has been a demon in the car with him on his way to work. All he knows is he feels normal once again; he is no longer depressed. John knows something has happened, although he isn't sure exactly what.

God's Spirit is pleased. John is learning something he needed to know to be the soldier He has wanted him to be. The Holy Spirit brings the simple words of a song to John's remembrance:

Now let us have a little talk with Jesus

Let us tell him all about our troubles.

He will hear our faintest cry

and He will answer by and by;

Now when you feel a little pray'r wheel turning

and you know a little fire is burning,

you will find a little talk with Jesus makes it right.[66]

As John sings this little tune that popped unexpectedly into his mind, he senses God is near. In that moment of closeness, God reveals the amount John and Marcia are to give toward the missionary's support. That settles the issue; John knows God's will. They will be giving the missionary one hundred dollars. He can't wait to call Marcia.

4.   Can a demon read our mind?

I am of the opinion that a demon cannot read a person's mind. The Scripture says that the LORD knows the thoughts of a man (Psalm 94:11). I'm not aware of any Scripture that says a demon can read our thoughts.

If there was a demon in the room where you were having a conversation with someone, the demon would hear what you were saying; they eavesdrop! They also observe us! They can see what we read and what we watch on TV and in movies.

Let's say you come home from work and say something to your wife, who has had a rough day. She hears your question, but she doesn't say a word. Instead, she rolls her eyes and produces a look of hostility, shakes her head in disgust, and stomps off.

Although she says nothing, do you think you would have any idea what she might be thinking? You might not know the exact words going through her mind, but you certainly would have an accurate indication of what kind of thoughts were there. You *can* read your wife's body language; a demon can do the same thing.

A demon may have been around and seen and heard all that had happened during her day. Being privy to this inside information, the demon would be able to design just the right thoughts for you to make her day even worse. From experience he would know just how to use her anger to trigger your wrong responses as well. A demon cannot read your mind, but he can interject thoughts into your mind without your knowing it. Then all he has to do is sit back and watch your body language.

For instance, you are in a convenience store and walk past a magazine rack that displays pornographic magazines. The demon suggests you pick up the magazine and look at it. There is no one else in the store except the clerk, but he is busy making a pot of coffee. You decide to open the magazine. What you see inside is different from anything you have ever seen before. You cannot believe pictures like this would ever be printed and presented to the public. You feel outraged and disgusted. You slam the book back onto the rack and shake your head in disbelief.

What do you think this demon has learned about you? Without you even speaking a word, he knows that if he's going to successfully tempt you, he must use another lure. The demon knows from watching your body language that you're not going to be easily tempted by pornography. This demon educated himself by watching your body language, not from reading your mind. But he has also planted a picture in your mind. In an opportune moment he may bring it back to your remembrance to test your response, to irritate you, or to make you feel guilty.

5.   What is generational sin?

In Exodus 20 verse 5 God said, " . . . I, the LORD your God, am a jealous God, visiting the iniquity of the fathers on the children, on the third and the fourth generations of those who hate Me."

Generational sin is sin that began in a bloodline but has never been rooted out by confession and repentance. People in a family tend to keep—or are bent toward committing—the same sin; they usually do not repent of it. The sin is continually modeled and passed down from one generation to the next. The only way to stop a generational sin is to confess it to God and turn from it. By example, we must repudiate it before our children.

6.   Why is the armor of God in Ephesians 6 so important?

This simple illustration may help us better understand the importance of our spiritual armor.

A Cold Hike

One morning you awaken and decide to go for a ten-mile hike in the country. You notice the thermometer reads 20°, so you grab a warm coat before you leave. The first mile is uphill; you begin to get warm and start to perspire. At the end of the next mile the wind begins to howl; a storm is heading your way. The temperature has dropped significantly. Although you do not know it, your thermometer at home now reads 10°. When you factor in the twenty mile per hour wind, the temperature stands at 25°

below zero! Your warm coat is not as warm as when you started. Your shirt, dampened by perspiration, is not helping keep you warm, either. The icy wind cuts through to the bone. Your boots are not insulated and your feet are getting cold. You have no hat and your thin gloves cannot keep your hands warm. The cold is like an ever-encroaching enemy, seeking to penetrate your inadequate clothing and steal your body heat.

You head back to the house. By the time you reach home, you are nearly frozen. If you had been forced to spend the night in this cold, you probably would not have survived. At best you would have experienced hypothermia or frostbite.

In this illustration, we easily note that cold temperatures can be hostile to ill-prepared hikers. The cold is impersonal. Whoever is caught in its grasp will be affected. Anyone not adequately protected, or unable to find warmth, will suffer. Unless shelter is quickly found, the person will soon become as cold as the surrounding temperature. The cold, without any concern, could drain the very life from its victim. Cold, however, doesn't have to be a deadly force; it can be neutralized. Though one may find himself in a sub-zero setting, all one must do is wear very warm clothing adequate for the temperature. By keeping the clothing dry and maintaining a proper expenditure of energy and food intake, the life-threatening cold will not constitute a risk to the person's life.

In this illustration, the hiker should have taken several layers of clothing including a warm parka, insulated boots, warm socks, insulated gloves, thermal underwear, and a warm hat. Then the cold would not have been of much concern at all.

The same is true in spiritual warfare. The enemy will continually try to invade our life, just as the cold does. Though the cold is not a living being, a demon is. A demon has desires and schemes. He purposes to steal, kill, and destroy. A demon loves to see believers without their armor; it is an easy thing to attack a defenseless Christian. Without his armor, a believer is as vulnerable to a demon as the hiker above was to the cold. Just as very cold temperatures can physically numb a person, so can a demon numb our spiritual sensitivity.

Though it might be wise for a hiker to be supplied with several layers of clothing, depending upon his need, we must always wear all our armor. Temperatures change as does the heat build-up during a hiker's activities. But the enemy never changes. He is never safe to be around, regardless of how comfortable circumstances may seem.

Since we are continually exposed to warfare in the spiritual realm, it is essential that we utilize the protection offered by the full armor of God. Using only part of His armor, however, leaves us vulnerable to spiritual attack in some area of our life.

7. **Why should we be concerned about getting rid of *any* oppressive demons? Wouldn't Satan just send more and keep us preoccupied chasing demons instead of doing the work of the Lord?**

Maybe another illustration will help.

Rabbits in the Garden

You have a garden in which you have planted fresh vegetables. As your garden grows, you diligently cultivate and water the tender plants. On one particular evening you go to bed very content and pleased with your gardening skills and the progress of your flourishing garden.

The next morning, however, you discover that sometime in the night, rabbits had feasted in your garden. Armed with this information you can choose to keep feeding the rabbits or you can do something to keep them out of your garden. Once an effective barrier is in place, it doesn't matter how many rabbits ogle at your garden—they can't get in.

The parallel is obvious. We need to take authority over all demons that have gained access to our lives. It is important for the believer to reclaim surrendered ground through confession and repentance. Once we accomplish that and cover ourselves with an effectual barrier, it doesn't matter how many demons Satan sends to afflict you. God's armor properly worn is an effective barrier against demonic enemies; it will protect His valuable property.

As we are being obedient to God, if another enemy with a new tactic approaches, God is faithful to train us to do battle against the new antagonist. By learning how to do effective spiritual warfare against spiritual enemies, we are better equipped to focus on the work of the Lord.

8. **Colossians 1:13 tells us that the Lord Jesus Christ delivered us from the domain of darkness. If that is true, why are Christians sometimes oppressed?**

When the Lord Jesus Christ delivered us from the domain of darkness, he purchased us and took us out of the realm of Satan's authority. Although believers come under God's authority and receive power to rule over demonic forces, Satan and his forces have the ability to oppress us. That leaves us with a choice: We can ignore or deny the reality and responsibility of spiritual warfare, or we can join the battle and learn how to be victorious over the enemy.

In various ways Scripture tells us repeatedly we are in a war and live in a combat zone. The enemy has the ability to oppress us, but we have been given the authority and power to defeat him. Perhaps the following will illustrate a believer's situation.

A Fly on the Prowl

During the summer, people enjoy themselves outdoors. At times, however, flying insects can become a nuisance. At such times, we often retreat into our homes where we are able to keep the majority of insects where they belong—outdoors. If an unscreened window or door is open, on the other hand, flies or other insects will enter your home and can become very annoying.

As homeowners, we generally try to discover how the insects are finding their way into our home. Once discovered, we seal off their entrance. At that point we can go about the task of removing any insects that remain. Later an occasional fly or two may slip in undetected through an open door. When that occurs, make sure there are no permanent points of entry available and grab your fly swatter.

In the spiritual realm, if we don't close all access points, demonic forces will find those remaining passageways. When they sense the time is right, they will attack, trying to plunder us in some way. Unconfessed sin gives demons access. Failing to put on the full armor of God provided in Christ Jesus also leaves us vulnerable. Our reception of their lies allows demons the freedom to build strongholds in our mind and emotions. As believers, we have the right and responsibility to eject our oppressors.

In Summary

As believers, we need to be aware that demons can oppress us. Their purpose is to steal, kill, and destroy. They intend to prevent us from being all God wants us to be. Their intent is to keep us out of the Promised Land. They do not want us to inherit the blessings God has in store for us. When they come to oppress, they do not usually come in such a way as to draw attention to themselves. They accomplish their work in a clandestine manner; they do not want us to be aware of what they are doing. They project the cause of our problems as being something else and hide behind their lies. They build and strengthen their strongholds upon lies generated and accepted by past generations. They desire to gain control of a person's thoughts and actions, which is their attempt to be like the Most High. They scoff at our feeble attempts to take authority over them in the flesh. They use Scripture against us to bring feelings of condemnation and hopelessness. Furthermore they never give up.

But remember this: God has not put us on Planet Earth to live in defeat. We are the beloved children and sons of the Most High God. Demons shudder when a believer learns to exercise authority over them in the name of the Lord Jesus Christ. When we learn to resist them with Scriptural truth, they flee in terror. Demons are no match for the obedient, alert, trained-for-battle, rhema-receiving believer dressed in the full armor of God. They stand no chance against that believer and they know it. Their lies cannot penetrate, nor can their schemes bring us down. In fact, God uses their efforts to train us to become more and more conformed to the image of Christ and to become like the Most High—which is a goal they will *never* attain! Take courage, fellow believers! God is on our side. He has already won the victory and wants us to join Him in His victory parade. Join the battle and fight for your loved ones. Put the enemy to flight and give him another mouthful of dust that God has promised him.

Deuteronomy 6 sums it up.

6:18   "And you shall do what is right and good in the sight of the Lord, that it may be well with you and that you may go in and possess the good land which the Lord swore to give your fathers,

6:19   by driving out all your enemies from before you, as the Lord has spoken."

Review: Questions and Answers

Here are the questions answered in this chapter:

1. Is there any authenticity to the book *This Present Darkness*?

2. If it is true that demons cannot take away a believer's salvation, why do they bother to oppress believers at all?

3. Can you give an example to show how a demon might put its thoughts into our mind or its feelings into our emotions?

4. Can a demon read our mind?

5. What is generational sin?

6. Why is the armor of God in Ephesians 6 so important?

7. Why should we be concerned about getting rid of *any* oppressive demons? Wouldn't Satan just send more and keep us preoccupied chasing demons instead of doing the work of the Lord?

8. Colossians 1:13 tells us that the Lord Jesus Christ delivered us from the domain of darkness. If that is true, why are Christians sometimes oppressed?

> Yet a little while and the wicked man will be no more;
> and you will look carefully for his place
> And he will not be there.
>
> Psalm 37:10

Appendix

The prayer of total commitment from Chapter 8 and the prayers used in Chapter 9 are placed in the Appendix for your convenience and easy access. You may wish to copy them from the book and keep them as a reference.

Total Commitment

Heavenly Father, I choose to totally commit my life to You. I choose to yield my will to You and to commit to Your will as You reveal it to me. I choose to yield all my rights to You. I choose to unconditionally surrender every part of my life—spirit, soul, and body—to anything You choose to do with it.

I recognize that my total commitment cannot be taken back. Thank You for being committed to my commitment.

All this I pray in the name, the power, and the authority of the Lord Jesus Christ.

Knitting-of-Souls' Prayer

Father, if my soul has been knit to the soul of any of the following people in any manner that would not bring glory and honor to the Lord Jesus Christ, I choose to loose my soul from the soul of each of the following: (Name them).

As best I know, I have chosen, or do now choose, to forgive them for any way they may have sinned against me. I bless them, and I ask You to bless them. If, according to Your wisdom and knowledge, I have not genuinely forgiven any of them, I'm asking You to reveal that to me and to prepare me and enable me to truly forgive each one of them. I choose to allow You to produce in me the attitude toward them that the Lord Jesus Christ wants me to have.

If I have listened to any lies that Satan or any demonic forces have given me concerning any of these people, I confess that as sin, and I ask You to forgive me. I put the blood of the Lord Jesus Christ between me and each person I have named and any demons that may be in or around them.

All this I pray in the name, the power, and the authority of the Lord Jesus Christ!

Iniquities-of-the-Fathers' Prayer

Heavenly Father, because of what I have learned from Scripture, I humble myself before You in prayer, and I confess that my father, his family and his ancestors; my mother, her family and her ancestors and I have sinned against You by not following after You fully. We have not kept Your commandments, nor have we walked fully in Your teaching. We have committed iniquity, acted wickedly, and rebelled against You and, as a result, we stand shamed before You. Because we have transgressed Your law and have not obeyed Your Word, and because You are righteous and keep the covenant You made with Abraham and his descendants, You have poured out the curse and brought great calamity upon us instead of Your blessing; thus You have confirmed Your words that You spoke against those that disobey You. You have kept this calamity in store for us and brought it upon us because You are righteous and we are disobedient. We have sinned, we have been wicked. (Be more specific here.)

Father, in accordance with Your righteous acts, I humbly request that You turn Your anger and wrath away from me that has come upon me because of the iniquities of my father, mother and our ancestors to the third and fourth generations and beyond. I'm asking You to hear my prayer, and I request that You review my situation, not because of any merit of my own, but because of Your great compassion, and I ask You to forgive and to take action on my behalf that I may be spared. All this I pray in the name, the power, and the authority of the Lord Jesus Christ!

Warfare Prayer

Father, in the name of the Lord Jesus Christ, I take authority over and bind this demon that is afflicting me, along with those under his authority. You evil, afflicting spirit, I bring the blood of the Lord Jesus Christ between you and me. Any negative words, thoughts, or feelings you have given or put upon me, I bind in the name of the Lord Jesus Christ. Any negative words, thoughts, or feelings you give _____ that are against me, I bind those words, thoughts, and feelings and put them back on you. I break any curse you've put upon me or that you are trying to carry out in my life, and I break any evil soul-tie between me and _____. I take back all the ground I have given you, and I confess my sins if I have listened to your lies, thoughts, or feelings. Now, you evil spirit from _____, I command you to go to the place the Lord Jesus Christ wants you to go. Be gone in the name of the Lord Jesus Christ!

Scripture Index

Subject Index

S

T

W

Bibliography

Vine, *Vine's Expository Dictionary of New Testament Words* (Oliphants, 1952).

James Strong, *Strong's Exhaustive Concordance Of The Bible* (New York: Abington Press, 1961).

Jack Samson, ed., *Man and Bear* (Clinton, New Jersey: Amwell Press, 2nd printing June, 1982).

Charles Caldwell Ryrie, *The Ryrie Study Bible* (Chicago: Moody Press, 1978).

Watchman Nee, *The Spiritual Man* (New York: Christian Fellowship Publishers, 1977), Vol. 1.

Watchman Nee, *The Spiritual Man* (Christian Fellowship Publishers, New York: 1968). Vol. 2.

Harold K. Moulton, *The Analytical Greek Lexicon, Revised* (Grand Rapids: Zondervan Publishing House, 1990).

Joseph Henry Thayer, *Thayer's Greek-English Lexicon of the New Testament* (Grand Rapids: Baker Book House, 1977).

Merrill C. Tenney, ed., *The Zondervan Pictorial Bible Dictionary* (Grand Rapids: Zondervan Publishing House, 1967).

The Concise Home Medical Guide (New York, Virtue and Company, Ltd., 1977).

Andrew Jukes, *The Names of God* (Grand Rapids: Kregel Publications, 1980).

Nathan Stone, *Names of God* (Chicago: Moody Press, 1944).

Bob George, *Classic Christianity* (Harvest House Publishers, 1989).

Francis Brown, *The New Brown-Driver-Briggs-Gesenius Hebrew and English Lexicon* (Peabody, MA: Hendrickson Publishers, 1979).

Jay Green, editor and translator, *The Interlinear Greek English Bible* (Layfayette, Indiana: Associated Publishers & Authors, Inc., 1981), Vol. 4.

Cleavant Derricks, A *Just a Little Talk with Jesus,*" *Songs Everybody Loves*, (Singspiration, Grand Rapids: Zondervan Publishing House), Vol. 1.

Endnotes

1. Most people usually cannot discern demonic forces with the senses. I have had people tell me they have smelled the presence of a demon. Fewer have told me they have seen them. Poltergeists—spirits which live in houses—have been seen at times and heard. People have told me that sometimes at night when no one is awake or no one is around, they will hear strange noises like doors closing, or footsteps in another room, or a knocking noise. Normally, however, people cannot detect the presence of a demon by the senses.

2. Vine, *Vine's Expository Dictionary of New Testament Words* (Oliphants, 1952), 143.

3. James Strong, *Strong's Exhaustive Concordance of the Bible* (New York: Abington Press, 1961), 40 #2616.

4. Unless otherwise specified, definitions used in this book can be found in *Webster's Encyclopedic Unabridged Dictionary of the English Language* New York: Portland House, 1989).

5. Anytime I give an example of any person I have counseled, I am not using that person's real name, nor am I giving any information that would disclose any person's identity.

6. Jack Samson, ed., *Man and Bear* (Clinton, New Jersey: Amwell Press, 2nd printing June, 1982), 114.

7. Charles Caldwell Ryrie, *The Ryrie Study Bible* (Chicago: Moody Press, 1978), 748.

    Job was not perfect in the sense of being sinless. The Bible teaches (and experience supports the fact) that every person falls short of God's standard of perfection (Rom. 3:23). The writer is asserting here that Job could not be justly charged with any moral failure by his fellow men. From the human point of view he was without blame.

8. Job 3:3

9. Job 3:4

10. Job 3:10

11. Job 3:11

12.   In Job 42:7 the Lord said to Eliphaz, "My wrath is kindled against you and your two friends, because you have not spoken of Me what is right as my servant Job has."

13.   James Strong, *Strong's Exhaustive Concordance of the Bible* (New York: Abington Press, 1961), 38 #2384.

14.   James Strong, *Strong's Exhaustive Concordance of the Bible* (New York: Abington Press, 1961), 558, #6663; 846, #6662.

15.   Note: The King James Version does not use quotation marks.

16.   See 2 Corinthians 5:21, Philippians 3:9, and Romans 10:4.

17.   Note: The Holy Spirit never leaves the New Testament believer. See Hebrews 13:5.

18.   Watchman Nee, *The Spiritual Man* (New York: Christian Fellowship Publishers, 1977), Vol. 1, 22, 33, 36–38.

19.   This legal ground for a demon to oppress a person can also come from the ancestral bloodline. See Chapter 9 of this book for more details.

20.   Charles Caldwell Ryrie, *The Ryrie Study Bible* (Chicago: Moody Press, 1977), 502. See note on 2 Samuel 24:10.

21.   Harold K. Moulton, *The Analytical Greek Lexicon, Revised* (Grand Rapids: Zondervan Publishing House, 1990), 299.

22.   Charles Caldwell Ryrie, *The Ryrie Study Bible* (Chicago: Moody Press, 1978), 549. See note on 1 Kings 22:17.

23.   Charles Caldwell Ryrie, *The Ryrie Study Bible* (Chicago: Moody Press, 1978), 502. See note on 2 Samuel 24:1.

24.   See 1 Kings 21:17–19.

25.   Joseph Henry Thayer, *Thayer's Greek-English Lexicon of the New Testament* (Grand Rapids: Baker Book House, 1977), 622, 623 #5087.

26.   Charles Caldwell Ryrie, *The Ryrie Study Bible* (Chicago: Moody Press, 1978), 1449. See note on Matthew 4:1.

27.   Charles Caldwell Ryrie, *The Ryrie Study Bible* (Chicago: Moody Press, 1978), 1842. See note on Hebrews 4:15.

28.   Merrill C. Tenney, ed., *The Zondervan Pictorial Bible Dictionary* (Grand Rapids: Zondervan Publishing House, 1967), 526.

29.   Vine, *Vine's Expository Dictionary of New Testament Words* (Oliphants, 1952), 70.

30.   Vine, *Vine's Expository Dictionary of New Testament Words* (Oliphants, 1952), 188.

31.   See 1 Corinthians 5:5 and 1 Timothy 1:20.

32.   See page 34 of this book.

33.   *The Concise Home Medical Guide* (New York, Virtue and Company, Ltd., 1977), 185.

34.   For more information concerning what the "flesh" is and how it works, read *The Handbook to Acceptance* and *The Handbook to Happiness* by Dr. Charles Solomon.

35.   Vine, *Vine's Expository Dictionary of New Testament Words* (Oliphants, 1952), 68.

36.   Vine, *Vine's Expository Dictionary of New Testament Words* (Oliphants, 1952), 298.

37.   Vine, *Vine's Expository Dictionary of New Testament Words* (Oliphants, 1952), 317.

38.   Merrill C. Tenney, ed., *The Zondervan Pictorial Bible Dictionary* (Grand Rapids: Zondervan Publishing House, 1967), 751.

39.   Vine, *Vine's Expository Dictionary of New Testament Words* (Oliphants, 1952), 317.

Vine says that, "Sanctification is God's will for the believer, 1 Thess. 4:3, and His purpose in calling him by the gospel, ver. 7; it must be learned from God, ver. 4, as He teaches it by His Word, John 17:17, 19; cp. Ps. 17:4; 119:9, and it must be pursued by the believer, earnestly and undeviatingly, 1 Tim. 2:15; Heb. 12:14. For the holy character, *hagiōsunē,* 1 Thess. 3:13, is not vicarious, i.e., it cannot be transferred or imputed, it is an individual possession, built up, little by little, as the result of obedience to the Word of God, and of following the example of Christ, Matt. 11:29, John 13:15; Eph. 4:20; Phil. 2:5, in the power of the Holy Spirit, Rom. 8:13; Eph. 3:16."

"The Holy Spirit is the Agent in sanctification. . . ."

40.   Vine, *Vine's Expository Dictionary of New Testament Words* (Oliphants, 1952), 71.

41.   Watchman Nee, *The Spiritual Man* (Christian Fellowship Publishers, New York: 1968), Vol. 2, 71.

"This spiritual sensing is called 'intuition,' for it impinges directly without reason or cause. Without passing through any procedure, it comes forth in a straight manner. Man's ordinary sensing is caused or brought out by people or things or events. We rejoice when there is reason to rejoice, grieve if there is justification to grieve and so forth. Each of these senses has its respective antecedent; hence we cannot conclude them to be expressions of intuition or direct sense. Spiritual sense, on the other hand, does not require any outside cause but emerges directly from within man."

42.   Joseph Henry Thayer, *Thayer's Greek-English Lexicon of the New Testament* (Grand Rapids: Baker Book House, 1977), 612 #4991.

43.   Andrew Jukes, *The Names of God* (Grand Rapids: Kregel Publications, 1980), 96.

44. Charles Caldwell Ryrie, *The Ryrie Study Bible* (Chicago: Moody Press, 1977), See note on Isaiah 14:4–11, 12 on p. 1033, 1034.

45. Charles Caldwell Ryrie, *The Ryrie Study Bible* (Chicago: Moody Press, 1977), 1034. See note on Isaiah 14:13, 14.

46. Nathan Stone, *Names of God* (Chicago: Moody Press, 1944), 38, 39.

47. Nathan Stone, *Names of God* (Chicago: Moody Press, 1944), 40.

48. Charles Caldwell Ryrie, *The Ryrie Study Bible* (Chicago: Moody Press, 1977), 794. See note on Job 40:6–14.

49. Charles Caldwell Ryrie, *The Ryrie Study Bible* (Chicago: Moody Press, 1977), 794. See note on Job 42:1–6.

50. Merrill C. Tenney, ed., *The Zondervan Pictorial Bible Dictionary* (Grand Rapids: Zondervan Publishing House, 1967), 460.

51. Charles Caldwell Ryrie, *The Ryrie Study Bible* (Chicago: Moody Press, 1978), 1708. See notes on Romans 4:25.

52. Charles Caldwell Ryrie, *The Ryrie Study Bible* (Chicago: Moody Press, 1978), 9.

    The name occurs 6,823 times in the O.T. and is especially associated with God's holiness (Lev. 11:44–45), His hatred of sin (Gen. 6:3–7), and His gracious provision of redemption (Isa. 53:1, 5, 6, 10).

53. Merrill C. Tenney, ed., *The Zondervan Pictorial Bible Dictionary* (Grand Rapids: Zondervan Publishing House, 1967), 408.

54. Nathan Stone, *Names of God* (Chicago: Moody Press, 1944), 25, 26.

55. Nathan Stone, *Names of God* (Chicago: Moody Press, 1944), 57.

56. Merrill C. Tenney, ed., *The Zondervan Pictorial Bible Dictionary* (Grand Rapids: Zondervan Publishing House, 1967), 357.

57. When a demon lies to us, he will very commonly speak in the first person singular: "I am worthless!"

58. Bob George, *Classic Christianity* (Harvest House Publishers, 1989), 170.

59. The prayers from this chapter have been included in the Appendix. You may copy them for quick reference should a need for them arise.

60. Francis Brown, *The New Brown-Driver-Briggs-Gesenius Hebrew and English Lexicon* (Peabody, MA: Hendrickson Publishers, 1979), 659–661.

61. Francis Brown, *The New Brown-Driver-Briggs-Gesenius Hebrew and English Lexicon* (Peabody, MA: Hendrickson Publishers, 1979), 905.

62.   Francis Brown, *The New Brown-Driver-Briggs-Gesenius Hebrew and English Lexicon* (Peabody, MA: Hendrickson Publishers, 1979), 823.

63.   Be specific. Name any sins known to cause problems in the bloodline such as alcoholism, anger, hate, incest, lust, rebellion, rejection, etc.

64.   Jay Green, editor and translator, *The Interlinear Greek English Bible* (Layfayette, Indiana: Associated Publishers & Authors, Inc., 1981), Vol. 4, p. 45.

65.   Merrill C. Tenney, ed., *The Zondervan Pictorial Bible Dictionary* (Grand Rapids: Zondervan Publishing House, 1967), 88.

66.   Cleavant Derricks, "*Just a Little Talk with Jesus,*" *Songs Everybody Loves,* (Singspiration, Grand Rapids: Zondervan Publishing House), Vol. 1, p. 35.

Contact author Areon Potter
or order more copies of this book at

www.adonairesources.org
areon@adonairesources.org

Adonai Resources
Attention: Areon Potter
P.O. Box 4289
Salem, Oregon 97302

or

TATE PUBLISHING, LLC

127 East Trade Center Terrace
Mustang, Oklahoma 73064

(888) 361 - 9473

Tate Publishing, LLC

www.tatepublishing.com